D1087579

Ethics Without Philosophy
Wittgenstein and the Moral Life

Ethics Without Philosophy
Wittgenstein and the Moral Life

James C. Edwards

A University of South Florida Book

UNIVERSITY PRESSES OF FLORIDA
famu / fau / fiu / fsu / ucf / uf / unf / usf / uwf

Tampa, St. Petersburg, Sarasota, Fort Myers

For the quotations appearing in this book from certain copyrighted works fully cited in the list of abbreviations (pages ix and x), the author gratefully acknowledges his thanks to the following proprietors:

Basil Blackwell, Publisher, Oxford, OX4 1JF, England, and Wittgenstein's literary executors for Wittgenstein's *The Blue and Brown Books*, "Lecture on Ethics," *Notebooks 1914–16, On Certainty, Philosophical Investigations, Philosophical Remarks,* and *Zettel;* and Friedrich Waismann's *Wittgenstein und der Wiener Kreis.*

Humanities Press, Inc., New Jersey 07716 (holder of U.S. rights), and Routledge & Kegan Paul, Limited, London E.C. 4 England (holder of world rights), for Wittgenstein's *Tractatus Logico-Philosophicus.*

Library of Congress Cataloging in Publication Data can be found on page 272.

This book is for some friends:
for Martha, of course, friend above all;
for Tom Turner, true friend of mind and heart;
and
for all the generations of the Soup Group,
the salt which has not lost its savor.

CONTENTS

ABBREVIATIONS

BB   *The Blue and Brown Books*. Oxford: Basil Blackwell, 1958.

F   "Bemerkungen über Fraser's *The Golden Bough.*" *Synthese* 17 (1967): 233–53. Page references will be to the translation by Rush Rhees in *The Human World,* 1971, pp. 18–41.

LC   *Lectures and Conversations on Aesthetics, Psychology and Religious Belief.* Edited by Cyril Barrett. Oxford: Basil Blackwell, 1966.

LE   "Wittgenstein's Lecture on Ethics," *The Philosophical Review* 74 (January 1965).

LLW   *Letters from Ludwig Wittgenstein*. With a memoir by Paul Engelmann. Oxford: Basil Blackwell, 1967.

ML   "Wittgenstein's Lectures in 1930–33." Recorded by G. E. Moore; reprinted in Moore's *Philosophical Papers*. London: Allen and Unwin, 1959. Page references are to its reprinting in R. Ammerman, ed., *Classics of Analytic Philosophy,* pp. 233–84. New York: McGraw-Hill, 1965.

NB   *Notebooks 1914–1916*. Translated by G. E. M. Anscombe. Oxford: Basil Blackwell, 1961.

OC   *On Certainty*. Translated by G. E. M. Anscombe and D. Paul. Oxford: Basil Blackwell, 1969.

PG   *Philosophical Grammar*. Translated by A. Kenny. Oxford: Basil Blackwell, 1977.

PI   *Philosophical Investigations*. Translated by G. E. M. Anscombe. Oxford: Basil Blackwell, 1953.

PR   *Philosophical Remarks*. Translated by R. Hargreaves and R. White. Oxford: Basil Blackwell, 1975.

RFM   *Remarks on the Foundations of Mathematics*. Translated by G. E. M. Anscombe. Oxford: Basil Blackwell, 1956.

RKM   *Letters to Russell, Keynes, and Moore*. Edited by G. H. von Wright. Oxford: Basil Blackwell, 1974.

TLP   *Tractatus Logico-Philosophicus*. Translated by D. F. Pears and B. F. McGuinness. London: Routledge and Kegan Paul, 1961.

WWK   Friedrich Waismann. *Wittgenstein und der Wiener Kreis*. Edited by B. F. McGuinness. Oxford: Basil Blackwell, 1967.

Z   *Zettel*. Translated by G. E. M. Anscombe. Oxford: Basil Blackwell, 1967.

PREFACE

WITTGENSTEIN'S work is both important and obscure. The true matter of his thinking, going as it does to the very heart of our culture, is difficult to grasp, yielding only to an effort of thinking that matches the original in courage and power. Why then publish this book, which certainly cannot pretend to such distinctions? What I have written here must be understood as a reaction to the kind of commentary Wittgenstein's work has so far received, and as a plea for another kind. A number of excellent introductions to his writings are in print—notably those by Kenny and Pears—but to my knowledge no books have yet focused upon the hidden, determining ground of Wittgenstein's thinking in its progress from the *Tractatus* to the notes *On Certainty*. What makes this progress (as I believe it to be) the moments of a *single work* of thinking, the various exemplary manifestations of a man's attempt to secure for himself and others the sound human understanding and life? Wittgenstein's voice, early and late, is utterly distinctive; from the *Notebooks* to the *Investigations* his remarks indelibly bear a stamp that is his alone. What gives his work this deep continuity? What is its animating, unifying vision? Such large and apparently unprofessional questions are not usually addressed by commentators on Wittgenstein, but they need to be, and they are the aim of what I have written here. Before he becomes merely a textbook figure, we need a second generation of attention to his work, attention which, however halting, partial, and violent, can prepare the ground for a better harvest.

In writing this book I have been aided by many people. Norman Malcolm is first due my thanks, because it was the chance reading in 1964 of his lovely and scrupulous *Memoir* that introduced me to Wittgenstein and confirmed me as a student of philosophy. Through the generosity of the National Endowment for the Humanities I was able to study Wittgenstein's works with Professor Malcolm at Cornell in the summer of 1974. Many thanks to Norman—and to my friend Philip Bennett, another member of the Cornell seminar—for encouragement and criticism.

The work of Stanley Cavell, encountered in graduate school in the late sixties, was fundamental for my thinking about Wittgenstein. In graduate courses at Chicago I read Wittgenstein with Robert Coburn; at Chapel Hill with Doug Long, Virgil Aldrich, and Jay Rosenberg. I am grateful to all these, but I am pretty sure none would approve of the way I proceed here.

Ever since he was my student at Furman in the early seventies, Tom Turner has been a constant companion in my thinking about Wittgenstein; indeed, on many of the matters discussed in this book it is impossible (and unimportant) now to distinguish my thoughts from his. The power of Tom's mind and the quality of his care have been of equally inestimable value to me. I am forever, and gladly, in his debt. Another happy debt is owed to my colleague Doug MacDonald, whose friendship over ten years has been a steady source of benefit, intellectual and moral. In recent days Dana Phillips has been both a discerning critic and a valuable friend; I am glad to thank him here for these good offices.

A first draft of this book was written in 1978, when I was on sabbatical leave from Furman University. I am extremely grateful to my *alma mater* for this benefaction; thanks especially to Dean John Crabtree, to Provost Frank Bonner, and to Tom Buford, my department chairman, for their continued support and encouragement. Crabtree was especially helpful in the last stages of writing and typing, arranging for very welcome forms of material assistance and, even more welcome, giving assurance and warm fellowship. Nancy Yacobi, Sylvia Livingston, and especially Kay Hudson were splendidly efficient and cheerful in preparing the typescript.

A complete revision of the manuscript was finished at Princeton in the summer of 1979, while I was a member of an NEH Summer Seminar directed by Richard Rorty. His influence and good judgment will, I hope, be obvious to my readers, but not everyone has had the good fortune to know first-hand his acute intelligence, his rare erudition, and, even rarer, his unstrained generosity. My thanks to NEH for the seminar, and my thanks to Dick and Mary Rorty for the summer. Another member of that seminar, Steve Turner of the University of South Florida, has been instrumental in the publication of the book. I thank him for his interest and his aid. In making this book, the staff of the University Presses of Florida have consistently exercised care, tact, and good judgment. I am indebted to them all.

To finish a book and see it before one in a neat pile of typescript—who knows whether it will ever be more?—is an odd experience. There, after all, is a year, or two years—or ten years—of one's life; sentences bled out of brain and bone, now lying crabbed and stricken on the page. "I did it," one says, feeling equal parts of pleasure and mortification. One is—I am—so aware of how richly one has fed on the graces of others, and of how poor the result of such generosity, that one is tempted just to chuck it all. So why doesn't one? Pure conceit and cussedness, in large part; but perhaps also something else, which one might dignify by calling *hope*. One cannot quite extinguish the glimmer of light that seems sometimes to flicker here and there among the pages: "Maybe, just maybe, I'm right. Maybe they'll see what I see too." It's delusion, probably; certainly it contains a large dose of pride; but maybe, just maybe . . .

James C. Edwards

CHAPTER 1

The recovery of Wittgenstein's thinking

AFTER DECADES of scrutiny Wittgenstein's thinking remains largely misunderstood. Since no other recent philosopher requires so explicitly that readers approach his work in a particular *spirit*, and since the spirit demanded is so foreign to our everyday sensibilities, it is not surprising that his work has failed to produce a deep change in our philosophical practice. He expected as much, of course. As early as 1930 he was wryly acknowledging his distance from his readers:

> This book is written for such men as are in sympathy with its spirit. This spirit is different from the one which informs the vast stream of European and American civilization in which all of us stand.[1]

And by 1945, anticipating publication of the book expected by his pupils to transform the face of philosophy, his own pessimism had become increasingly profound and unrelenting.

> I make [these philosophical investigations] public with doubtful feelings. It is not impossible that it should fall to the lot of this work, in its poverty and in the darkness of this time, to bring light into one brain or another—but, of course, it is not likely.[2]

In these later remarks we hear not only his conviction that his work is likely to be misunderstood in these black times; we also catch there some of his bleak assurance that philosophers in particular belong to the company of those outside, those who—for all their cleverness and expertise—see without perceiving and hear without understanding.

Most philosophers have ignored the warnings implicit in these passages; it has been widely assumed that we are, without any special preparation, able to understand, appreciate, and criticize Wittgenstein's work. When considered at all, his own worries are put down to the workings of his self-protective temperament and are thereby discounted. Such optimism has the advantage of unfreezing one's exegetical and critical capacities, capacities which would perhaps be daunted by the conviction that one is facing a body of work written for a radically different sensibility. But what if the warnings with which Wittgenstein prefaced his books are not mere epiphenomena but point to something essential to understanding his thinking? What if philosophers really are outside the pale and Wittgenstein's texts must be read with an eye for their very darkness? A nicely domesticated Wittgenstein stands before us; gallons of ink have been spilled explicating and reëxplicating his philosophical themes and arguments. He has been accommodated, and now he is being dismissed: "Wittgenstein is long dead, and philosophers have recovered their nerve."[3]

This book attempts to reclaim Wittgenstein's work from the abyss of trivializing misunderstanding into which it has fallen and to restore its intended power to rebuke and to cleanse. The animating spirit of his work is both prophetic and evangelical. Like a prophet, he constantly proclaims and demonstrates the corruption of the present; he forces us again and again to see the pernicious absurdity of many of our familiar patterns of thinking and of the forms of life consonant with them. At the same time he gestures toward a way out; he intimates a gospel that can free us from the rat runs of fantastic philosophy and can restore to us the sound human understanding and the sound human life.

This spirit—since it pertains to the discernment of good and evil in thought and life one can properly call it *moral;* perhaps in its depth and intensity even *religious*—has been lost in our contemporary appropriation of Wittgenstein's work. Part of the explanation for this loss is, no doubt, the captivity of philosophy by the modern university, an exile that has brought increasing professionalization, technicality, and spurious objectivity. But part of the loss must be accounted to difficulties internal to Wittgenstein's conception itself. He does not—*deliberately* does not—make it easy for us to follow him; he demands that in our thinking we too "go the bloody *hard* way." [4] Without the difficulty, the desired and necessary enlightenment is not possible to achieve. To be efficacious, a philosophical remark must be thought, not just heard: "I should not like my writing to spare other people the trouble of thinking. But, if possible, to stimulate someone to thoughts of his own." [5] But even these necessary difficulties can be mitigated; we can approach Wittgenstein's work in such a way that inessential impediments to understanding are removed. We can, to use his own word, approach it in the right *spirit,* acknowledging both the necessary darkness of the texts and our necessity to read them with understanding as a ransom from the darkness of this time.

But how are we to understand that unfamiliar spirit and make it our own? How can we penetrate to the true significance of Wittgenstein's work? A necessary precondition for such penetration will be our ability to see that work as a whole, early and late. I do not mean, of course, that the *Tractatus* and the *Philosophical Investigations* are to be construed as supporting pillars in a grand philosophical architectonic; certainly not. There can be no doubt that Wittgenstein came to reject the *Tractatus* as fundamentally flawed, but there can also be no doubt that its author continued to see it as a work of fundamental significance. Wittgenstein's thinking certainly went beyond the *Tractatus,* but to follow that way beyond one must first pass *through,* just as—to use his own image—the only way to reach a higher place is up a ladder, even if, distrusting it, one kicks it away as soon as the ascent has safely been made (TLP 6.54). His own most explicit hermeneutical suggestion about the *Investigations* makes clear its intimate connections to the early work.

Four years ago I had occasion to re-read my first book (the *Tractatus Logico-Philosophicus*) and to explain its ideas to someone. It suddenly seemed to me that I should publish these old thoughts and the new ones together; that the latter could be seen in the right light only by contrast with and against the background of my old ways of thinking. (PI, p. x)

The *Investigations*, then, is a response to the *Tractatus;* it is an attempt at criticism, at just assessment, not of that particular book alone, but of the whole philosophical tradition of which it is, in Wittgenstein's view, the apotheosis. And the later work is, as well, an attempt to make good on an ambition at the very heart of the *Tractatus* and its tradition. It is, to put it cryptically, an attempt to do justice to that ambition without acknowledging it as such, or (even more cryptically) to recover that ambition for philosophers without making it a subject for philosophy. So there are at least two ways in which Wittgenstein's life work is a unity: the later writing is an attempt to take the measure of the earlier, and hence of the tradition which it culminates; and the later work tries to recast, to transmute, the ambition that gives rise to the tradition itself, to fulfill that ambition in spite of itself.

The argument of this book is that the fundamental intention of Wittgenstein's thinking, in both its periods, is its attempt to incarnate a vision of the healthy human life; the transmission of a moral vision—the attempt to reveal its character and to make it potent—is the true burden of all his philosophical work. Wittgenstein's own conception of the sound human understanding and life was not, of course, static; in the course of our examination we will mark the fundamental changes that occur between the *Tractatus* and the *Investigations*. Nevertheless, in both periods his essential ambition is an ethical one: to locate the sense of life; to answer the question of human being. Throughout his life he was deepening his insight into the nature of that ethical demand, exploring and establishing its connections to the philosophical tradition he had inherited. Early and late his texts intend to show, through the medium of philosophy, the possibility of sound thinking and living.

A serious misunderstanding must be averted here at the outset, if possible. I am not claiming that Wittgenstein's "hard" philosophical work—the picture theory of the *Tractatus,* or the remarks in the *Investigations* on the privacy of experience, for example—is somehow negligible in our understanding of his deepest intentions, nor am I suggesting that he was not quite serious in his agonies with problems about the nature of logical truth or the significant proposition. Quite the contrary, the recognizably "analytical" and "philosophical" discussions are essentially connected to the moral vision that holds them in place. Neither part of Wittgenstein's work can be neglected: without the explicit connections to the philosophical tradition, the vision remains ghostly and impotent, the spiritual tic of an individual; without the moral vision, the philosophical remarks are diffuse and lack the weight necessary to work a permanent alteration in sensibility. Up till now, however, our philosophical community has almost totally failed to reckon with the moral ideal that animates and unifies his work, and this failure has consigned that work to increasing trivialization and indifference.

This introduction is not the place to anticipate in detail the argument of the book, but it may be helpful to indicate its general direction. The argument will turn upon several key notions, notions which (in different ways) function in both the earlier and the later work and which provide clear entry into the works' underlying visions. The first of those is the notion of *the unsayable*. It is commonly known that in the *Tractatus* Wittgenstein explicitly calls attention to the importance of what cannot be expressed in language:

6.522   There are, indeed, things that cannot be put into words. They *make themselves manifest*. They are what is mystical.

7   What we cannot speak about we must pass over in silence.

The display of silence as a proper end for philosophical activity, familiar to us from the *Tractatus*, is also a fundamental theme of the later work; it thus helps to substantiate a claim of significant unity throughout Wittgenstein's thought. Part of the argument of this book will be an attempt to reveal the crucial role of silence in the later work. Intimately connected to these matters is the important distinction between what can be *said* and what must be *shown*. This distinction, originating in the *Tractatus*, can be found, in a significantly transmuted form, in the later work as well. Both the fundamental significance of silence and the necessity of what must be shown are basic components of the moral visions claimed here to be essential to understanding the spirit of Wittgenstein's thought.

A second key notion is the use of 'nonsense' as a fundamental term of philosophical criticism.[6] In both the *Tractatus* and in the later works Wittgenstein uses 'nonsense' as an epithet to condemn certain philosophical contentions and arguments. By tracing the force of that word as a term of criticism, and by seeing how the basis on which such criticism rests is radically altered after 1929, one can see the stubborn persistence of a fundamental and liberating insight throughout his thought; one can also see how that insight appeared to him differently at different stages of his philosophical development.

This attempt to lay bare the moral visions underlying Wittgenstein's work is conceived historically. It will be impossible to keep biography completely at arm's length, but every effort will be made to document my claims by appeal directly to the philosophical writings. The *Tractatus* is, obviously, the first major landmark to be surveyed, since that book is the first finished product of Wittgenstein's attempt to weld his ethical insights to traditional philosophical concerns.

In chapter two I will argue that the *Tractatus* is a book of radically divided sensibility: on the one hand, its author is theoretically committed to a conception of human nature (and thus, implicitly, of human excellence) that I call *rationality-as-representation;* on the other hand, he cannot easily live with some of the consequences of that powerful and philosophically traditional conception. The tension at the core of the book, manifest in the doctrine of showing and in the mute appeals to *das Mystische* and to "what is higher," springs from this conflict. Having sharply drawn the distinction between "rational" thought and "mystical" will, Wittgenstein finds himself forced to discount thought's intrinsic worth (and also the worth of the world that thought represents) and to advert to a sort of silent, willful mysticism in order to consolidate and protect his insights into the sense of life. Chapter three focuses upon the unjustly neglected "Lecture on Ethics" and shows that the quasi-solipsist conceptual structure adumbrated in the *Notebooks* and presupposed by the Tractarian ethical remarks persisted until the late twenties. Thought and will, rationality and action, remained, from a theoretical perspective, unconnected with one another.

In chapter four I show how this tension is resolved when rationality-as-representation loses its former hold and becomes for Wittgenstein the very mark of the diseased understanding. I will demonstrate how some of the most familiar and puzzling Wittgensteinian notions of the later work—language-game, perspicuous presentation, grammatical picture—function within a way of thinking undetermined by rationality-as-representation, and thus radically unphilosophical. In the later work Wittgenstein is struggling to criticize philosophy from a perspective not itself philosophical; indeed, he is trying to identify and to root out the very impulse to philosophizing itself, thereby making his work distressing and unsatisfactory to most philosophers. In this fourth chapter I try to provide a hermeneutic for reading the later work, one that makes intelligible its characteristic rhetorical devices and preserves its self-professed evangelical intention.

Chapters five and six connect Wittgenstein's therapeutic philosophical practice to a distinctive form of life, first by contrasting him with Descartes and then, more directly, by trying to describe some salient features of the radically nonphilosophical sensibility that Wittgenstein believes to be the hallmark of the sound human understanding and life. These last chapters bear most of the burden of my claim that the point of the later work is, like the earlier, the manifestation of a vision of human life properly called *moral*. It is here that one finally gets ethics without philosophy.

One might naturally wonder whether an attempt like this one to uncover a writer's hidden sensibility and to use it as a key to his work is not doomed to failure, especially in the case of a philosopher. After all, philosophy is *argument;* and the interest of a philosopher's work for other philosophers resides in the objective quality of the arguments he propounds, not in some ghostly "spirit" that allegedly hovers around those chains of inference. The philosophical wheat can and should be threshed from the "historical" or "biographical" chaff. So speaks our analytical superego. Furthermore, what are the standards to be employed in trying to say something about the spirit of Wittgenstein's work? Will not dispute inevitably reduce to matters of "feeling" or "interpretation," rather than hard evidence? And will not such interpretation do violence to the texts themselves, forcing them to say what we wish to hear?

In fact, these quite legitimate qualms cannot be settled in advance of the attempt itself. What is needed, I believe, is a kind of philosophical criticism relatively unfamiliar in the English-speaking philosophical community of today; such criticism of philosophers is usually practiced by Nietzsche or Kierkegaard and their followers. It is not clear that it can fruitfully be applied to a figure like Wittgenstein. But very real risks of failure, clearly apparent, need not paralyze: "Sin boldly!" is sometimes good advice, even in philosophy. Responding to criti-

cisms of his controversial attempts to make sense of the first *Critique,*
a contemporary philosopher has written:

> Nevertheless, an interpretation limited to a recapitulation of
> what Kant explicitly said can never be a real explication, if the
> business of the latter is to bring to light what Kant, over and
> above his express formulation, uncovered in the course of his
> laying of the foundation. To be sure, Kant himself is no longer
> able to say anything concerning this, but what is essential in
> philosophical discourse is not found in the specific propositions
> of which it is composed but in that which, although unsaid as
> such, is made evident through those propositions. . . . It is true
> that in order to wrest from the actual words that which these
> words "intend to say," every interpretation must necessarily re-
> sort to violence. This violence, however, should not be con-
> fused with an action that is wholly arbitrary. The interpretation
> must be animated and guided by the power of an illuminating
> idea. Only through the power of this idea can an interpretation
> risk that which is always audacious, namely, entrusting itself to
> the hidden inner passion to get through to the unsaid and to try
> to find expression for it. The directive idea itself is confirmed
> by its own power of illumination.[7]

Wittgenstein is not Kant, perhaps, and I certainly am not Heidegger;
but in Wittgenstein's work too there is the "hidden inner passion" of a
fundamental thinker. To reveal that passion—perhaps even to make it
our own—is worth the risks taken in the attempt.

A more troubling issue is the propriety of trying to reveal the pos-
tulated Wittgensteinian vision in the face of his own unwillingness to
speak of it. At the best, is not this book a temptation to avoid the
"bloody *hard* way" he insisted upon? At the worst, is it not, to para-
phrase Frank Ramsey, an absurd attempt to *whistle* what one insists
cannot be said? Perhaps. In the case of Wittgenstein there *is* the powerful temptation to remain silent, to insist that the work itself is complete
and that to say anything about what it "means" is certainly impudent
and probably an impediment to understanding. Here again, the proof
of the pudding is in the eating; but it may alleviate some of our worries
to recall a remark from the *Philosophical Investigations:*

127.   The work of the philosopher consists in assembling reminders for a particular purpose.

This book is an assemblage of reminders, nothing more. Its particular purpose is that one see Wittgenstein's work in a new light. The argument of the book is a series of *gestures,* pointing the reader back to the work itself. The worth of a gesture is not in the gesture itself but in what it accomplishes. To point well is to direct attention away from oneself to what is pointed at. What is said here about Wittgenstein's vision is, paradoxically enough, itself an attempt to show what cannot properly be said.

CHAPTER 2

Ethics in the *Tractatus:* showing and saying

N ow I'm afraid you haven't really got hold of my main contention to which the whole business of logical propositions is only corollary. The main point is the theory of what can be expressed (*gesagt*) by propositions, i.e., by language (and, which comes to the same thing, what can be thought) and what cannot be expressed by propositions, but only shown (*gezeigt*); which I believe is the cardinal problem of philosophy.

—Wittgenstein writing to Russell, 1919

I

WHILE NOT an entirely seamless garment, the *Tractatus Logico-Philosophicus* is very closely sewn; so in order to understand its remarks on ethics and its distinction between what can be said and what must be shown, one must first understand the basic features of the philosophical position worked out in the book.

The author's preface makes quite clear Wittgenstein's fundamental aim: "The whole sense of the book might be summed up in the following words: what can be said at all can be said clearly, and what we cannot talk about we must pass over in silence." He then goes on to say:

> Thus the aim of the book is to set a limit to thought, or rather—not to thought, but to the expression of thoughts; for in order to be able to set a limit to thought, we should have to find both sides of the limit thinkable (i.e., we should have to be able to think what cannot be thought).
>
> It will therefore only be in language that the limit can be set, and what lies on the other side of the limit will simply be nonsense. (TLP, p. 3)

These remarks set the book firmly within the transcendental conception of philosophy dominant in the West since Kant. The *Tractatus* is essentially a transcendental critique of the concept of representation: through a critical scrutiny of language, the philosopher can elucidate the necessary conditions of representation itself; and to discover the nature of representation is thereby to discover the boundaries of all thinking, to "set a limit to thought" (preface). By putting thought in its proper place, Wittgenstein's transcendental critique wants both to preserve the legitimate role of thinking in natural science and to prevent its encroachment into territory reserved to other human interests, much as Kant wanted his critique to limit knowledge in order to make room for faith. For Kant and for Wittgenstein some things must be passed over with that pregnant silence which indicates that representation is out of its depth.

The result of the Tractarian critique of representation was, of course, the "picture theory" of the proposition, an account which purported to reveal "the incomparable essence of language" (PI, sec. 97) by "explaining the essence of the proposition" (NB, p. 36). A brief review of its main points will be helpful to our discussion.

The picture theory attempts to specify the necessary conditions for something's being a proposition, i.e., for being the linguistic representation of a possible situation; its crucial insight is the comparison of the elementary proposition to a picture (*Bild*), the most familiar and most general instance of representation. But how is it that a picture is capable of representing something? On analysis one discovers two sorts of structural features necessary to *any* picture, says Wittgenstein; these features give it its representational capability. First, the picture must be structurally complex ("logically segmented"), so that in the picture there are distinguishable picture elements that can be made to go proxy for the objects constituting the situation which the picture is intended to represent (TLP 2.13; 2.131). In a realistic pen-and-ink drawing of a house and barn, for example, the components of the picture are indeed "logically segmented": that is, they are discrete combinations of lines, iconically correlated with the roof of the house, the front door, the barn roof, the hayloft entrance, and the like. Second, in any picture there must be a distinguishable relationship among its picture elements that is mathematically capable of representing a relationship among the objects of the situation that the picture intends to depict (TLP 2.14; 2.15; 2.151; 2.17; 2.18). That is, in the pen-and-ink drawing the relationship between the drawn house and the drawn barn (e.g., that the former is to the left of the latter) must be capable of being mapped onto the spatial relationship of the real house and the real barn (e.g., that the former is to the left of the latter).

Because of these structural features, pictures make it possible for us to represent, truly or falsely, the existence of states of affairs.

2.1   We make for ourselves pictures (*Bilder*) of facts.

· · ·

2.202   A picture represents a possible situation in logical space.

Now Wittgenstein directly approaches the topic of language. Elementary propositions, the logically basic units of language, are capable of representation because they are themselves a kind of picture. Just as in an ordinary iconic picture there are distinguishable picture elements that represent the objects in the state of affairs meant to be depicted, so too in an elementary proposition there are proposition elements— names—correlated with objects (TLP 3.2; 3.202; 3.22; 4.22). This crucial semantic relationship between name and object, corresponding to the more general relationship between picture element and object, is not the only parallel between elementary propositions and pictures. There is also the parallel of complex internal structure. Any picture must be articulated, i.e., it must be structurally so complex that it is possible that a relationship among its parts could be mapped onto a relationship among certain objects in the world. This requisite complexity, by means of which a given picture can depict a given situation, Wittgenstein called, generically, *logical form*. Elementary propositions, as a sort of picture, must have this complexity too. An elementary proposition must share logical form with the state of affairs (configuration of objects) it depicts (TLP 3.21; 3.22; 4.032; 4.04).

Wittgenstein believed that these two structural and semantic features of elementary propositions—that names name objects and that configurations of names depict possible configurations of objects—constitute the essence of language itself. Since elementary propositions are configurations of names (and thus possible pictures of states of affairs), and since all propositions are either elementary propositions or truth-functions of elementary propositions (TLP 5), and since the totality of propositions is language (TLP 4.001), one now has a way of plotting the limits of language and of thought. Now, in theory at least, one can look at what purports to be a specimen of significant discourse and see whether or not it is sense or nonsense. Is the specimen either (*a*) an elementary proposition, consisting of an immediate concatenation of names for objects and functioning as asserting the existence of a determinate state of affairs, or (*b*) a truth-function of such elementary propositions? If so, it is a genuine piece of language and is the expression of a genuine (even if false) thought. If not, then the utterance is shown to be a piece of nonsense and thus not a thought at all.

Even this brief recapitulation of the picture theory immediately shows how rigidly Wittgenstein conceived the limit of thought that the *Tractatus* was seeking to present. Thought functions to represent configurations of objects, nothing more. Outside of thought there is only nonsense. Already one can sense the difficulty to be faced in trying to fit ethics into such a straitjacketed conception of rationality.

II

THE ETHICAL vision of the *Tractatus* can best be approached through an investigation of Wittgenstein's distinction between what can be said and what must be shown. He uses forms of 'show' (*zeigen*) in at least twenty-three numbered sections of the *Tractatus,* along with additional appeals to the notion expressed in other ways (e.g., TLP 4.124); it is possible, however, to group the categories of things that must be shown under four broad headings: (1) showing and the specimen proposition (logical form as shown, propositional sense as shown, formal properties and relations as shown);[1] (2) showing and the truths of logic (logical truths as shown, logical inference as shown, mathematics as shown);[2] (3) showing and the possibility of laws of nature (6.36); and (4) showing and the realm of the ethical-mystical.[3] Even a cursory look at these passages will make clear a common feature of the things that must be shown: showing is an escape hatch from the realm of nonsense.

We have seen how Wittgenstein wanted to limit thought by delimiting meaningful language and thus shutting out nonsense; the picture theory of the proposition, grounded in a general theory of representation, seemed to satisfy these goals. Apparently it demonstrates the nonsensical character of many traditional philosophical problems and metaphysical doctrines. But this very success soon became problematic, since the canons of the theory were seen to menace more than just metaphysics. While some traditional topics of philosophical discourse could joyfully be given up as confused nonsense, this certainly could not be allowed to happen to logic or to ethics. If the picture theory of the proposition consigned these topics to the realm of nonsense, then the theory itself was thereby reduced to absurdity. It was immediately clear to Wittgenstein that, strictly speaking, the claims of logic or ethics, since they are not assertions of the existence of contingent states of affairs, are *not* propositions sanctioned by the picture theory. The truths of logic, manifesting the formal relationships of language and world, depict no particular states of affairs at all and thus are not genuine propositions. The claims of ethics are equally not picture-theory propositions, for ethical insights intend to vouchsafe the necessary sense of the world; and that sense must, he believes, lie outside the world (6.41), outside the sphere of what can be represented. Ethics, like logic, is a condition of the world (NB, p. 77); both deal with necessities, not contingencies. But no one, certainly not Wittgenstein, could therefore dismiss the utterances of the logician or the moralist because the picture theory pronounces them "nonsense." Must the theory then go? The notion of showing, rooted in the logical theories of Frege and Russell, was seen as a way of keeping both the picture theory and the indispensable but problematic sorts of insights: these things, although they could not be said, could be *shown*.

It is not difficult to describe the historical origin of Wittgenstein's interest in the notion of showing. As is well known, when as a young man he became interested in topics in the philosophy of mathematics, he went (apparently at Frege's suggestion) to study with Bertrand Russell at Cambridge. For some years both Frege and Russell had been deeply involved in the attempt to found mathematics on a purely logical basis. Frege's *Die Grundgesetze der Arithmetik* and Russell and Whitehead's *Principia Mathematica* both claim to show, as a test case of the logicist program, that arithmetic can be built up out of purely logical axioms and concepts, without the importation of any notions that are peculiarly "mathematical."[4]

Central to any such logicist analysis of arithmetic is, of course, the concept of *number.* How can the notion of number—which seems so inherently "mathematical"—be constructed from purely logical elements?

Frege had the brilliant idea that numbers could be defined solely in terms of the logical notion of class membership. A number, on his analysis, is a class of classes; the number two is defined as the class of all pairs, the number three is the class of all triples, etc. An obvious difficulty is how to avoid vicious circularity in such a definition; but it is not necessary here to examine in detail Frege's ingenious attempt to do so, since the notion of class membership itself was to prove troublesome enough.[5] If the Fregean analysis of number makes sense, then apparently it also makes sense that a class can be a member of itself. (After all, a number is a class of classes; and the class of classes is a class, i.e., a member of itself.) Of course, most classes are clearly not members of themselves (the class of all penguins, for example, is not a penguin).

This division of classes into two sorts—those that *are* members of themselves and those that are *not*—leads to what seems a fatal paradox. Russell, who first saw the paradox and after whom it is named, realized that a hidden incoherence was involved in a procedure that allowed classes to be formed out of other classes as easily as out of individuals like penguins, pens, and parkas. For consider the class of all classes that are not members of themselves: it *is* a member of itself if and only if it is *not* a member of itself; and if it is *not* a member of itself, then it *is*. This elegant paradox is remarkable for the fact that its construction employs only the notions of *class* and *class membership;*

and, since these notions are essential to Frege's and Russell's attempts to found arithmetic on logic, its discovery caused great consternation. Frege, when informed of the paradox by Russell himself, is reported to have said: "Arithmetic totters." In an appendix to the second volume of the *Grundgesetze* he bravely tried to defuse the paradox, but Russell's own salvage attempt attracted more of Wittgenstein's attention.

Russell sought to block the paradoxical implications of the Fregean account of number by the employment of his Theory of Types. He saw that if classes could be freely constructed from other classes, then paradox was inevitable; so in the Theory of Types he set out strict limits on what sorts of elements can be used to make up a genuine class. The Theory insisted that classes are different in logical type from the individuals of which they are composed; they belong to different levels in the logical hierarchy, so to speak. Thus "the class of all classes not members of themselves" is a piece of nonsense, according to the Theory, since in its formulation it inexcusably mixes up quite distinct logical types or levels by forming a class whose elements are other classes. If different logical levels are recognized and heeded, Russell believed, then the paradox he had discovered could not arise to menace a logicist analysis of number: arithmetic no longer totters.

"Logic must take care of itself." [6] This brave declaration, the first sentence in Wittgenstein's surviving 1914 philosophical notebook, shows very clearly his profound dissatisfaction with Russell's Theory of Types as a solution to the paradox. While Wittgenstein was sympathetic to the logicist program advanced by Frege, and while he was of course bothered by Russell's Paradox and the threat it posed to that program, he was convinced that the Theory of Types was a cure worse than the disease, worse because it compromised the integrity of logic as an autonomous system of thought. That is, the statements in the Theory that specify the different types or levels, and thus prevent paradoxical combinations like "the class of all classes not members of themselves," do not seem to be themselves truths of *logic;* they are not purely *formal.* Such statements appear to be prescriptions that set extrinsic limits on logic; prescriptions that, however "self-evident," do not belong to logic itself. So the logicist program is saved only by undercutting logic's autonomy.

As is shown by the *Notebooks,* the "Notes on Logic" of 1913, and the notes dictated to Moore in 1914, a great deal of Wittgenstein's early philosophical work was directed toward securing the integrity of logic while avoiding paradoxes like Russell's. [7] The doctrine of showing in the *Tractatus* was the culmination of those efforts. By the time of the *Tractatus* he had demonstrated to his own satisfaction that a theory of logical types was not only a threat to logic's integrity; it was also utterly superfluous.

> 4.1213   Now, too, we understand our feeling that once we have a sign-language in which everything is all right, we already have a correct logical point of view.

That is, Wittgenstein had become convinced that once one had a logically perspicuous symbolism, a symbolism which in itself clearly marked the differences between names of individuals, classes, relations, and the like, the nonsensical combinations of such symbols would *show* themselves to be nonsensical. There would be absolutely no need for a *theory* to be appealed to in order to prevent paradoxes; the perspicuous symbolism itself would immunize the system against hidden incoherence. Of course, a logically perspicuous symbolism is possible to construct (or recognize) only after the essential nature of the proposition, and thus of language, has been revealed by philosophical reflection. The *Tractatus*, Wittgenstein believed, provides that philosophical basis: so a symbolism understood in terms of its syntactic and semantic principles removes any need for a Theory of Types and, furthermore, demonstrates that the sentences of that theory are themselves logically faulty. They are attempts to *say* what can only be shown: "What expresses *itself* in language, *we* cannot express by means of language" (TLP 4.121). In that remark is the very heart of the notion of showing: the conception that the formal properties of a symbolism can in themselves vouchsafe "insights" not themselves capturable in the symbolism.

These purely logical considerations connected with the attempts of Frege and Russell to set mathematics on a basis of pure formal logic provided the initial impetus to Wittgenstein's formulation of the doctrine of showing; and, while their importance certainly cannot be overlooked, it would be a bad mistake to limit the significance of showing to these contexts.[8] The Wittgenstein of 1914 was most concerned about certain problems in logic. But the author of the *Tractatus* reckoned by twin stars, logic *and* ethics; and, since he appealed to the notion of showing in both contexts, it is worthwhile to attempt a unified account of the use of the notion of showing. It is easy to see that the first three

Tractarian applications of the doctrine of showing (set out in section one of this chapter) develop directly from its origin in logical problems; it is not so easy to see its connection to the realm of the ethical-mystical. How can the development of a logically perspicuous symbolism have anything to do with the discovery of the sense of life? Thus it has typically been assumed, if not argued, that the doctrine of showing was adventitiously employed there in order to help create the illusion of intrinsic connection between the ethical *obiter dicta* and the coherent philosophy of language of the bulk of the book.

III

IN ORDER to demonstrate an intrinsic connection between Wittgenstein's use of the notion of showing in logical contexts and his use of the same notion in the realm of the ethical-mystical, it will be necessary for us to penetrate to the very deepest level of his thinking. The doctrine of showing originated, as we have just seen, in the desire to have logic "take care of itself" and in the necessity to preserve the integrity of logic and ethics from the threats of the picture theory; but tracing these immediate sources of the doctrine still leaves a great deal mysterious. It leaves the *Tractatus* a book without coherence—a great deal of incisive and fruitful philosophy of language, roughly tied to a few remarks about ethical values and the meaning of life—and, more important, it leaves one without any interesting explanation of why this apparent incoherence is present. Why would a philosopher as astute and self-critical as Wittgenstein have thought that these quite disparate topics go together? And why would he have seized upon this notion of showing as a way of combining them?

To answer these complex questions it will be necessary to penetrate to the very heart of Wittgenstein's book; we must begin to reflect upon not just the philosophical statements themselves but also the deep assumptions from which those statements proceed. We need to uncover those largely unremarked channels in which Wittgenstein's early philosophical thinking naturally flowed, later to issue in the explicit doctrines of the *Tractatus*. One of those channels—perhaps the most important—was a powerful and philosophically traditional self-understanding, a picture of the nature of thought and thinker. This picture, the self-understanding of Western philosophy, we may call rationality-as-representation.

What is it to be a human being? This question, so embarrassing to professional philosophers when asked so bluntly, nevertheless has fair claim to be *the* question of Western philosophy, since it was the question of human being—what is it? what is its characteristic excellence?—that drew the Greek Sophists away from the naturalistic speculations of the Ionian and Eleatic thinkers, thus preparing the way for Socrates, the critic and the fulfillment of the Sophists.[9] And, for better or worse, the Socratic-Platonic answer to the question of human being stressed our capacity for *thinking,* conceived as accurate representation of the real: knowledge is (our) virtue; and knowledge is knowledge of universal definitions, re-presentations of the eternal Forms of which we here and now see only the shadows. Our characteristic excellence is our capacity for such accurate representation and for the kind of action that must (on the Socratic conception) inevitably follow from that knowledge.

This emphasis on our (apparent) capacity to represent the real became definitive for philosophical self-consciousness in the West. To be a human being is to be a rational creature; and to be a rational creature, to engage in thought, consists in pursuing and having true representations of what is the case. Thought, therefore, is identified with rational intellect; to think is to try to represent in some medium the real. To use Locke's trope, mind is the mirror of nature.[10]

This intellectualist picture of rationality, although it began with the Greeks and reached a definitive expression in Descartes, is by no means a historical artifact. It is alive and well in this characteristic expression of contemporary philosophy:

> *The* essential and characteristic human activity is representation—that is, the production and manipulation of representations. Except for the new-born and the severely brain-damaged, all humans, of whatever time and culture, engage in it, and, insofar as we can now say with confidence (the verdict on dolphins and the data on Martians not yet having come in), only humans do.[11]

Kant is for two (related) reasons an especially crucial figure in the philosophical history of rationality-as-representation. First, frightened awake by the specter of Humean skepticism, he began to recognize that the nature of representation itself had to be elucidated before particular representations could be pronounced trustworthy or not; thus, the transcendental turn in his thinking made possible the question that is the true problematic of the *Tractatus*: How is representation possible? What are its necessary conditions? And second, in Kant's architectonic account of the human faculties one gets the paradigmatic separation of representation and will, a separation which poses immense difficulties for ethics conceived as an instance of practical reason. How is it possible that reason be practical? This Kantian question—which, as we shall see, is a terrible puzzle for the early Wittgenstein as well—can only arise with its characteristic force because the conception of rationality-as-representation is so firmly entrenched. Because we thinkers are so sure that thinking consists merely in the production and manipulation of representations, we find it difficult to understand how there could be such a thing as *ethical* thinking, i.e., thinking that is intrinsically tied to *action* in service of the Good.

When taken seriously as a picture of thought's essence, rationality-as-representation leads naturally to an infatuation with the ideals of a traditional "scientific" metaphysics: if the task of thought is to (try to) represent things as they are, then the pinnacle of thought, metaphysics, is the representation of things as they ultimately are *sub specie aeternitatis*. After all, if the *telos* of thought is representation, then once it occurs to one that some representations seem more comprehensive, more accurate—"truer," in other words—than others, it seems only natural that thinking should aim at the production of these more satisfactory sorts. Representation has, it seems, an inner impetus toward an ideal: representation *sub specie aeternitatis;* the re-presentation in thought of the world as it really is, without error or partiality. Philosophers thus become obsessed with a system of representation which is Nature's own, one which is utterly nonconventional. The empiricists sought such "natural" representation in a pure observation of language; the rationalists looked for the *characteristica universalis,* the pure language of the mind inherent in all natural languages.[12]

It is this pursuit of representation *sub specie aeternitatis* that connects rationality-as-representation to a certain conception of objectivity, one which seeks understanding through the loss of a subjective point of view. Thomas Nagel has well described this ideal:

> The pursuit of objectivity therefore involves a transcendence of the self, in two ways: a transcendence of particularity and a

transcendence of one's type. It must be distinguished from a different type of transcendence by which one enters imaginatively into other subjective points of view, and tries to see how things appear from other specific standpoints. Objective transcendence aims at a representation of what is external to each specific point of view: what is there or what is of value in itself, rather than *for* anyone. Though it employs whatever point of view is available as the representational vehicle—humans typically use visual diagrams and notation in thinking about physics—the aim is to represent how things are, not *for* anyone or any type of being.[13]

Thus, under the spell of rationality-as-representation the thinker becomes the seeing eye, trying with all its might to represent things as they purely are; and the search for the objective understanding, the representation *sub specie aeternitatis,* impels the seeing eye to try to transcend its own perspective, to become the *limit* of the world, not a part of it. We shall see how precisely this movement toward objectivity is present in the *Tractatus*.

Finally, a picture of rationality (because, as we have noted, that characteristic seems the distinctively human excellence) adumbrates as well a concept of the *person* and is thus inescapably (even if only implicitly) a *moral* ideal. It specifies, if not particular modes of conduct, the form of life out of which those modes naturally issue. It specifies an ideal for human being, and in the pursuit of that ideal it encourages certain kinds of activity over others. It is not too much to claim that a given picture of rationality implies a *social* ideal as well: Plato's ideal Republic is partly the result of taking a particular conception of human rationality with ultimate seriousness. As we shall see later in this chapter, rationality-as-representation does carry moral baggage, and that poses great difficulties for Wittgenstein.

So, in summary, rationality-as-representation is a powerful and philosophically traditional picture of the nature of thought and thinker. According to it, rationality, the exercise of thought, is ultimately representational. To be a rational creature consists in pursuing and having true representations of what is the case; and the pinnacle of rationality, indeed, in some sense the pinnacle of personhood, is the pursuit of representation *sub specie aeternitatis*.

Even a cursory look at the *Tractatus* will show the determining presence there of rationality-as-representation. In the preface Wittgenstein says that the purpose of his book is to set a limit to thought by setting a limit to the medium of thought's expression, *language*. Thought and language are thus immediately identified as coextensive realms. In the book itself this identification between thought and language is further hammered home:

4   A thought is a proposition with a sense.
4.001   The totality of propositions is language.

Furthermore, the Tractarian image of language is certainly the image of representation. Propositions, the constituent parts of language, are representations of the possibilities of existence and nonexistence of contingent states of affairs (2.210). Thus, since thought is meaningful language and language is representation, for the author of the *Tractatus* rationality—the exercise of thought itself—is ultimately representational.

The deepest tension of the *Tractatus* results from Wittgenstein's theoretical captivity to the picture of rationality-as-representation and, at the same time, from his inability to live happily with the final consequences of that picture. With one part of his mind—the part shaped by theoretical philosophy—he readily identified thought and representational language; with another he sensed that some essential ways of thinking and speaking about the deepest human concerns are not representational at all. He implicitly *knew* this—that there is practical rationality as well as representational—but the grip of the intellectualist picture was too strong to allow this knowledge its full scope in the *Tractatus*. The doctrine of showing is, at bottom, an attempt to relieve this tension at the center of the book, a way for Wittgenstein to eat his cake and have it too. The passages already cited indicate that the author of the *Tractatus* was theoretically committed to the picture of rationality-as-representation; to show that he was simultaneously (if only tacitly) aware of the unacceptable implications of that picture it will be necessary to demonstrate the centrality of ethical considerations in his thought and life of that time. We will begin in this section with attention to his life, and in section four of this chapter a systematic account of his ethical remarks will be attempted.

As is well known, the text of *Tractatus* is an arrangement of some of the remarks Wittgenstein wrote in his philosophical notebooks. He faithfully carried these notebooks all through his service in the Austrian armed forces; and by August of 1918 he had, according to a letter he wrote Russell, finished a book "containing all my work for the last six years. I believe I've solved our problems finally. This may sound arrogant but I can't help believing it." [14] Through the diplomatic intervention of John Maynard Keynes the manuscript of the *Tractatus* was sent to Russell from the prisoner of war camp at Monte Cassino, where Wittgenstein had been held since November, 1918; he was anxious that Russell should see it before publication and wanted very much that they be able to discuss it face to face. The desired meeting took place in The Hague in the middle of December, 1919. A letter Russell wrote on 20 December 1919 to Lady Ottoline Morrell describes the encounter, and part of this letter bears quoting:

> I had felt in his book a flavour of mysticism, but was astonished when I found that he has become a complete mystic. He reads people like Kierkegaard and Angelus Silesius, and he seriously contemplates becoming a monk. It all started from William James's *Varieties of Religious Experience,* and grew (not unnaturally) during the winter he spent alone in Norway before the war, when he was nearly mad. Then during the war a curious thing happened. He went on duty to the town of Tarnov in Galicia, and happened to come upon a bookshop, which, however, seemed to contain just one book: Tolstoy on the Gospels. He bought it merely because there was no other. He read it and re-read it, and thenceforth had it always with him, under fire and at all times. But on the whole he likes Tolstoy less than Dostoewski (especially Karamazov). He has penetrated deep into mystical ways of thought and feeling, but I think (though he wouldn't agree) that what he likes best in mysticism is its power to make him stop thinking. I don't much think he will really become a monk—it is an idea, not an intention. His intention is to be a teacher. He gave all his money to his brothers and sisters, because he found earthly possessions a burden. I wish you had seen him. [15]

Although they had been in correspondence, Russell had not seen Wittgenstein since the autumn of 1913; the letter makes clear that profound changes were perceived by Russell to have taken place in the meantime. (It is perhaps worth noting that Wittgenstein had much earlier noticed "enormous differences" between himself and Russell.)[16] These movements in the direction of what Russell took to be a sort of mysticism coincide with the period in which the *Tractatus* was being composed, and it is crucial to recognize the fundamental importance of such themes in the book. It is not, despite its appearance, just a theory of language with ethical dark sayings appended. Its author himself insisted on the book's singular ethical intention.

Writing to Ludwig von Ficker, editor of the periodical *Der Brenner,* in hopes of getting his help in publishing the *Tractatus,* Wittgenstein tried to mitigate the editor's anticipated incomprehension and (perhaps) impatience.

> You see, I am quite sure that you won't get all that much out of reading it. Because you won't understand it; its subject-matter will seem quite alien to you. But it really isn't alien to you, because the book's point is an ethical one. I once meant to include in the preface a sentence which is not in fact there now but which I will write out for you here, because it will perhaps be a key to the work for you. What I meant to write, then, was this: My work consists of two parts: the one presented here plus all I have *not* written. And it is precisely this second part that is the important one. My book draws limits to the sphere of the ethical from inside as it were, and I am convinced that this is the ONLY *rigorous* way of drawing those limits. In short, I believe that where *many* others today are just *gassing,* I have managed in my book to put everything firmly into place by being silent about it. And for that reason, unless I am very much mistaken, the book will say a great deal that you want to say. Only perhaps you won't see that it is said in the book. For now, I would recommend you to read the *preface* and the *conclusion,* because they contain the most direct expression of the point of the book.[17]

In the preface he had written:

> If this work has any value, it consists in two things: the first is that thoughts are expressed in it, and on this score the better the thoughts are expressed—the more the nail has been hit on

the head—the more will be its value. —Here I am conscious of having fallen a long way short of what is possible. Simply because my powers are too slight for the accomplishment of the task. —May others come and do it better.

On the other hand the *truth* of the thoughts that are set forth seems to me unassailable and definitive. I therefore believe myself to have found, on all essential points, the final solution of the problems. And if I am not mistaken in this belief, then the second thing in which the value of this work consists is that it shows how little is achieved when those problems are solved.

And from the book's "conclusion":

6.522   There are, indeed, things that cannot be put into words. They *show* themselves. They are what is mystical.

. . .

6.54   My propositions serve as elucidations in the following way: anyone who understands me eventually recognizes them as nonsensical, when he has used them—as steps—to climb up beyond them. (He must, so to speak, throw away the ladder after he has climbed up it.)

He must transcend these propositions, and then he will see the world aright.

7   What we cannot speak about we must pass over in silence.

The point of the book, then, is an "ethical" one; its aim is that one "see the world aright."

What is one to make of the startled reaction of Russell and of the elucidative remarks to von Ficker? Both point inexorably to the conclusion that Wittgenstein's "mysticism," far from being just a proud idiosyncrasy, in fact is central to understanding the *Tractatus;* that the oracular tone of the preface and the conclusion is not a negligible affectation, but rather an attempt to communicate a vision that is of profound moral and spiritual significance to the author. In the happy phrase of Janik and Toulmin, the *Tractatus* is fundamentally an *ethical deed;*[18] to fail to see this is to falsify and, in Wittgenstein's own view, to trivialize the book. The author of the *Tractatus* is not just the legitimate heir of Frege and Russell; he belongs as well to the evangelical tradition of Kierkegaard and Tolstoy. This ethical intention of the book clearly stands in some immediate opposition to its tone of uncompromising philosophical rigor and purity. Rationality-as-representation, through the picture theory, exclusively emphasizes the mind's power to represent contingent reality, with language as the primary medium of such representation. But ethics deals, not with representable, contingent facts, but with necessities, with eternal meanings, with good and evil, and with the world-penetrating will. Thus another aspect of the tension at the center of the *Tractatus:* it is an ethical deed; worked, however, in a philosophical medium inherently hostile to such considerations.

In view, however, of the work's relative scarcity of ethical remarks in comparison to those concerning language and logic, one might wonder why Wittgenstein, if indeed he did intend to write a book with an ethical point, did not just *do* that. Why should he feel it necessary to wrestle with the logical problems of Frege and Russell? Tolstoy and Kierkegaard, after all, never felt the necessity to discover the foundations of mathematics or to plot the limits of thought. Why not just follow in their footsteps?

Part of the answer is, I believe, simply personal. The young Wittgenstein was intrinsically fascinated by the philosophical interests of Frege and Russell, and a man as proud and touchy as he was must have been eager to try his hand at the problems that had consumed and baffled his teachers. It is only natural that he would have wanted to publish his successes. But a more important part of the answer is alluded to in Wittgenstein's letter to Ludwig von Ficker, quoted above. There he bluntly expresses his distaste for *gassing,* loose talk about good and evil. He wants, in contrast, *rigor* to be the distinguishing mark of his ethical contribution, and he believes that the only way to get such rigor is to follow through to the bitter end the Kantian program of specifying the necessary conditions of representation itself.

So the logical bulk of the book is for Wittgenstein a necessary condition of its ethical intention. Our philosophical tradition has been defined since Plato by the primacy of reality-as-representation; and the transcendental logic of the *Tractatus,* by showing how far rationality-as-representation can go toward answering the Socratic question of human being, is in the view of its author the "final solution" (preface) of the tradition's fundamental query. The logic of the *Tractatus* puts the ethical "firmly into place by being silent about it" (letter to von Ficker); that logic is not just an accidental accretion on the book's ethical point, any more than the ethical remarks are an appendage to its philosophy of language. Both must be present in Wittgenstein's conception: the ladder of the *Tractatus* must be climbed to the higher place (TLP 6.54).

Once it is clear that the primary burden of the *Tractatus* is ethical, it becomes crucial to determine the form and content of the moral vision it seeks to communicate. Two sorts of sources may be consulted for the lineaments of that vision: first, there are the *Tractatus* itself and the surviving *Notebooks* from the period 1914–16; second, there are various biographical indications of Wittgenstein's views and their influences. While neither source is as ample or as clear as one would wish, taken together they present a fairly coherent conception of human good and evil. Consider, first, some of the biographical indications.

Others have described in some detail the culture of late nineteenth-century Vienna and the social and intellectual role of the Wittgenstein family in that city; it will not be necessary to duplicate their efforts.[19] It is sufficient here to note that Ludwig Wittgenstein was raised in a family remarkable for both its wealth and its artistic and intellectual inclinations. According to G. H. von Wright, the first philosophy Wittgenstein read seriously was Schopenhauer's *Die Welt als Wille und Vorstellung,* and in the *Notebooks* there are remarks clearly due to the influence of this early infatuation.[20] Schopenhauer's pessimism, his recognition of the necessity of suffering, his Kantian insistence on the separation of the realms of fact ("representation") and value ("will"), all these struck responsive chords in the young Wittgenstein. As will be seen later in this chapter, the elements of Schopenhauer's philosophy provided something of the form of the ethical vision of the *Tractatus;* the content, such of it as can be determined, came from other sources—in particular, from some unorthodox Christian thinkers.

Russell's letter to Lady Ottoline, quoted above, tells of Wittgenstein's dramatic discovery of Tolstoy's revision of the Gospels. This little book had, it seems, an enormous influence on his thinking; it is said that he was known among his fellow soldiers as "the man with the Gospels" because he constantly had the book with him. He is also reported to have said that the book had "saved his life."[21] (By this time two of his brothers had already committed suicide.)

The Gospel in Brief was published by Tolstoy in 1883. It is an attempt to free the message of Jesus from the "false Church interpretations" with which, he believed, it had been overlaid, and thus to restore its power to give meaning to life.[22] In *A Confession* Tolstoy had movingly recounted his own loss of faith and meaning, his strong temptations to suicide ("It was then that I, a man favoured by fortune, hid a cord from myself lest I should hang myself from the crosspiece of the partition of the room where I undressed alone every evening, and I ceased to go out shooting with a gun lest I should be tempted by so easy a way of ending my life."), and his recovery of life's meaning through a vital, if un-Orthodox, Christian faith.[23] Wittgenstein's similarity to Tolstoy's spiritual travail is striking: he is another, ostensibly "favoured by fortune," tormented by a sense of moral and spiritual despair and haunted by thoughts of suicide. And like Tolstoy he said that the Gospels had "saved his life."

What did these men see there to save them? Tolstoy believed that the "sense of the teaching" of Jesus could be expressed in twelve chapters, the meaning of which he summarized thus:

1. Man is the son of an infinite source: a son of that Father not by the flesh but by the spirit.
2. Therefore man should serve that source in spirit.
3. The life of all men has a divine origin. It alone is holy.
4. Therefore man should serve that source in the life of all men. Such is the will of the Father.
5. The service of the will of the Father of life gives life.
6. Therefore the gratification of one's will is not necessary for life.
7. Temporal life is food for the true life.
8. Therefore the true life is independent of time: it is in the present.
9. Time is an illusion of life; life in the past and in the future conceals from men the true life of the present.
10. Therefore man should strive to destroy the illusion of the temporal life of the past and future.
11. True life is in the present, common to all men and manifesting itself in love.
12. Therefore he who lives by love in the present, through the common life of all men, unites with the Father, the source and foundation of life.[24]

We shall see that several of the themes of this summary bear striking relationships to the ethical remarks of the *Notebooks* and the *Tractatus*.

Both Tolstoy and Wittgenstein agree that a radical re-visioning of self and world is necessary to a life of secure meaning; and, in spite of their very different intellectual makeups, their re-visions overlap in significant respects.

A second Christian thinker must be mentioned in connection with the content of Wittgenstein's ethical vision: Søren Kierkegaard. In his letter to Lady Ottoline, Russell mentions Kierkegaard by name (along with Angelus Silesius) as someone who is being read by the new "mystical" Wittgenstein. It has not been determined exactly what works of Kierkegaard's he had been reading before the meeting with Russell (Malcolm reports that at some point Wittgenstein had read the *Concluding Unscientific Postscript*—but found it "too deep"),[25] but it can be reasonably inferred what it was in the Danish writer that appealed to him.

Like Tolstoy and Wittgenstein, Kierkegaard had personally known despair; in his authorship he took for granted that the standard moral and spiritual certainties of Christianity, appropriated in the standard way, had lost their powers to provide a sense to life. His problem as a writer was to recover the content of the doctrines and thus to restore their capacities to challenge and to save. Also like Tolstoy, he had the conviction that the simple (though extraordinarily demanding) message of the Gospel was being distorted by the dominant ecclesiastical bodies. What is needed is to scrape away the centuries of conventional understanding so that the words of Jesus can once again be heard for what they were and are; as it is now, the various corruptions of our culture have created the *illusion* in us that we have heard, understood, and obeyed.

Kierkegaard explicitly faced, in a way Tolstoy did not, the problem of how to combat the common illusion of having *understood* the Gospel. Tolstoy, at least in *The Gospel in Brief,* apparently thought it sufficient to harmonize the writings of the four evangelists into one coherent narrative, to restate Jesus' words in slightly different terms, and then to trust those words to do their task. Kierkegaard, on the other hand, was much more pessimistic; he believed that various forces in our culture have conspired to make it next to impossible for the average person (or, at least, the average intellectual) to hear the words of the Gospel with their true intentions. Our culture is shot through with *illusion,* illusions which are so powerful that any direct statement of the Gospel will fail to penetrate them undistorted. The Gospel, Kierkegaard believed, must be heard and received in *inwardness;* it must be appropriated in an extraordinary act of will by *one individual* for himself or herself; it is subjective, that is, directed to a subject of will and passion, and it is to be received as is proper by such a subject. But our culture has lost the capacity for inwardness and subjectivity; instead it exalts objectivity and abstraction.

> My principal thought was that in our age because of the great increase in knowledge, we had forgotten what it means to exist, and what *inwardness* signifies, and that the misunderstanding between speculative philosophy and Christianity was explicable on that ground.[26]

Since the spirit of the age is antithetical to the proper appropriation of the Gospel, extraordinary means must be taken to offset the effects of the illusions and to allow the message to be heard.

> No, an illusion can never be destroyed directly, and only by indirect means can it be radically removed. If it is an illusion that all are Christians—and if there is anything to be done about it, it must be done indirectly, not by one who vociferously proclaims himself an extraordinary Christian, but by one who, better instructed, is ready to declare that he is not a Christian at all.[27]

Kierkegaard, of course, seized upon the indirect method for the destruction of the illusions that beset Christian faith in his time. The whole of his pseudonymous authorship is an attempt to communicate indirectly: it tries to preach the Gospel without proclamation, without the direct address that lends itself to being swept up into an abstract, objective way of thinking. In order that the message really be heard, the message itself is never boldly proclaimed. Instead, silence, doubt, humor, and literary artifice all combine to direct one's attention away from the obvious and to that which is never spoken, to that which lies outside the boundary of what can (at least *now*) be said: the good news. Like the author of the *Tractatus,* Kierkegaard put the real point of his efforts firmly into place by being silent about it. And as we shall see, Kierkegaardian emphases on subjectivity and on the inward flash of individual will (the "leap of faith") have counterparts in the fabric of Wittgenstein's ethical conception.

Obviously, much more could be done to make clear connections of detail between Schopenhauer, Tolstoy, Kierkegaard, and Wittgenstein; the most effective way to do this is to turn directly to the Wittgensteinian texts and to delineate the account of the ethical life found there.

IV

FOR THE author of the *Tractatus* the subject matter of ethics is significantly different from what is now commonly assumed. Most people think that the study of ethics is the concrete investigation and critique of certain modes of conduct: business ethics is an investigation of what kinds of professional behavior are right and wrong for corporation executives; medical ethics has to do with determining what is proper and improper action for doctors and nurses; and so forth. Philosophers, on the other hand, conceive ethics as the abstract and theoretical determination of the principles that underlie modes of conduct, along with the examination of the concepts and arguments alleged to justify or undermine those principles. For both groups, philosophers and non-philosophers, problems of conduct form the basic matter of ethical thinking. Wittgenstein did not exclude problems of conduct from the scope of ethics, of course; but he conceived the true center of ethical interest to be elsewhere. In its most fundamental signification, ethics is the investigation of "the meaning of the world," a meaning that is immediately perceived by us to be "problematic." [28] For Wittgenstein the real matter of ethics is indistinguishable from considerations usually deemed religious; both religion and ethics have to do with discovering the fundamental sense of the world and of life, a sense without which human existence is insupportable. Issues of conduct, the traditional province of ethics, clearly may have some connection with the discovery of the meaning of the world and the resolution of its problematic character, but the latter concerns take clear precedence in Wittgenstein's conception. Only when the world's true meaning is grasped and despair is overcome can one hope to know how to live in that world. That is (at least part of) the reason he writes:

> Ethics does not treat of the world. Ethics must be a condition of the world, like logic. [29]

It is useful to begin an account of the ethical vision of the early Wittgenstein by examining a remarkable notebook entry of 11 June 1916. Most of the fundamental ethical themes of the *Tractatus* are arranged there like the bare bones of a skeleton; in the six months that follow this summary, the *Notebooks* entries reveal a process of expansion and gradual elucidation. By the time the *Tractatus* was put together the skeleton had become—at least for Wittgenstein himself—a living, breathing person. Here is the entry itself.

11.vi.16

What do I know about God and the purpose of life?
I know that the world exists.
That I am placed in it like my eye in its visual field.
That something about it is problematic, which we will call its meaning.
That this meaning does not lie in it but outside it.
That life is the world.
That my will penetrates the world.
That my will is good or evil.
Therefore that good or evil are somehow connected with the meaning of the world.
The meaning of life, i.e., the meaning of the world, we can call God.
And connect with this the comparison of God to a father.
To pray is to think about the meaning of life.
I cannot bend the happenings of the world to my will: I am completely powerless.
I can only make myself independent of the world—and so in a certain sense master it—by renouncing any influence on happenings. (NB, pp. 72–73)

Our analysis of this programmatic statement of Wittgenstein's ethics must start with his conception of the self. At 5.641 of the *Tractatus* one reads:

The philosophical self is not the human being, not the human body, or the human soul, with which psychology deals, but rather the metaphysical subject, the limit of the world—not part of it.

Ordinarily, of course, one thinks of oneself as a part of the world: I am here, in this place at this time, writing these words; I am *in* the world. Wittgenstein thinks otherwise; to conceive of oneself as *in* the world is necessarily to conceive of oneself as some sort of object, either physical ("body") or psychological ("soul"). And, "The I is not an object" (NB, p. 80). There must, therefore, be some way of conceiving the self nonobjectively.

> Thus there really is a sense in which philosophy can talk about the self in a non-psychological way. What brings the self into philosophy is the fact that 'the world is my world'. (TLP 5.641)

The nonobjective self which makes the world "my world" is not a *part* of that world, of course.

> 5.632   The subject does not belong to the world: rather, it is a limit of the world.
> 5.633   Where *in* the world is a metaphysical subject to be found?
> You will say that this is exactly like the case of the eye and the visual field. But really you do *not* see the eye.
> And nothing *in the visual field* allows you to infer that it is seen by an eye.

In the 11 June 1916 notebook entry he says "I am placed in the world like my eye in its visual field." That is, I am not *in* the world at all; I am in the world's boundary.

Why cannot the self be considered a part of the world? Wittgenstein's reasoning seems to turn upon his conviction, itself predicated on his account of the elementary proposition, that there is no a priori order among things (5.634). The world is the totality of existing states of affairs (2.04), and:

> 2.061   States of affairs are independent of one another.
> 2.062   From the existence or non-existence of one state of affairs it is impossible to infer the existence or non-existence of another.

If, *ex hypothesi,* the self were a part of the world—if, so to speak, the eye were inescapably a part of its own visual field—there would be in the world an a priori order; this would destroy the independence of all states of affairs. Whatever else the self is for Wittgenstein, it first of all is the center of consciousness, the locus of representation; and the world is *my* world (5.62, 5.641), the world that the self represents to itself. Without the representing self, there would be no world. "I am my world" (5.63). (This Wittgensteinian "solipsism" will be examined in more detail below.) The world is composed of states of affairs; if the self were a part of the world it would therefore be a state of affairs, or a set of them. So if the self were a part of the world, i.e. a state of affairs, then the existence of all the other states of affairs would depend upon *that* state of affairs, thus giving the world an a priori order and destroying the independence of states of affairs. No longer would it be the case that "Whatever we can describe at all can be other than it is" (TLP 5.632).

But if the self cannot be a part of the world, it likewise cannot be doubted that there is indeed a self.

The world is *my* world: this shows itself in the fact that the limits of *language* (the only language I understand) mean the limits of *my* world. (TLP 5.62).[30]

To put the issue somewhat crudely, there is necessarily a "point" of consciousness from which the world is viewed. (Of course, as we have just seen, this "point" of consciousness cannot be a *part* of the world.) Any set of propositions that completely and truly describes the states of affairs that compose the world must issue from *somewhere:* that is, the senses of these propositions must be "thought out" by someone in order that the propositional signs have projective relations to the world (cf. TLP 3.11, 3.12). The world revealed in propositions is always my world, for these are always *my* propositions that picture it. The world thus *shows itself* to be my world. I am the world's necessary limit.

There is another important sense in which for Wittgenstein "the world is *my* world." The world is my world, he believes, in the sense that it is "penetrated" by *my will* (NB, p. 73).

The world is *given* to me, i.e., my will enters into the world completely from outside as into something that is already there. (NB, p. 74)

The nature of this world-penetrating will becomes a great puzzle for Wittgenstein, as will be seen in the detailed discussion below; but it is important to note at the outset this connection between the world as irreducibly mine and the will, since it is the will that is fundamentally the bearer of good and evil (NB, p. 76).

Wittgenstein's account of the metaphysical subject as the limit of the world, not a part of it, has, as he himself noticed, strong affinities to philosophical solipsism. Solipsism is a congeries of different philosophical doctrines; perhaps it is best for our expository purposes to focus attention on an exemplary instance of the solipsist. In the middle of the Second Meditation, having recognized the certainty of his own existence and having at the same time divined his essential nature as a *res cogitans,* Descartes is a classical solipsist. Certain only of his own existence as a thinking thing, as a center of consciousness, he knows everything else only as modifications of that consciousness. The world of independently existing things—rocks, birds, persons—has become the world of ideas, of *my* ideas (thinks Descartes); the self—the "I"— is the only substance known to exist.

Characteristically, the *Tractatus* approaches solipsism by reflecting on the nature of language.

> 5.6   *The limits of my language* mean the limits of the world.
>
>   . . .
>
> 5.62   This remark provides the key to the problem, how much truth there is in solipsism. For what the solipsist means is quite correct; only it cannot be *said,* but shows itself. The world is my world; this shows itself in the fact that the limits of *language* (of the only language I understand) mean the limits of *my* world.

Obviously, the picture theory will not allow traditional solipsism to be formulated in meaningful propositions; it is one of those philosophical problems that gets discussed only because "the logic of our language is misunderstood" (preface). Nevertheless, what the solipsist *intends* by his nonsensical doctrine shows itself in the world's necessarily being *my* world, and in the fact that the language in which the world is pictured is necessarily *my* language ("the only language I understand"). The self, the "I," is the necessary condition of the world. Without the re-presenting self, without that "I" which makes for itself pictures of facts, there would be no facts in logical space, i.e. no world (1.13; 2.11). Any visual field must have an eye, even if it can never see itself and thus remains only an invisible *limit* to what is seen. And this invisible seeing eye must be *single*.

But this Wittgensteinian solipsism has some interesting and radically untraditional consequences:

5.631   There is no such thing as the subject that thinks or entertains ideas.

If I wrote a book called *The World as I Found It,* I should have to include a report on my body, and should have to say which parts were subordinate to my will, and which were not, etc., this being a method of isolating the subject, or rather of showing that in an important sense there is no subject; for it alone could *not* be mentioned in that book. —

5.64   Here it can be seen that solipsism, when its implications are followed out strictly, coincides with pure realism. The self of solipsism shrinks to a point without extension, and there remains the reality co-ordinated with it.

Solipsism and realism, perhaps because the doctrines have most often arisen in epistemological contexts, have usually appeared to be competitors for the philosopher's allegiance. But the kind of solipsism that shows itself in the doctrines of the *Tractatus* coincides with its erstwhile alternative. Realism is incorporated in the book *The World as I Found It:* any language—any totality of propositions—is an attempt to write that book. Any Tractarian language is a world-story, complete or incomplete, accurate or inaccurate. And the world I describe is *given* me: I do not create it; it is already there to be described (NB, p. 74). But the title of that book of Realism must always be the same; it must never fail to indicate that the world that is given is also the world found and depicted by *me*. "The world is *my* world" (TLP 5.62), and that is what the solipsist meant to say all along. Of course, the philosophical self that shows itself in the title can never appear in the book itself; it is not a part of the world. In Wittgenstein's brand of solipsism, the self is not some substantial entity that knows itself as a *res cogitans* ("the subject that thinks or entertains ideas"), as in Descartes. The metaphysical subject of the *Tractatus* can never catch itself in its own vision any more than the eye can see itself in its visual field; the self is always jumping back behind itself, never an object of its own scrutiny, never a part of the world. It is never, as in Descartes, the substantial center of the world (of its ideas), known to itself as that center. Rather, as Wittgenstein says, it shrinks to an "extensionless point"—a mere boundary to experience—and the reality (independent and alterable states of affairs) remains.[31]

So much for an account of the metaphysical subject operating in the ethical vision of the *Tractatus;* it is now time to connect the philosophical self with good, evil, and the meaning of the world. As has been shown, Wittgenstein wanted to reject the substantial spectator self of the post-Cartesian philosophical tradition: "There is no such thing as the subject that thinks or entertains ideas" (TLP 5.631). Nevertheless, the philosophical self—the limit of the world—is in its own way quite real. So, what is the nature of this necessary metaphysical subject? If the self is not a mere spectator, what is he? The answer which Wittgenstein gave to this question, an answer profoundly influenced by his reading of Schopenhauer, is intimated in the notebook entry of 11 June 1916: "My will penetrates the world." Two months later he expanded his insight:

> The thinking subject is surely mere illusion. But the willing subject exists.
> If the will did not exist, neither would there be that centre of the world, which we call the I, and which is the bearer of ethics. (NB, p. 80)

The philosophical self is the will, the will which penetrates the "problematic" world and which (in part) makes it *my* world. But how can this be reconciled with the statement later in the 11 June 1916 entry: "I cannot bend the happenings of the world to my will: I am completely powerless"? What sense does it make to identify the metaphysical subject with the will if that will is "completely powerless"? How could a "powerless" will be a *will* at all, much less "the centre of the world" which is also "the bearer of ethics"?

The notebook entry that immediately follows the long summary statement of 11 June 1916 begins:

> The world is independent of my will.
> Even if everything we want were to happen, this would still only be, so to speak, a grace of fate, for what would guarantee

it is not any logical connexion between will and world, and we could not in turn will the supposed physical connexion. (NB, p. 73)

These sentences, with only minor changes, appear as 6.373 and 6.734 of the *Tractatus*. Ordinarily a philosopher thinks of the will as a faculty of *agency,* effecting some sort of "necessary" connection between someone's desires and some event in the world. If, for example, I want to reach a jar of peanut butter high on the pantry shelf, the traditional account has it that I *will* my arm to rise and my fingers to grasp, and, lo, I have the jar in my hand. (I do, that is, if nothing goes wrong.) The will—my act of willing—translates (some of) my desires into action. It can seem to us, moreover, that the will-established connection between my wanting the peanut butter and my having the jar in my hand must be a "necessary" connection of some kind; after all, it does not seem to me an *accident* (a "grace of fate") that I end up with my fingers around the jar. And since my holding the jar is an event "in the world," the will thus quite naturally appears to be that faculty which, through the medium of the body, throws up a causal bridge between the desires, intentions, etc., of the subject and the physical states of affairs comprising reality.

Two problems are apparent to Wittgenstein in this picture of will-as-agency. First, the causal "necessity" attaching to this concept of the will seems nonsensical to him. Given the nature of the elementary proposition as a concatenation of names for simple objects, given the world as comprised of states of affairs consisting of constellations of these simple objects, and given the independence of these propositions, or states of affairs, there can be no necessary connection between the occurrence of one state of affairs and the occurrence of another.

6.37   There is no compulsion making one thing happen because another has happened. The only necessity that exists is *logical* necessity.[32]

Obviously, there is no *logically* necessary connection (in the *Tractatus* sense) between my wanting a peanut butter sandwich and my hand taking the jar down off the shelf; thus there is no power in my will as it is ordinarily conceived (i.e., as effecting "necessary," nonaccidental, connections between events). The only possible connections between

my wanting the peanut butter and my subsequent handling of the jar
are purely accidental, Humean ones.

Moreover, the common account of will-as-agency makes a particular body, which I call *my body,* the intermediary between will and the
world: I will that *my arm* rise, that *my fingers* grasp, to get the jar of
peanut butter off the shelf. But this is unacceptable to Wittgenstein.

> For the consideration of willing makes it look as if one part
> of the world were closer to me than another (which would be
> intolerable). (NB, p. 88)

If "my" body—particular, contingent states of affairs—is "closer" to
me than other parts of the world, that makes me seem somehow a *part*
(even if only a *ghostly* part) of the world. Will-as-agency is inconsistent with the Tractarian notion that the philosophical self is the *limit* of
the world—all the world, not just some particular part of it.

So on both these grounds, the impossibility of causal "necessity"
and the incoherence of "my" body as intermediary, the standard philosophical conception of the will is faulty. Thus it is that for Wittgenstein
the world is independent of my "will": the ordinary conception of the
causally efficacious will, will-as-agency, is nonsense.

But if the old conception of the will has got to go, what *is* the will
that helps to make the world *my* world? Many of the most obscure
notebook entries wrestle with this question. It was clear to Wittgenstein from early on that the will is the essential ethical notion: "I will
call 'will' first and foremost the bearer of good and evil" (NB, p. 76).
There still remained, however, the problem of how good and evil could
have any intelligible connection to a will that was "completely powerless" to effect causal change. Was the key to identify goodness with the
renunciation of will in the old causal sense? Was Wittgenstein being
led into a kind of latter-day Spinozism which venerated *acquiescence*
to whatever happens as a "grace of fate"? The following notebook entry (29 July 1916) shows both his temptations and his resistance:

> For it is a fact of logic that wanting does not stand in any
> logical connexion with its own fulfillment. And it is also clear
> that the world of the happy man is a *different* world from the
> world of the unhappy.
> Is seeing an activity?
> Is it possible to will good, to will evil, and not to will?

Is only he happy who does *not* will?

"To love one's neighbor" means to will!

But can one want and yet not be unhappy if the want does not attain fulfillment? (And this possibility always exists.)

Is it, according to the common conceptions, good to want *nothing* for one's neighbor, neither good nor evil?

And yet in a certain sense it seems that not wanting is the only good.

Here I am still making crude mistakes! No doubt of that! (NB, pp. 77–78)

One can see Wittgenstein tempted to identify the good life with the renunciation of desire ("not wanting is the only good"), a Schopenhauerian influence; yet he never finally succumbs. " 'To love one's neighbor' means to will!" The Christian influence of Tolstoy, calling him to a life of active love of the least fortunate of men, is stronger than the advice of Schopenhauer to turn away from wanting any alteration in the necessary fabric of things. Moreover, as the above *Notebooks* entry remarks, the passive acceptance of not-willing does not seem to make sense of a fundamental datum of moral phenomenology: "The world of the happy is a different world from that of the unhappy." A world totally without willing (of some sort) would be a world *without ethics,* rather than the world of the happy person (NB, p. 77). And yet, how could a will without causal power—as ours is—ever be a happy will? How could it be a *will* at all, happy or unhappy? It seems that by default one is brought back to a notion of will as causally efficacious, in spite of its difficulties.

Wittgenstein resolves these puzzles to his own satisfaction by coming to an alternative conception of the will as the bearer of good and evil, an account in which the will is not identified with a causal faculty of agency. Here are the crucial remarks:

It is clear, so to speak, that we need a foothold for the will in the world.

The will is an *attitude* of the subject to the world. (NB, p. 87; my emphasis)

Will-as-agency has been dismissed; will-as-attitude has taken its place.[33]

The *Notebooks* offer no substantial account of will-as-attitude, probably because no such conception can be made coherent, especially within the boundaries he has already established. He does try in a few remarks to make clear the sense in which his attitudinal protoconception of the will is, while not the idea of a causal faculty, still connected to action:

> The act of will is not the cause of the action but is the action itself. (NB, p. 87)
>
> . . .
>
> The fact that I will an action consists in my performing the action, not in my doing something else which causes the action. (NB, p. 88)

But he is hampered here by his conception of the self as mere limit to the world. That picture of the self makes any connection to the happenings of the world mysterious and merely accidental; there is no room for giving a coherent sense to the notion of *performing* an action. As much as he wishes to reject the substantial spectator subject to traditional solipsism and to identify the self with will instead, his own fundamental assumptions about the nature of thought and language offer no foothold to his protoconception. Like it or not, given his account of the elementary proposition and the atomism that it entails, he is forced back to the self conceived as world-limiting eye; and in that conception will becomes merely a mode of that eye's vision: an "attitude." The good will becomes, as we shall see in more detail later, a way to "see the world aright" (TLP 6.54). Will becomes a way to view the world; it is an affective perspective toward whatever is there to be seen. It has nothing to do with altering the actual structure of what is viewed.

So far, then, Wittgenstein has rejected the traditional account of the philosophical self and has tried to substitute a conception of the self as willing subject instead. This willing subject is, of course, the *limit* of the world, not *part* of it, as the eye is the limit of the visual field. Further, he has attempted to intimate a picture of will-as-attitude to substitute for the ordinary philosophical picture of will-as-agency. Will has become, not a faculty of agency, but a mode of the self's vision of the world, an attitude, happy or unhappy, toward that world represented in the self's propositions. With these intellectual movements completed, he was ready to connect his vision of good and evil to the fabric of the *Tractatus*.

Because the philosophical self is in no way a part of the world and because language always pictures the world, "It is impossible to speak about the will in so far as it is the subject of ethical attributes" (TLP 6.423). And because the will (understood as attitude, as a mode of "vision") is powerless to affect the world, the ethical attributes of that will are completely internal.

> 6.43   If the good or bad exercise of the will does not alter the world, it can only alter the limits of the world, not the facts—not what can be expressed by means of language.
>
> In short, the effect must be that it becomes an altogether different world. It must, so to speak, wax and wane as a whole.
>
> The world of the happy man is a different one from that of the unhappy man.

In the summary notebook entry of 11 June 1916, Wittgenstein had said that the meaning of the world—the center of ethical interest—is problematic, that the meaning of the world must lie outside the world, and that through the will the notions of good and evil are connected to the world of facts. What is it that lies outside the world? Only the philosophical self, the willing subject that is the limit of the world. So the meaning of the world, the resolution of its problematic aspect, lies in the self whose world it is. As 6.49 puts it, only the limits of the world—the philosophical self—can be altered by willing. The facts cannot be changed by the self (the causally efficacious will of philosophical theory is superstition); but the attitude of the self to those facts is somehow within the self's power. The sense of the world is determined by the will of the self. Good willing resolves the world's problematic aspect; bad willing leaves it untouched.

At 6.43 Wittgenstein further says that the effect of good or bad willing must be that the world becomes an altogether different one: "It must, so to speak, wax and wane as a whole." There is no possibility that a *part* of the world could become happy while some other part remained problematic. Since the key to resolving the unhappy world into the happy lies in the self which is the boundary of the *whole* world, the whole world must be altered with the self's alteration toward good willing. "The world of the happy man is a different one from that of the unhappy man" (6.43). The *whole world* is different—is viewed differently—as a result of good willing.

But what *is* the good willing that gives the world a meaning that is not problematic? What is its nature? By the strict canons of the *Tractatus* there is, obviously, no answer to this question.

> 6.421   It is clear that ethics cannot be put into words. Ethics is transcendental. (Ethics and aesthetics are one and the same.)

Only that which occurs in the world can be pictured in propositions; since the willing subject is not a part of the world, nothing that has to do with that subject can be captured in language. Thus ethics must be left to silence. In the *Notebooks,* which were not intended for publication, Wittgenstein is not quite so reticent. There one can see his struggles to understand the process by which, by changing one's will, one can change the meaning-aspect of the world. Much of his thought has distinct Stoic and Spinozistic themes:

> In order to live happily I must be in agreement with the world. And that is what "being happy" *means.* (NB, p. 75)

But what brings this sense of agreement?

> How can man be happy at all, since he cannot ward off the misery of this world?
> Through the life of knowledge.
>
> . . .
>
> The life of knowledge is the life that is happy in spite of the misery of the world.
> The only life that is happy is the life that can renounce the amenities of the world.
> To it the amenities of the world are so many graces of fate.
> (NB, p. 81)

This sounds very much like Spinoza: once one has recognized one's inability to effect alteration in the natural flow of things (once one has reached "the life of knowledge"), one resigns oneself to bear with equanimity whatever it is that fate puts in one's way.

There are other marks of good willing mentioned in the *Notebooks,* ones which probably owe more to the influence of Tolstoy than to that of anyone else. The profound impact on Wittgenstein of *The Gospel in*

Brief has already been mentioned, and Tolstoy's twelve-statement summary of the true meaning of the Gospel was set out.[34] His sixth statement in that summary is: "Therefore the gratification of one's will is not necessary for life." The Wittgenstein of the *Notebooks* and the *Tractatus* would doubtless agree, even if for somewhat different reasons. Since the world is independent of my will (i.e., independent of any causal connection to the metaphysical subject), and since the problematic aspect of the world's meaning can yet somehow be overcome by me, the gratification of my "will" (i.e., the gratification of my wants and wishes) is irrelevant to that conquest. A change in my attitude toward the world—a movement from bad to good willing—does not depend on anything that happens within the world; it depends only on me. "How things are in the world is a matter of complete indifference for what is higher" (TLP 6.432). There is an even more apparent Tolstoyan influence in Wittgenstein's insistence on the importance of life in the present, an insistence found in this *Notebooks* passage.

> A man who is happy must have no fear. Not even in the face of death.
> Only a man who lives not in time but in the present is happy.
> For life in the present there is no death. (NB, pp. 74–75)

According to Tolstoy, the Gospel claimed that the temporal life lived by most—i.e., the life that takes account of the glories and burdens of the past or the hopes and fears of the future—must be only "food" for the true life. "Therefore the true life is independent of time: it is in the present. Time is an illusion of life; life in the past and future conceals from men the true life of the present."[35] The true life in the present manifests itself in love and is common to all men.[36] To live this life is to unite oneself with the infinite source of all life, thus removing any fear of death. So too Wittgenstein:

> If we take eternity to mean not infinite temporal duration but timelessness, then eternal life belongs to those who live in the present. (TLP 6.4311)

In the *Tractatus* the nature of the good willing that gives a true sense to the world is passed over in (almost total) silence: "Propositions can express nothing that is higher" (6.42). Nevertheless, some things are said:

6.432   How things are in the world is a matter of complete indifference for what is higher. God does not reveal himself *in* the world.

. . .

6.52   We feel that even when *all possible* scientific questions have been answered, the problems of life remain completely untouched. Of course, there are no questions left, and this itself is the answer.

6.521   The solution of the problem of life is seen in the vanishing of the problem.

(Is this not the reason why those who have found after a long period of doubt that the sense of life became clear to them have been unable to say what constituted that sense?)

6.522   There are, indeed, things that cannot be put into words. They *show themselves*. They are what is mystical.

Nothing substantial can be said about the way the world acquires meaning; all one can say, as a result of noting the essential nature of language revealed in the perspicuous Tractarian account, is that this accession of meaning (cf. NB, p. 73) has nothing at all to do with the "scientific" questions and answers that can be formulated in propositions.

At this point *the mystical* (*das Mystische*) plays its crucial role in the *Tractatus*. The things that show themselves and thus make clear the sense of life that had been obscure—those belong to *das Mystische*.

6.44   It is not *how* things are in the world that is mystical, but *that* it exists.

6.45   To view the world *sub specie aeterni* is to view it as a whole—a limited whole.

Feeling the world as a limited whole—it is this that is mystical.

There is an important connection in Wittgenstein's mind between feeling the world as a limited whole and seeing the sense of that world. That connection is, obviously, the philosophical self, as conceived in the *Tractatus*. To feel the world as a limited whole it is necessary first to feel its limit, i.e., to be aware of *oneself* as that limit of the world. It is to be aware of the "godhead" of the "independent I" (NB, p. 74). And this awareness brings the further insight (at the level of something like *feeling* now) that the world is *my* world; the sense of the world, which must lie outside it, must therefore lie in the self whose world it is. That the world exists at all is seen to be inseparable from the necessity that it be *my* world—this feeling of necessary interpenetration of self and world is a feature of *das Mystische*.

> 5.63   I am my world. (The microcosm.)

Once this insight is combined with the notion of the philosophical self as the willing subject, it is possible that by good willing "one see the world aright" (TLP 6.54). Once one has come to see that as a self one is only will, i.e., only an attitude toward what is factually given as a grace of fate, then it becomes possible for one's attitude toward the "given" world to change. The world of the unhappy man can become the completely different world of the happy man. But this accession of meaning cannot occur until one has gained the particular self-consciousness furnished by the *Tractatus*. Until one's attention has been directed to oneself as the willing self at the limit of one's world, a gesture accomplished by the perspicuous symbolism of Tractarian language, it is impossible for good willing to occur. Only then can the sense of life show itself to the philosopher; only then can the world-transforming import of *das Mystische* be felt. What cannot be said, mystically shows itself.

It is notorious that the philosophical propositions of the *Tractatus* do not meet the stringent conditions for meaningfulness that they themselves set out:

> 6.54   My propositions serve as elucidations in the following way: Anyone who understands me eventually recognizes them as nonsensical, when he has used them—as steps—to climb beyond them. (He must, so to speak, throw away the ladder after he has climbed up it.)
>
>   He must transcend these propositions, and then he will see the world aright.

Although Wittgenstein does not use 'show' or its cognates in this passage, he might well have done so. There is something to be gained from understanding the *Tractatus*, even if the benefit of that understanding cannot be captured in a picture-theory-licensed proposition. One uses the propositions of the book to climb beyond them. Significantly, Wittgenstein's metaphor for the book as a whole is a ladder, not a picture. One *uses* the book to gain a new standing; the book does not represent.

> 4.112 Philosophy aims at the logical clarification of thoughts.
> Philosophy is not a body of doctrine but an activity.
> A philosophical work consists primarily of elucidations.
> Philosophy does not result in 'philosophical propositions,' but in the clarification of propositions.
> Without philosophy thoughts are, as it were, cloudy and indistinct: its task is to make them clear and give them sharp boundaries.

Philosophical (hence ethical) enlightenment does not consist in possessing a *statable, true theory* of language or of life. Since language, thought, and world are coextensive, to sharpen the boundaries of thoughts (which are propositions about the world) is at the same time inevitably to highlight the philosophical self which is the boundary of that world pictured in thought. Philosophy, by making the boundaries of the thought-world sharp and distinct, inevitably directs our attention beyond that world to the self for which it is "problematic" and in whose power the resolution of that problematic aspect rests. All philosophy is in this sense a branch of ethics. The progress of the *Tractatus* is intended to be the gradual but inexorable direction of one's attention to that which lies beyond the world, the self—to see and feel the world as a limited whole, *sub specie aeterni:* the advent of *das Mystische*. All the remarks of philosophy, including the sentences of the *Tractatus,* fall into the class of those things that (try to) say what must be shown.

V

AT THE beginning of section three of this chapter I claimed that understanding the real significance of the distinction between showing and saying depended upon seeing its connection to the picture of rationality functioning in the *Tractatus*. Having gotten a somewhat firmer grasp on the main ethical conceptions of the *Tractatus*, it is now time to return to the doctrine of showing and draw together the somewhat frayed threads of our discussion.

The form of Wittgenstein's early ethical vision is now clear: the task of ethics is the restoration of meaning to my problematic world, a meaning that lies outside that world, in the philosophical self which is my world's limit. This self is the willing subject; and good willing, which is to adopt a certain attitude toward the world, changes the problematic world into the world of the happy man. To have a happy world is essentially connected to feeling the world as a limited whole; the problems of life can then disappear and the sense of life can come clear. This sense cannot be talked about, nor can it be said what exactly is the nature of good willing that makes it clear. These things belong to the realm of *das Mystische:* they *show* themselves. The *Tractatus,* by demonstrating clearly what can and cannot be said, makes it clear how impotent thought (language) is when it comes to the really important things in life. Silence, the silence in which *das Mystische* shows itself, is the paradigmatic response of the enlightened philosopher who has kicked away the ladder of philosophy after he has climbed up it.

The doctrine of showing is obviously an essential component in this conception: it is the way the unsayable vouchsafes itself to the subject. We have so far determined the contexts in which the doctrine of showing is invoked; we have said something about its origins and about the use to which it is put in the book.[37] But these determinations still have left mysterious the "mechanisms," so to speak, of showing. What is it for something to be shown? And what, if anything, is the connection of ethical showing to the showing that occurs in strictly logical contexts?

The *Tractatus* gives no explicit answer to these questions. Nevertheless, answers can be extracted from the book's subtext. An important part of that subtext is, as we have seen, a certain picture of rationality, a picture of what thought is, and what it can and cannot do. In summary, this intellectualist conception of rationality insists that thought and language are mutually coextensive realms: "A thought is a proposition with a sense" (TLP 4). Since, according to the picture theory, a proposition can do nothing more than depict the possibility of the existence of a contingent state of affairs consisting of a constellation of objects, the utter limit of thought's power is the representation of reality. Thought is ultimately and finally representational; all it can do is picture, truly or falsely, the way things contingently are.

This intellectualist picture of rationality helps to make plausible a passive conception of the subject. The self becomes a camera; or, rather, in Wittgenstein's metaphor it becomes the seeing eye, viewing its world spread out before it, representing this world to itself. It is not an accident that this powerful picture of the self recommended itself to Wittgenstein: influenced by his reading of Schopenhauer, the comparison of the self to the eye appears in the *Notebooks* entry of 11 June 1916 and remains a crucial part of the *Tractatus* (see 5.633, for example). According to this historically honored conception, thought is the activity of a spectator.

Obviously, if thought can reach no further than the representation of contingent reality, then ethics, which has to do with discovering the noncontingent *meaning* of those contingencies, has nothing to do with thought. And with that realization the picture of rationality-as-representation begins to chafe a bit. Here one can begin to see something of the profound tension at the heart of the *Tractatus:* on the one hand, Wittgenstein is committed in theory to rationality-as-representation; on the other, he cannot live with some of the most central consequences of that commitment. Although the intellectualist picture of the self as the passsive seeing eye is enormously attractive, and squares neatly with the enticing Tractarian account of thought and language, he knows too that the world is penetrated by *will;* the world is always happy or unhappy, meaningful or senseless for the eye which views it. The "I" yearns for the happy world, for the life whose sense is not problematic. How can the will, the bearer of ethical attributes, be accommodated in the intellectualist account? The yearning will must obviously be something entirely different from representational thought, but what? It is not some faculty of causal agency; in that sense, the world is utterly independent of my will. So in Wittgenstein's thinking the will must itself become a mode of the spectator self's "vision"; it must be some sort of affective attitude toward the world that is given it, an attitude that identifies the self with certain actions and which somehow makes it possible for the unhappy, "problematic" world to become the happy, meaningful one. Ethics is a matter of will, not of thought—even if the willing involved is nothing more than a mysterious movement within the willing (attitudinal) self.

This notion of will as a mode of the self's "vision" helps to explain

Wittgenstein's frequent identifications of ethics and aesthetics (TLP 6.421; NB, pp. 77, 86, 83). Just as aesthetic perusal of an object is defined by a certain way of viewing it (what Wittgenstein calls seeing it *sub specie aeternitatis*), so also is the ethical stance a way of viewing the world *sub specie aeternitatis* ("as a limited whole") (NB, p. 83). Both ethics and aesthetics are conditions of the world; the aspect of the world—whether ethical or aesthetic—is conditioned by the self, which is its necessary limit. The will, which is the bearer of good and evil, is thus the condition of the self, a way of looking at the world spread out before one; will, like aesthetic contemplation, becomes a passive mode of vision, not an active principle of change.

But a huge mystery remains. How is it that bad willing (the unhappy world) becomes good willing (the happy world)? One's attitude toward the world changes, but how and why? What makes the change possible? One might think that Wittgenstein would have to believe that the change is utterly capricious: after all, if will has absolutely nothing to do with thought (rationality, language, knowledge), then any change of will must be purely arbitrary and accidental, mustn't it? It happens because it happens; the change is in no way explicable by reference to any sort of *insight*. Nothing that belongs to the realm of thought can have anything to do with an alteration of the will.

But this is *not* Wittgenstein's view, in fact. On the contrary, he believes that what can be said can also serve to communicate an ethically powerful (even if itself unsayable) insight. In a letter to his friend Paul Engelmann, who had sent him a poem by Uhland, he wrote:

> The poem by Uhland is really magnificent. And this is how it is: if only you do not try to utter what is unutterable then *nothing* gets lost. But the unutterable will be—unutterably—*contained* in what has been uttered.[38]

Obviously, there is no way directly to say what cannot be said. But there are things that can be said which will "contain" the unsayable: to say these things is somehow to communicate what is in itself unsayable. A poem is an example of this phenomenon: it can communicate some ineffable truth about life while talking about the growth of a sprig into a hawthorn bush.[39] A poem may alter one's whole view of the world, making happy what was unhappy; and it is no *accident* that the poem makes the change possible. Perhaps without the poem the alteration would never have occurred. When Wittgenstein said that Tolstoy's book on the Gospels had saved his life, he was affirming a mysterious but real connection between reading that book and the alteration of his sensibilities. By reading one of Jesus' stories—frequently just a description of a familiar empirical phenomenon, like a storm washing away a house built on sand, to which description is appended an injunction like "He who hath ears to hear, let him hear"—one's attitude toward one's world can be radically changed. So a change from bad to good willing is not merely capricious; rather, it is typically mediated through something that is explicitly and legitimately said.

It is just here that the doctrine of showing comes into play in ethics. What is said can be the vehicle for *showing* something that is unsayable. What is shown in ethics is *das Mystische,* and it is this which makes possible the good will that solves the problems of life. *In ethics the doctrine of showing is fundamentally Wittgenstein's attempt to connect the will to thought;* it is his attempt to make explicable the way in which what can be said (thought, known, represented) can illuminate what cannot.

Thus we see in another way how closely the doctrine of showing is bound up with the picture of rationality-as-representation, for it is that intellectualist conception that makes it seem impossible directly to connect thought and will. Thought has as its only *telos* the representation of what is there, the picturing of facts. How can thought—the eye which blankly sees—have anything to do with an attitude of happiness or unhappiness to what is seen? It was clear to Wittgenstein, however, that the world could change its meaning-aspect for a self; in his own life there had been the overcoming of despair, the movement from the unhappy world to the happy. And it was equally clear to him that this movement of his was not just an accidental, capricious incident; it was connected to his reading of (*inter alia*) *The Gospel in Brief,* the book that had saved his life. Something had been given him in that book; he had been changed, and so had his world. He had moved (at least for a while) from bad willing to good. But how, given his philosophical conclusions, could he make sense of that movement? How could anything which he *read*—something that must, it seems, belong to the realm of language-thought—the picturing of contingent states of affairs—have anything to do with the happy life of the good will? To put it in Socratic terms, how could knowledge have any connection to virtuous action? According to the *Tractatus,* text and subtext, these questions have no legitimate answers: they are nonsense. But for Wittgenstein himself, the issue couldn't be left there, in spite of his own admonitions to remain silent. The doctrine of showing, by means of which the ineffable could be communicated "indirectly" (think of Kierkegaard), was his bridge built to span the chasm between the will and thought.

According to this doctrine, there are things which can be attended to by us that cannot be captured in representational propositions. When a logically perspicuous symbolism of the *Tractatus* variety shows one the sense of a certain proposition, that sense is then an object of one's attention—even though the sense itself cannot be represented in a proposition. When a poem or a parable shows one the sense of life, that sense also is an object of one's attention. Ordinarily, one would not hesitate to say that the sense of a proposition or the sense of life is something that one could *learn* under the proper circumstances, and this perfectly ordinary way of speaking exhibits a natural connection between what is shown and what is known. All the members of the class of Tractarian things that are shown are, in our ordinary ways of thinking and speaking, actual or possible items of *knowledge*.[40] Take the propositions of logic, for example. The proposition '$p \vee \sim p$' cannot be a piece of vicious nonsense because, as we would ordinarily say, we know '$p \vee \sim p$' to be true. The same point holds for the sense of a proposition, or its logical form. We can know, on occasion, what the sense of a given proposition is; and we also can know what its logical form is. (To be able to learn, and thus to know, the logical form of a proposition is a necessary condition for speaking and understanding a language.) But since these are items of knowledge (ordinarily speaking) that cannot have been captured in Tractarian propositions, our knowledge must have been gained in another way, i.e., it must have been *shown* us.

At this point there can arise with great persuasive force a certain picture of what it is to know something. The picture is roughly and partially this: to know something is to stand in a certain relation to a particular brute fact, specifically the relation of giving justifiably wholehearted assent—tacit or explicit—to the proposition that models that fact. Such an epistemology is the product of rationality-as-representation, of course, and in the *Tractatus* Wittgenstein succumbs to its charm. Given this picture, talk about learning or knowing something that is not capturable in a proposition is sure to seem muddled. Wittgenstein felt the weight of this ostensible muddle, so he wanted to draw down tightly the limits of language and of thought: rationality-as-representation. But he was unable to go the full distance with the positivist and dismiss as vicious nonsense and illusion all nonpropositional "knowledge." Thus the doctrine of showing.

But of course there is no reason to succumb to a caricature of knowledge like the one sketched above. Only when one nourishes oneself with a very one-sided diet of examples is one tempted to insist that all one knows must be capable of being modeled in a proposition. There is a very familiar kind of knowledge that cannot be completely exhibited in propositions; it is *practical* knowledge, knowledge of how to do something. Knowing how to do something is *an ability to do something intelligently,* and it is clear that acquiring such an ability cannot always be reduced to giving justifiably wholehearted assent to a proposition or a set of propositions. Think of knowing how to ride a bicycle, or how to discriminate by taste twenty-three varieties of red wine. To know how to do something like that is not just to be able to represent certain facts as a spectator; it is to possess an ability, connecting insight to action, thought to will. And it is these connections, of course, that are such mysteries in the *Tractatus*.

Here, then, is the fundamental connection of the doctrine of showing and knowing how to do something: in the *Tractatus* Wittgenstein uses showing as a way of making sense of *knowing how to do something,* instances of knowledge made incoherent by the complete separation of thought and action demanded by rationality-as-representation. Since he was in the grip of a picture of human rationality that identified thought and language and that focused on theoretical reasoning and knowledge to the almost total exclusion of the practical sort, the doctrine of showing was a necessity to save the entire program from a *reductio*. The examination of two main contexts of showing in the *Tractatus,* the logical and the ethical, will support this interpretation.

Consider, as a first example, the doctrine of showing and the truths of logic. Three distinct themes are found there: logic as mirror of the formal properties of language and world; logical inference as shown; and mathematical truth as shown. Take first the Tractarian assertion that logic mirrors the formal properties of language and the world. What does this come to? At 6.12 Wittgenstein says that the fact that the propositions of logic are tautologies shows something about language and world. That is, something is learned by noting this fact, but the knowledge gained is not knowledge about the possible existence of a contingent state of affairs. It seems plausible to claim that what is gained here is a kind of practical knowledge, the knowledge of how to do something. The knowledge afforded by the fact that the propositions of logic are tautologies is, first of all, knowledge of how to operate with certain symbols:

> The fact that a tautology is yielded by *this* particular way of connecting its constituents characterizes the logic of its constituents.
> If propositions are to yield a tautology when they are connected in a certain way, they must have certain structural properties. So their yielding a tautology when combined in this way shows that they possess these structural properties. (TLP 6.12)

Recognizing that '$p \lor \sim p$' is a tautology teaches one something about the structural relationships of 'p' and '$\sim p$', i.e., it teaches one how one can combine propositional variables in series with the logical constants, and how one cannot. At 4.4611 Wittgenstein says that a tautology, while it says nothing, is not nonsensical, because it is a "part of the symbolism," like the '0' (zero) in mathematics. A tautology is part of the symbolism because by considering it one learns something of *how to operate with* its constituent symbols. And, since these symbols represent propositions, one at the same time learns something of how to operate in the world. That's what is meant at 6.12 when he says that logic mirrors the formal properties of the *world,* as well as those of language. A tautology does not depict the world of contingent states of affairs; yet it conveys knowledge of the formal structure of language and the world. The knowledge it communicates is practical knowledge; the tautology functions instrumentally by inculcating certain abilities in symbol—and proposition—manipulation. Here one sees something fundamental to the doctrine of showing in all its contexts—the use of language in an instrumental, rather than descriptive, capacity.

The second theme of this heading, logical inference as shown, follows fairly closely the last point. At 6.1201 Wittgenstein writes: "The fact that the propositions '$p \supset q$', 'p', and 'q', combined with one another in the form '$(p \supset q) \cdot (p) :: (q)$' yields a tautology shows that q follows from p and $p \supset q$." Here it is quite clear that what is shown, viz., the possiblity of an inference, is a bit of practical knowledge. In learning how to make inferences one learns how to operate with certain symbols; and because these symbols are propositional variables, ranging over propositions which are, if true, pictures of states of affairs, one thus learns how to operate with the world as well. An inference is a bit of practice; it is something one does. What is shown by an "inferential" tautology like the one at 6.1201 is something of how the practice of inference is intelligently done. What is shown is a bit of practical knowledge.

Showing and the truths of mathematics, the third theme of the heading, is very helpful to our attempt to connect the doctrine of showing with practical knowledge. Because of his logicist conviction that the truths of mathematics are really just truths of logic, Wittgenstein believes that their function is ultimately the same:

> 6.22   The logic of the world, which is shown in tautologies
>   by the propositions of logic, is shown in equations by
>   mathematics.

Thus, like logic, mathematics is intended to show the formal properties of language and world; the discussion above has shown how this is a kind of practical knowledge. The following striking remark substantiates that interpretation:

> 6.211   Indeed in real life a mathematical proposition is never
>   what we want. Rather we make use of mathematical
>   propositions only in inferences from propositions that
>   do not belong to mathematics to others that likewise do
>   not belong to mathematics.
>   (In Philosophy, the question 'What do we actually use
>   the proposition for?' repeatedly leads to valuable insights.)

This is an important passage because here one sees Wittgenstein focusing on the "non-informative" propositions of mathematics as *instruments,* as having a *use.* He says "we make *use* of mathematical propositions. . . ." They do not state facts, but they are nonetheless connected to one's action in the world. They show how to do something, how to perform a certain operation, namely, how to get safely from this nonmathematical proposition to that one. And sometimes the ability to move from proposition to proposition is just what one needs in order to accomplish one's ends. The "logic of the world" shown in mathematical propositions is part of the practical knowledge one needs in order to get around intelligently in the world. Given the close connections in Wittgenstein's thought between mathematics and logic, it is clear he believed the latter had an "instrumental" role as well. Both logic and mathematics show one something of the nature of things; both give practical insight into how some operations within the world are intelligently performed.

Thus all three types of cases falling under the heading of showing and the truths of logic can be plausibly construed as cases of practical knowledge. In all three, some insight is given as a result of paying attention to a logically perspicuous symbolism; that insight is thus a recognition of the formal properties of language and world. But that insight, which seems in some way naturally to belong only to the passive realm of representational thought, actually has to do with our *practice*. It is knowledge of how to *do* something (even if just to do it in thought, within the Tractarian self). The doctrine of showing, the way these logical insights are transmitted, is thus intimately bound up with the connection of thought and will, with representation and (some form of) action.

This same connection is present when the doctrine of showing is employed in ethical contexts. The discussion in this chapter of Wittgenstein's ethical vision has already pointed out a fundamental difficulty for that account: how is it that good willing takes the place of bad? The problems of ethics, since they have to do with the world's problematic sense, cannot be solved merely by knowing *that* such-and-such is the case: rather, they are solved by acquiring a new way of willing, a new sort of practice. They are solved by knowing *how* to make the world a totally different one (TLP 6.43). The remarks of ethics, which literally cannot be said, thus are attempts to convey a sort of practical knowledge. They are attempts to show one how to *do* something. They aim at changing one's attitude toward the world ("will"), not at changing one's beliefs. The ethical insight that sometimes gets shown in such a remark is practical knowledge; it is a knowledge of how to live so as to give a sense to the world. The successful ethical remark functions instrumentally. Although as a proposition it may function representationally (describing the hawthorn bush, for example), as ethical remark its *telos* is the will, not the intellect. Philosophical enlightenment gives one a certain power: the power to will the world to be a happy one.

Thus in the ethical context as well the doctrine of showing is an attempt to connect thought and action. Something—some insight—is given when, for example, one hears a perceptive ethical remark or reads with understanding one of the *Twenty-Three Tales* of Tolstoy; but this insight, since it goes beyond the mere recognition of the accidental existence of a state of affairs, cannot belong solely to the realm of representational thought. It must somehow belong to the will, which, in good or evil willing, determines the meaning of the world. Nevertheless, the ethical insight is *really* there; the movement of the will from evil to good willing is not an accident, but is the result of what is shown in the remark or the story. Strictly speaking, of course, any non-accidental connection between thought and will in the *Tractatus* account is incoherent: nothing could be learned (known, thought, attended to) that could have any intrinsic connection to a change in will. But Wittgenstein, however great his theoretical captivity to rationality-as-representation, could not live with an absolute separation of thought and action. He knew—from personal experience—that in some way that which is captured in language can have an intrinsic connection with the solution of life's problems; the doctrine of showing is his attempt to make sense of that connection. The self's power to alter the meaning-aspect of the world is vouchsafed through what is shown in what is legitimately said.

Here one can again see the fundamental role of the picture of rationality-as-representation, for it is the presence of that picture in the *Tractatus* that renders the connection of thought and will apparently incoherent. Without his captivity to that intellectualist conception, and to the picture theory of the proposition which is its legitimate offspring, he would not have excluded practical knowledge, knowledge of how to do something, knowledge that sometimes cannot be reduced to a recipe of fact-asserting propositions. The doctrine of showing thus can be seen as a stab at a fuller conception of rationality, one which would allow an intrinsic connection between thought and practice. What is shown in the *Tractatus* is in every case practical knowledge, the ability to do something intelligently. Unfortunately, the primacy of rationality-as-representation reduced the doctrine of showing to a collection of dark sayings and prevented Wittgenstein himself from seeing its true nature and significance.

Earlier in this chapter I claimed that the author of the *Tractatus* navigated by the twin stars of logic and ethics and that there should be some explanation for his use of the doctrine of showing in both these contexts. The elements of that explanation should now be clear. The picture of rationality-as-representation is the key: because of that picture no coherent connection of thought and will is possible; the notion of showing is a way to try to forge that ethically necessary connection nevertheless. In all the cases of showing—logical as well as ethical—the connection of thought and action is problematic; all the things that are shown are instances of what we would call *practical knowledge*. Of course, the issue could not present itself to Wittgenstein in these terms. He could not see the connection between showing and practical knowledge, because at this time his sensibility was really a divided one. Theoretically, he was genuinely committed to rationality-as-representation. Although he knew that there had to be some intrinsic connection between thought and will, his captivity to the intellectualist picture would not allow it to surface; and that is why the shown insights that follow from seeing the world as a limited whole, that solve life's problems by changing bad willing to good, must belong to the unutterable *das Mystische*. The connection between thought and will cannot take place in the full light of day; it must be shoved up into the murkiness of *das Mystische*.

And just here the division in Wittgenstein's sensibility becomes acute, for, having sharply drawn the boundary between "rational" thought and "mystical" will, he now must cherish the latter over the former. Because of his conception of rationality-as-representation, he finds himself forced sharply to discount thought's intrinsic worth and to plunge into a sort of mysticism. In the Preface to the *Tractatus*, having lamented that the expression of his philosophical thoughts in the book is not as powerful as it might have been, he writes:

> On the other hand the *truth* of the thoughts that are here set forth seems to me unassailable and definitive. I therefore believe myself to have found, on all essential points, the final solution of the problems. And if I am not mistaken in this belief, then the second thing in which the value of this work consists is that it shows how little is achieved when these problems are solved. (TLP, p. 5)

"How little is achieved." In this connection it is useful to remember the remark to Ludwig von Ficker to the effect that the unwritten part of the *Tractatus* is the really important one. In that same letter to von

Ficker Wittgenstein said that his book had drawn the boundary of the sphere of the ethical "from the inside as it were," the only rigorous way of drawing it. The "sphere of the ethical" lies outside the range of thought. Thus thought and will ("the bearer of ethical attributes") can have only a boundary as their connection; in no way do the realms interpenetrate. And, of course, it is the ethical realm that is really important. Thought is ultimately important only for what it shows, not what it says. The formal structure of thought shows the world-limiting self upon which meaning depends; particular thoughts (like those constituting the poem or the parable) may somehow show that self how to will the world to be a happy one. In neither case does the actual accomplishment of rationality itself—the representation of the real—finally and directly serve "what is higher" (TLP 6.42). Rationality, like the *Tractatus* itself, is to be kicked away like the ladder already climbed; it is rationality itself which finally must be transcended in order to see the world aright. Not, of course, that there is some real alternative to rationality; just that it is firmly put in its proper place. Rationality, which had seemed so intrinsically powerful and valuable, is finally shown to be just an instrument on which one climbs to the realm of the good will. And it is an instrument used *indirectly* (as if one used a marble statue of Aphrodite as a ladder), since its defining intention—representation of contingent reality—has no place in that higher realm. So what one ultimately sees in the *Tractatus* is the devaluation of rationality (i.e., a certain picture of rationality: rationality-as-representation) in the service of a profound and transforming ethical vision. The initial adoption of an uncompromisingly intellectualist conception of rationality, and the brave sallies against the vicious nonsense spawned by other philosophies, lead finally to the denigration of rationality itself and to mute gestures at the all-important, unutterable *das Mystische*.

VI

THUS FAR in this chapter the focus of attention has been the *form* of the ethical vision of the *Tractatus* and the connection of that vision to the distinction between saying and showing; it is now time to try to say something about the content of the vision. Since a defining feature of his conception removed ethics from the sphere of what can be said, one cannot rely directly on Wittgenstein's own ethical pronouncements; instead, one must look first to his life to see there his determining moral commitments. The most obvious features of that life, understood in the light of influences known to be operating, reveal the elements of his vision of the good life.

The most striking episode in Wittgenstein's life around the time of the completion of the *Tractatus* was his abandonment of philosophy in favor of elementary-school teaching. This event can be understood only in conjunction with another: the surrender of his large fortune.

Wittgenstein's father, who had died in 1912, had been a wealthy industrialist; naturally his son Ludwig inherited a considerable fortune from his estate. The money seems always to have been an embarrassment to the son. Before the war he had made a large anonymous grant to aid artists and writers (the poets Trakl and Rilke were among the beneficiaries).[41] After the war he gave away the remainder of his fortune and began to live a life characterized by simplicity and frugality.[42] The influence of Tolstoy in this seems clear, especially the Tolstoy that comes through in his redaction of the Gospels. Neither wished to live off the fruits of another's work. Just as Tolstoy rejected a system of serfdom that allowed the landowner to feed off the labor of his peasants while contributing nothing, so Wittgenstein rejected his father's fortune in order to make his life his own.

Having completed his war service, and having disposed of his fortune, Wittgenstein faced the decision of what to do with himself. With the enthusiastic support of Russell and others, he would have had little trouble securing a prestigious academic post and thus beginning a life of security, position, and relative ease. Instead, he enrolled in a teacher-training school in Vienna and, having completed his certification, began to teach the children in remote villages in Lower Austria. Familiarity should not blind one to the striking character of this decision: here is a man of culture, wealth, and substantial original philosophical achievement who turns his back on all his prospects in order to teach the children of peasants in a remote section of his country. And this was not just the summer job or "interim year" of a concerned college student: in 1919 Wittgenstein was already thirty years old; he spent at least a year training for the work; and he remained a teacher for six years, until a crisis precipitated his resignation.[43] The decision to spend his life in this way—for that was what the commitment meant to him—must undoubtedly carry a great deal of ethical significance.

What can one learn about Wittgenstein's moral vision from this sequence of events? Like all important choices, it was both a rejection of some things and an affirmation of others. In the first place, it was a rejection of the life of "the world." That life exalts ease, glory, affectation; and for these things is needed wealth. But wealth does not come by magic. It is always produced through the labor and suffering of many, and the one who becomes wealthy is thus feeding off the lives of others. His life is a robbery of the lives of others.

> I turned from the life of our circle, acknowledging that ours is not life but a simulation of life—that the conditions of superfluity in which we live deprive us of the possibility of understanding life, and that in order to understand life I must understand not an exceptional life such as ours who are parasites on life, but the life of the simple laboring folk—those who make life—and the meaning which they attribute to it.[44]

That is Tolstoy, but it could equally be Wittgenstein in 1920. In the movement to Trattenbach and the other isolated and poor villages of Lower Austria, he was rejecting a life of superfluity and parasitism. The life of wealth and ease in Vienna or Cambridge was for him an insuperable barrier to the good will.

> It is not possible to serve two masters at once—God and riches: the will of your Father and your own will. You must serve either one or the other.[45]

But in going to the mountains Wittgenstein was not rejecting just a particular set of economic and social realities; he was also rejecting a much deeper conception of the life of virtue. One might say, somewhat misleadingly, that he was rejecting the life of thought; he was abandoning the hope that any "scientific" discoveries—whether they belong to natural science proper or to philosophy—can go any distance toward solving the deepest and most important problems of life. That is not to say, of course, that he quit thinking, nor that he wanted others to. He was, after all, a teacher; and there is evidence that as such he was exceptionally hard-working and successful.[46] What he was rejecting was not thought itself, but a virulent idolatry of a certain kind of thinking. This idolatry expresses itself in the view that the key to virtue, to the good life, lies in some form of "scientific" knowledge. Like any deep conception of rationality, rationality-as-representation adumbrates an ideal of the person, and hence a moral ideal as well. It holds up certain forms of life as peculiarly human, thus implying a conception of human virtue. According to this conception, science—either concrete, like chemistry; or abstract, like philosophy—can answer the fundamental questions of human life and can direct human energies toward the true good; thus, a life devoted to science (the more abstract the better) is the highest form of human life. Man is the rational animal, and the key to his destiny lies in his rationality, in his capacity for representation of the way the world is. Knowledge is virtue.

Like Tolstoy and Kierkegaard, Wittgenstein despised this idolatry of science, concrete and abstract. Kierkegaard delighted in caricaturing the "objective tendency, which proposes to make everyone an observer, and in its maximum to transform him into so objective an observer that he becomes almost a ghost."[47] He wanted instead a person of inwardness and subjectivity, capable of feeling and acting as well as thinking. Tolstoy was even more direct in his conviction that any form of science was incapable of resolving the problematic world:

In my search for answers to life's questions I experienced just what is felt by a man lost in a forest.

He reaches a glade, climbs a tree, and clearly sees the limitless distance, but sees that his home is not and cannot be there; then he goes into the dark wood and sees the darkness, but there also his home is not.

So I wandered in the wood of human knowledge, amid the gleams of mathematical and experimental science which showed me clear horizons but in a direction where there could be no home, and also amid the darkness of the abstract sciences where I was immersed in deeper gloom the further I went, and where I finally convinced myself that there was, and could be, no exit.[48]

The "wood of human knowledge" was for Wittgenstein also a place where home was not to be found. Whatever the values of concrete or abstract science—and for Wittgenstein these *are* valuable in certain ways—they cannot provide the really valuable things to a person; they cannot reveal (except, perhaps, by contrast) the pearl of great price for which everything should be sold. However valuable the written part of the *Tractatus* is, the *really* important things are found in the part that cannot be written.

It is clear, of course, that rationality-as-representation plays the fundamental role in this rejection of the way of knowledge, since it is the operation of that conception in the *Tractatus* that restricts thought to the mere representation of contingent facts. If that's all that human intelligence can provide, it's no wonder that it is inconsequential to the life that nourishes the soul with real food. Thus we see the central role of rationality-as-representation in the content of Wittgenstein's ethical vision, as well as its form.

For Kierkegaard and Tolstoy, the life to be affirmed is, rather than the life of knowledge, the life of faith, or at least their idiosyncratic versions of what they took to be Christian faith. For Kierkegaard, Christian faith is an evident absurdity, a stumbling block to the spectral "objective observer." The doctrines of Christianity contain contradictions (e.g., that the eternal entered time) that make them unacceptable to reason; yet they must be affirmed nevertheless by faith. What cannot be accepted objectively must somehow be believed subjectively, with "fear and trembling." For Tolstoy, faith is also a sort of nonrational affirmation of certain doctrines. The key to being able to understand and to accept these scandalous propositions is turning away from the parasitical life of superfluity to the real life of the working people.

For Wittgenstein, on the other hand, his affirmation was not the affirmation of doctrines, rational or irrational. He really believed that *das Mystische* cannot be spoken of, not even in the vocabulary of faith. "What you cannot say, you cannot say; and you cannot whistle it either."[49] The content of his ethical affirmation was wholly in his actions, and in the meaning they had for him. His life shows his affirmation of simplicity, frugality, and effective, direct service to the less fortunate. It shows the rejection of abstract and concrete science in favor of the practical application of intelligence to immediate problems. What matters is not what is *said* or *thought,* but what is *done.*

One thinks here of "The Three Hermits," one of Tolstoy's *Twenty-Three Tales,* a book that Wittgenstein greatly admired.[50] A party of pilgrims, a bishop among them, is sailing to visit the shrines of the Solovetsk monastery; in route they pass an island where three hermits are said to live, mostly in silence, praying for the salvation of their souls. The bishop, proudly aware of his role as a teacher of God's poor, decides to visit the hermits and instruct them. Landing on the island, he finds them lamentably ignorant ("We do not know how to serve God. We only serve and support ourselves, servant of God") and praying a strange prayer ("Three are ye, three are we, have mercy upon us").

The bishop patiently explains to them the details of the Gospel and the doctrine of the Trinity, and finally he teaches them the Lord's Prayer to substitute for their own. Because they are old and unlettered, the instruction is long and laborious, but finally it is completed and the bishop reboards the ship and resumes his pilgrimage. A good wind fills the boat's sails, and by nightfall they are making swift progress.

But the bishop cannot sleep; he sits on the deck thinking of the old men and how pleased they were to be taught the Lord's Prayer. Suddenly, far off the stern, he sees something—perhaps a sail, or a bird. The mysterious shape grows as it quickly gains on the ship, and the bishop inquires of the steersman what it might be:

> The steersman looked, and let go the helm in terror.
> "Oh Lord! The hermits are running after us on the water as though it were dry land."
> The passengers, hearing him, jumped up and crowded to the stern. They saw the hermits coming along hand in hand, and the two outer ones beckoning to the ship to stop. All three were gliding upon the water without moving their feet. Before the ship could be stopped, the hermits had reached it, and raising their heads, all three as with one voice began to say:
> "We have forgotten your teaching, servant of God. As long as we kept repeating it we remembered, but when we stopped saying it for a time a word dropped out, and now it has all gone to pieces. We can remember nothing of it. Teach us again."
> The Bishop crossed himself, and leaning over the ship's side, said:
> "Your own prayer will reach the Lord, men of God. It is not for me to teach you. Pray for us sinners."
> And the Bishop bowed low before the old men; and they turned and went back across the sea. And a light shone until daybreak on the spot where they were lost to sight.[51]

Whether or not this story, written in 1886, was already known to Wittgenstein in 1919, it captures something essential to his ethical vision of that time. For a prayer to reach the Lord it is not necessary that it be composed of the right words, nor does it need to issue from a basis of correct theological understanding; what is necessary is just that it be prayed in a spirit of humility and trust, and that it issue from a

life lived for the salvation of souls rather than for ease and self-aggrandizement. What matters in Wittgenstein's lived ethics is not thought,
either in the sense of correct world-representation or of abstract doctri-
nal rectitude, but a mode of action that identifies one's energies with
the common life of all. Returning to an earlier theme of this chapter,
the things that are shown and that make it possible for one's world to
be the happy world are items of *practical knowledge*. They show one
how to live; they are sources of energy for the form of life that is life in
the happy world. The things that are shown are not mystical *doctrines*
that must be appropriated in some arcane way, like the truths of Kierkegaardian faith. Rather, they have to do with the will—the philosophical self—and with its (mysterious) capacity to alter the meaning-
aspect of the world.

In summary, the content of Wittgenstein's ethical vision in 1920 is
just what one most obviously sees in the contours of his early life: the
rejection of wealth and ease, and the corresponding rejection of disinterested thought, in favor of direct involvement with the fate of the unfortunate. The hallmarks of that life are simplicity, selflessness, and an
abhorrence of "gassing": loose talk about good and evil. *Wovon man
nicht sprechen kann, darüber muß man schweigen.*

VII

IS THERE any connection between the philosophical form of the ethical
vision found in the *Notebooks* and the *Tractatus* and the actual character of the life Wittgenstein was living in the early twenties? Did his
solipsist account of the powerless willing self that is the limit of the
world simply evaporate when it touched moral reality? Or was that account always promulgated just for philosophical consumption, having
even for Wittgenstein himself no real connection to what he was doing
with his life in Vienna and Trattenbach?

Both suggestions ignore what we know of Wittgenstein's character
at that time. The *Tractatus* was composed and submitted for publication over a number of years, years in which the Tolstoyan-"Christian"
views had taken strong root in his life. To have published philosophical
doctrines that he knew to be unrelated to or inconsistent with those
views would have demanded more double-mindedness and self-aggrandizement from him than we actually see in his deeds. The prin-
cipled surrender of his fortune, for instance, is sharply at odds with his

coolly putting his name to positions he did not hold. Furthermore, as we shall see in the next chapter, there is textual evidence that those philosophical conceptions persisted in his thinking until the late twenties. So for him there must have seemed some connection between ethical form and content. But what was it? By raising and answering this question we will also be led to formulate another: What, finally, is the significance of the *Tractatus*—for its author, first of all; and then for us, who can stand on his shoulders to look at it? What, if anything, does the book mean?

It is clear now that the *Tractatus* is fundamentally an ethical deed, its writing and publication just as much an act of conscience as was the move from Vienna to Trattenbach. Any conception of good and evil deep enough to have produced the *Tractatus* will be set, however implicitly, within a narrative image; it will presuppose some story—heroic, tragic, even comic—of how evil is to be conquered and how good is to be achieved. To put it bluntly, any profound moral philosophy, and any extraordinary moral life, will be the amplification of some myth; and Wittgenstein's is no exception. It is in that myth that the true significance of the *Tractatus* may be located and its connection to Wittgenstein's deeds found.

With some compression and loss of detail we may recapitulate the ethical vision of the book as the constellation of three mythic motifs: self-consciousness; ascent; the hero-god. The protagonist of this moral drama is the metaphysical self, the center of will for whom the sense of the world is problematic. The progress of the *Tractatus* is the gradual awakening of this self to full and true self-consciousness, a self-consciousness that, when complete, vouchsafes the sense of life.

According to the *Tractatus* the self is the limit of the world, not part of it (TLP 5.641). Since the world is already the world of facts, not of things (1.1), and since that means that the world is the world that shows itself in propositions, and since the self is a necessary condition of propositional representation, then the self is the necessary condition of the world itself. "The world is *my* world" (TLP 5.62). But this transcendentally necessary self is merely the *limit* of the world, the seeing eye that is never a part of the visual field it surveys (5.633).

The philosophical self which limits the world is, however, also a center of ethical affection, or, as Wittgenstein puts it, a center of *will*. Not, of course, that the will is a faculty of agency; the metaphysical self is completely powerless to alter the world's contingencies (6.373).

The self is a center of will only in that it views the world with a certain (happy or unhappy) attitude (NB, p. 87). The world of the happy self is a different world from that of the unhappy (TLP 6.43). Will is a mode of the metaphysical self's vision, staining the world with either despair or bliss; and the discovery of the sense of life—the answer to the ethical question—will be marked by that change in the self's willing that allows the unhappy world to become the happy one.

How can the self move from bad willing to good, from despair to bliss? If the self is, as the *Tractatus* says, merely a powerless limit of the world, unable to create or to alter states of affairs, must it not also be attitudinally powerless, dependent for its happiness or unhappiness upon whatever contingently happens, upon the graces of fate? But that would mean that ethics itself was ultimately futile; there would then be no sense of life that could give to human being a stable and enduring ground. The "problematic" character of our life would become patently absurd.

The early Wittgenstein is unwilling to assent to such absurdity. The self *can*, he believes, make its world a happy one. The key to this transfiguration lies in the self itself, and the real drama of the *Tractatus* is found in its exemplification of that achievement: the book is the self's ladder to climb to the place from which its view is a happy one.

Here we approach the heart of the *Tractatus*, its animating myth of salvation. Salvation is achieved through heroic ascent to a godlike self-consciousness. Only when the self has abandoned its traditional but degrading self-understanding, only when it has won through to the recognition of itself as the "godhead of the independent I" (NB, p. 74), will it be possible for the self to achieve that permanent good willing which is the aim of ethics.

This achievement has the form of an ascent. Ordinarily I view myself as a part of the world, a physical body and/or a psychological consciousness equally subject to happenings at the level of states of affairs. Because I am part of the world, I am either its fair-haired child or its victim. If as a part of the world I try to secure my happiness *within* that world, adopting the world's standards (affectation, ease, power) and tying the sense of life to such ephemera, I am bound to fail. Within the world my happiness or misery will depend upon the graces of fate; and, powerless to stop the wheel of fortune, I must thus despair of any permanent health of soul.

But as a result of reading the *Tractatus* my ordinary self-understanding is replaced with another. I come to see that I am not just one part of the world among others; I am the world's necessary limit, the eye which views it and without the view of which the world is not. On the ladder of the *Tractatus* I rise above the ordinary human self-consciousness and achieve a view of the world *sub specie aeternitatis.* Only from the perspective of that higher place is it possible for me to will the good, thus to make the world a happy one. *Das Mystische* makes itself felt only when the ascent is completed; only, in other words, when one has become a god: the "independent I" (NB, p. 74) who has come to see the world as a limited whole.

Two distinct aspects comprise that godlike self-consciousness. First, I have recognized the world's necessary dependence upon me; without me there is no world.

> 5.62 . . .
> The world is *my* world: this shows itself in the fact that the limits of *language* (the only language that I understand) mean the limits of my world.
>
> 5.621 The world and life are one.
>
> 5.63 I am my world. (The microcosm.)

And second, as the godlike I, I am nevertheless independent of my world, both in that I am powerless to influence the world's happenings and, more importantly, in that I have recognized that my happiness has nothing essentially to do with those happenings, since I am not a part of the world at all. A god is unaffected by what happens *in* the world: "*How* things are in the world is a matter of complete indifference to what is higher" (6.432). The sense of life must lie outside of life, i.e. in oneself as limit of world. The independent I is, through the grace of *das Mystische,* the maker of the world's meaning. (There is an important connection here to the feeling of absolute safety which Wittgenstein mentions in the "Lecture on Ethics"—to be discussed in the next chapter.) The metaphysical self revealed by the *Tractatus* is, therefore, a "godhead" in two senses: the world cannot exist without it (6.431); and the meaning of the world is conferred by it alone.

Both in theory and in practice Wittgenstein's quest for salvation through self-consciousness is *heroic* in form. To be able to rise in thought through the levels of the *Tractatus* and thus to be able to see the world (*my* world) *sub specie aeternitatis:* this vision-quest pits one against overwhelming obstacles and demands heroic applications of industry, intelligence, and courage. *Das Mystische,* the power to move from bad willing to good, is the healing boon granted to the hero once he attains his godlike perspective. The image of the soldier with his philosophical notebooks in his knapsack is an image of a hero of the intellect, pursuing his goal of truth against all odds, even in the cannon's mouth. Then, after all that, to kick away the ladder of thought one has climbed up: that demands an even more heroic, an even more godlike, renunciation. And just that is demanded of Wittgenstein, as we have seen.

In his going to the mountains to teach in the peasant schools there is, I believe, a corresponding *practical* attempt heroically to ascend from the normal human condition and to put on the attributes of a god. The image that springs immediately to mind is the *imitatio Christi.* Not only does his life in the mountains reflect that service to the poor and humble which Jesus (and Tolstoy) urged; it represents Wittgenstein's own self-conscious attempt to become perfect, to become a god. It is his attempt to become Spirit, not flesh; to abandon the normal human cravings for affectation, ease, power. To abandon the world and become a god is to abandon the flesh, to deny or turn aside from all the desires normal to human beings, and, instead, to pursue their opposites. If human beings naturally want comfort and power, then the life of the Spirit demands humility and self-abasement. If money is naturally wished for, then Wittgenstein will choose to forfeit his wealth. If there is a natural human prompting to procreation and the establishment of a family, he will become a solitary.

In all of this Wittgenstein shows the characteristic lineaments of a hero. He must courageously rise above the ordinary demands and graces of the human perspective; he must renounce them in favor of the perfection of Spirit. No compromise with the world is acceptable to the hero. Since any imperfection, any humanness, will imperil the finding of the Grail, it is all or nothing. The hero must emulate the perfection of the god he seeks; he must reënact—indeed, *become*—that god.

To speculate on the psychological roots of the hero's attempt to become perfect, "as your Father in heaven is perfect," would be both insulting and fruitless: Wittgenstein is not a case history, nor does the reality of soul-making reveal itself in the gross etiologies and discriminations of such an approach. What is to the point here is just to note an important similarity: in both his writings and his life the early Wittgenstein shows an impetus toward the godlike. He is living out there a certain myth of the hero. As in thought he tried to reach the view *sub specie aeternitatis,* to realize himself as the godlike self which limits the world, so also in his life he sought to abandon the merely human in order to emulate the divine. Reared in a Christian culture, saved from confusion and despair by his encounter with Tolstoy and Kierkegaard, it was entirely natural that Wittgenstein's *imitatio* should take the form of a heroic renunciation of the world of corruption and compromise. The god to be emulated was, obviously, Jesus Christ, as interpreted by Leo Tolstoy and Søren Kierkegaard; and that emulation required the heroic renunciation of the "world" and of pure representational rationality. Leaving rich Vienna and Cambridge Wittgenstein went instead to the mountains of Lower Austria to teach the children of peasants. However idiosyncratic his particular form of life, it must nevertheless be recognized that the early Wittgenstein's infatuation with the heroic image is not philosophically anomalous. Ever since the Socratic-Platonic answer to the question of human being became definitive for Western self-consciousness, heroic ascent from error and illusion by dint of intellectual effort has been the norm. One way or another, Western philosophy has continually reënacted the heroic ascent out of the Cave; rationality-as-representation, especially its apotheosis in metaphysics, is itself a heroic conception. Thus the *Tractatus* can be seen as the culminating effort in the heroic struggle of rationality-as-representation. It can be seen as the place where, for good or for ill, the Socratic-Platonic conception of human excellence comes to fruition. By revealing the powers and limits of representation (hence *thought*) itself, the *Tractatus* once and for all shows the role thought can play in the discovery of the sense of life and world. And that role is necessary but finally inadequate. Thought is the medium for the heroic self's ascent, the ladder he must climb; but this ladder finally brings him to a place where what he sees first and foremost is himself. That is, he sees that the sense of life resides in him, in his mysterious (even mystical) power to change his attitude toward the world.

So the outcome of the *Tractatus* (and ultimately of rationality-as-representation) is narcissistic: the self is the maker of meaning. We escape from the shadows of the Cave only to find, not some Reality which gives our lives meaning, but only ourselves: heroic will. I believe that Wittgenstein's continuing fascination with the *Tractatus* derives from his perception of it as the logical result of Western philosophy. Its inhumanity is the inhumanity of philosophy itself. The movement to metaphysics culminating in the *Tractatus* is itself a manifestation of heroic self-assertion; it is, as Heidegger later points out, the truest exemplification of the will to power. And, in the end, once the ladder is kicked away, only naked will remains. In this book rationality-as-representation has its best shot, and the outcome is clear: a clock that consistently tells the wrong time.

The key, early and late, to seeing the connection between the form and substance of Wittgenstein's ethical vision lies in his pursuit of the godlike. In the early work, the mythical mode of his ethical vision is the heroic quest, and the godlike is seen through the image of *height:* to become a god is to *ascend* (the *Tractatus* is a ladder, remember) above the normal human perspective. It is to see the world *sub specie aeternitatis,* as a valueless whole limited by the godlike self itself; and it is to go up into the mountains, leaving behind all one's achievements and prospects, abandoning the "world" of abstract thought and glory and ease. In the later work, as we shall see, the heroic mode loses its dominance, and the godlike comes to be seen through the image of *depth,* not height. The elevated view *sub specie aeternitatis* is replaced with an acknowledgment of mystery in every single thing, a mystery which, as Heraclitus says of the soul, is so deep that you could not find the end of it, though you traveled every way (fragment 47).[52]

VIII

EVEN IF it were possible, it would not be useful to try to summarize this long chapter. Perhaps it would be worthwhile, however, to close it by reminding the reader of its place within the general scheme of the book and to call attention to the appearance of some themes that will become increasingly important as the argument of the book proceeds.

Chapter one asserted that the fundamental intention of Wittgenstein's work—in both its incarnations—was the transmission of a vision of the sound human life. One can now see how this is true for the *Tractatus;* and in its attempt to manifest its moral vision, that book makes use of several notions that are important for the later philosophy as well. The most obvious is, of course, the distinction between what can be said and what must be shown. Another is the intellectualist picture of rationality-as-representation. A third is the notion of nonsense. In the *Tractatus* Wittgenstein's ethical vision is, so to speak, attached to traditional philosophical concerns through the medium of these three conceptions: because of the hold of rationality-as-representation (and its offspring, the picture theory), ethical matters lie outside the realm of thought—are, therefore, a sort of nonsense—and must be *shown* rather than *said*. These same concepts (transmuted, to be sure) function in the later work as well, for there also is an attempt to reveal and empower a vision of the good life.

CHAPTER 3

The "Lecture on Ethics"

I CAN ONLY describe my feeling by the metaphor, that, if a man could write a book on Ethics which really was a book on Ethics, this book would, with an explosion, destroy all the other books in the world.

— Wittgenstein in the "Lecture on Ethics"

I

IN 1929 Wittgenstein returned to Cambridge and to sustained research in philosophy. For six years after 1920 he had taught the children of peasants in Lower Austria, living a frugal and simple life, and devoting himself to the Tolstoyan ideal of humanly useful work. While philosophy occasionally invaded (Frank Ramsey made visits in 1923 and 1924), most of his thinking was directed toward the concrete problems faced by his pupils and their parents. (He published a *Wörterbuch für Volksschulen* in 1926, and there is a wonderful story of how he repaired the steam engine of the wool factory in Trattenbach. In lieu of payment he directed that the owners distribute woolen cloth to the needy children of the village.)[1] This period of retreat, so reminiscent of Tolstoy's decision to teach in the peasant schools of his country, came to an abrupt and unhappy end in 1926 when Wittgenstein was let go from his position as schoolmaster. For a time he served as a gardener's assistant at a monastery near Vienna, but in the autumn of 1926 he undertook to design and supervise the building of a house in the Kundmanngasse for his sister, Mrs. Margaret Stonborough. This task, to which he brought his characteristic energy, dedication, and genius, was completed in 1928; the house that resulted is "free from all decoration and marked by a severe exactitude in measure and proportion. Its beauty is of the same simple and static kind that belongs to the sentences of the *Tractatus.*"[2]

It was through his sister Margaret that Wittgenstein met the philosopher Moritz Schlick. Schlick introduced him to other members of the Vienna Circle, notably Friedrich Waismann; Wittgenstein attended a few meetings of the Circle, finding the atmosphere philosophically and personally oppressive. But whatever his reaction to the philosophers he was meeting, his interest in philosophy itself was at this time being rapidly rekindled. There is a rumor that hearing a lecture given in Vienna in 1928 by the intuitionist mathematician L. E. J. Brouwer was the immediate cause of his philosophical renascence. Wittgenstein himself said merely that he returned to philosophy because he thought he could again do creative work there.[3] In light of his bold remark in the preface of the *Tractatus* that in his book the problems of philosophy are in their essentials finally solved, a feeling that for him creative philosophical work was again possible must indicate a recognition (or at least a fear) that the clean and imposing structure of the *Tractatus* is neither as strong nor as complete as it might appear.

When he returned to Cambridge early in 1929, he immediately plunged into philosophical thinking and writing. On arrival he had registered as a research student; but university regulations permitted that he count his prewar studies as residence toward the Ph.D., and the already famous *Tractatus* could legitimately be submitted as his thesis. After an oral examination administered by Moore and Russell, the degree was awarded in June, and in 1930 he was made a Fellow of Trinity College. Once again his lot was cast with philosophy.

The contours of Wittgenstein's philosophical thinking at this time can be observed in the *Philosophical Remarks*. This was a long type-script constructed by him out of passages written in his notebooks between 2 February 1929 and 24 April 1930 (PR, p. 347). It is clearly a transitional work. Most of its fundamental ideas derive from the *Tractatus;* in the *Remarks* Wittgenstein appears to believe that the philosophical difficulties that had recently presented themselves to him can, with slight alterations, be accommodated within the conceptual structure of his earlier book. Yet there are, at the same time, intimations of those images and ideas that mark the "later" Wittgenstein.

The continuity of the *Tractatus* is clearest in the retention of the comparison of propositions and pictures. In his book the individual *Satz* ('proposition', or 'sentence') was a picture of the reality it modeled: if it was an elementary proposition, it was a concatenation of names whose relationship depicted the relationship of the simple objects named by them; if not an elementary proposition, it was a truth-function of elementary propositions. Conjoined with this picture theory in the *Tractatus* was a theory of inference and an atomistic ontology that insisted upon the complete independence of elementary propositions: from the truth or falsity of one elementary proposition, nothing can be inferred about the truth or falsity of any other elementary proposition. The constituent propositions of language are inferentially discrete, just as the constituent states of affairs of the world are existentially discrete (TLP 5.134; 2.061; 2.062).

This linguistic and ontological atomism has a certain theoretical appeal, but it runs into difficulty when applied to some simple and familiar phenomena. Consider an ordinary color attribution: one points to a (red) object and says, "This is red." It is hard to imagine a proposition less likely to be a truth-functional construction from other propositions, so the color proposition is a prime candidate for being an elementary proposition of the Tractarian sort. Yet it is not inferentially discrete, for if it is true (at t_1) that the object pointed to is red, then it is false (at t_1) that the same object is blue. Color words form a system; if a color is (truly) predicated of an object at a given time, then it can be inferred that none of the others can be predicated of that object at that time. From "This [object O] is red" it can be inferred that "This [object O] is not blue"; "This is not green"; "This is not yellow"; and so forth. These inferences, completely familiar to us from everyday life, tend to undermine the Tractarian assurance that elementary propositions are logically independent of one another.

In the *Philosophical Remarks* Wittgenstein responds to these difficulties by altering one of his fundamental images in the *Tractatus:*

> I once wrote: 'A proposition is laid like a yardstick against reality. Only the outermost tips of the graduation marks touch the object to be measured.' I should now prefer to say: a *system of propositions* is laid like a yardstick against reality. What I mean by this is: when I lay a yardstick against a spatial object, I apply *all the graduation marks simultaneously.* It's not the individual graduation marks that are applied, it's the whole scale. If I know that the object reaches up to the tenth graduation mark, I also know immediately that it doesn't reach the eleventh, twelfth, etc. The assertions telling me the length of an object form a system, a system of propositions. It's the whole system which is compared with reality, not a single proposition. If, for instance, I say such and such a point in the visual field is *blue,* I not only know that, I also know that the point isn't green, isn't red, isn't yellow, etc. I have simultaneously applied the whole color scale. (PR, p. 317)

By drawing attention to the systematic relationships among some propositions, he has widened the scope of the comparison of propositions and pictures. Without giving up the doctrine that individual propositions depict reality, he adds the insight that *systems* of pictures are sorts of pictures too: "It's the whole system that is compared with reality, not a single proposition" (PR, p. 317). So, "the concept of an 'elementary proposition' now loses all its earlier significance" (PR, p. 111).

This instance is typical of the *Remarks:* a fundamental Tractarian theme, its difficulties recognized, is modified in the direction of the ideas and techniques that come to fruition in the *Philosophical Investigations.* The comparison of individual propositions and pictures, so crucial in the *Tractatus,* is deëmphasized in the *Remarks* in favor of the importance of systems of propositions (or, as he sometimes says, "coordinates of description"). This focus on systems, rather than on individual sentences, foreshadows the notion of a language-game which will become so important in the *Brown Book,* dictated just a few years later.

The *Philosophical Remarks* has a strong tinge of verificationism:

The meaning of a question is the method of answering it: then what is the meaning of 'Do two men really mean the same by the word "white"?'

Tell me *how* you are searching, and I will tell you *what* you are searching for. (PR, pp. 66–67)

. . .

To understand the sense of a proposition means to know how the issue of its truth or falsity is to be decided. (PR, p. 77)

The interest in verification is connected to a more general interest in the *Remarks* in epistemological issues. The *Tractatus* contains almost no epistemology; its focus is meaning, not knowledge. In the *Philosophical Remarks* one sees that Wittgenstein is no longer confident that these two notions are quite so distinct from one another as he had believed. In fact, this growing concern with epistemology is symptomatic of a more profound alteration in Wittgenstein's perspective. Reading the *Tractatus* one can sometimes forget that language has to do with living and breathing human beings; it seems somehow independent of, even superior to, human interests like knowledge and opinion, certainty and doubt, will and action. In the *Remarks,* however, the idea of language has become less transcendent; there is more attention to its role in everyday human life.

An important instance of the "humanizing" of the idea of language is found in Wittgenstein's reflections in section two on the connection between language and action. In the *Tractatus* language is conceived from the perspective of a spectator, not that of an agent. The fundamental image of language as a picture was presented there in ways that emphasized the static, purely pictorial, qualities of the depiction relationship. The picture-proposition was understood to be a model of reality, but in the *Tractatus* there is little indication of what use such models might actually have for human beings. The depicting proposition assumes something of the aspect of a landscape painting hanging in a museum; it models reality, all right, but what—past viewing—is one to do with it? Here one can see in another way the grip of Wittgenstein's thinking of the conception we called "rationality-as-representation" in chapter two: language-thought can do no more than represent reality.[4]

In the *Philosophical Remarks* Wittgenstein's thinking about language gives much more attention to its connection to action. The match of a picture-proposition with reality, conceived pictorially and

statically in the *Tractatus,* here has to do with the actions that the picture-proposition initiates or underwrites.

> If you think of propositions as instructions for making mod-
> els, their pictorial nature becomes even clearer.
> Since, for it to be possible for an expression to guide my
> hand, it *must* have the same multiplicity as the action desired.
> (PR, p. 57)

In the *Tractatus* the identity in mathematical multiplicity necessary to
the picturing relationship is shared between the proposition and the
state of affairs; there is no indication that picturing has to do with anything other than passive representation of reality (cf. TLP 4.04). But in
the *Remarks* multiplicity itself is connected to agency:

> Language must have the same multiplicity as a control panel
> that sets off the actions corresponding to its propositions.
> Strangely enough, the problem of *understanding* language is
> connected with the problem of the Will.
> Understanding a command before you obey it has an affinity
> with willing an action before you perform it.
> Just as the handles in a control room are used to do a wide
> variety of things, so are the words of language that correspond
> to the handles. One is the handle of a crank and can be adjusted
> continuously; one belongs to a switch and is either on or off; a
> third to a switch which permits three or more positions; a
> fourth is the handle of a pump and only works when it is being
> moved up and down, etc.; but all are handles, are worked by
> hand.
> A word has meaning in the context of a proposition: that is
> like saying only in use is a rod a lever. Only the application
> makes it into a lever.
> Every instruction can be construed as a description, every
> description as an instruction. (PR, pp. 58–59)

In these passages one gets the sense that Wittgenstein has started to
break the paralyzing hold of rationality-as-representation. Although he
is still clinging desperately to the comparison of propositions to pictures, he is beginning explicitly to recognize that the representation of

reality may not be the (sole) *telos* of language-thought. He is on the verge of making room *within* thought for some of the practical knowledge that had to be so mysteriously shown in the *Tractatus*. Language and thought are being demythologized; they are becoming human again.

These movements away from the rigidities of the *Tractatus* are certainly not consolidated in the *Philosophical Remarks;* it remains only a transitional work in the career of Wittgenstein's thought. Nevertheless, it is important for indicating the kinds of dissatisfaction he felt with his early work when he began to write philosophy again. By contrast, it forces one to see again the central and unquestioned place of rationality-as-representation in the subtext of the *Tractatus;* and it shows that Wittgenstein himself was slowly coming to recognize inadequacies in his earlier attempts to evade the sterilities of that conception.

II

THE "LECTURE ON ETHICS" (the title is not Wittgenstein's own; the manuscript itself is untitled) was written in Cambridge sometime between September 1929 and December 1930.[5] It was probably read to a society known as "The Heretics"; and, so far as is known, it was the only popular lecture Wittgenstein ever wrote or presented. It is also, after the *Tractatus,* the only one of Wittgenstein's writings explicitly concerned with ethical matters. In light of my own book's argument that *all* Wittgenstein's work has an ethical intention, and in light of the Lecture's proximity both to his ten-year sojourn outside academic philosophy and to the radical turn in his thought, it is worthwhile to analyze it in some detail.

Since it was a popular lecture directed toward an audience not especially familiar with current philosophical thinking, it is not surprising that none of the new themes of the *Philosophical Remarks* are clearly in evidence. But there is, nevertheless, some tentative movement away from the *Tractatus,* especially in what the "Lecture on Ethics" omits. In it one finds, for example, no explicit reference to solipsism, nor to the "powerless" will as the bearer of ethical attributes. As in the *Remarks,* there is also a clear tendency away from that earlier book's oracular tone; instead, one gets the sense of a man speaking to men, trying to do justice to a phenomenon that is important and familiar to them all. This change of tone, seemingly insignificant, actually marks the beginning of an alteration in Wittgenstein's sensibility, an alteration with the most profound philosophical consequences. To mark these changes is not to say, however, that the Lecture is in its essentials free of the *Tractatus;* indeed, as will be argued below, its central themes are understandable only if the viewpoint of the *Tractatus* is presupposed. The Lecture, like the *Remarks,* remains a transitional work.

The "Lecture on Ethics" begins with a specification of the subject matter of ethics. In *Principia Ethica* G. E. Moore had defined it thus: "Ethics is the general inquiry into what is good."⁶ Wittgenstein is content to adopt Moore's phrasing as a summary explanation of the term; but in the Lecture he intends to use 'Ethics' in a wider sense than is usual, "in a sense in fact which includes what I believe to be the most essential part of what is generally called Aesthetics" (LE, p. 5). In order to indicate that wider sense he proposes to put before his audience a series of "more or less synonymous expressions, each of which could be substituted for the [Moore] definition" (LE, p. 5).

> [B]y enumerating them I want to produce the same sort of effect which Galton produced when he took a number of photos of different faces on the same photographic plate in order to get the picture of the typical features they all had in common. And by showing to you such a collective photo I could make you see what is the typical—say—Chinese face; so if you look through the row of synonyms which I will put before you, you will, I hope, be able to see the characteristic features they all have in common and these are the characteristic features of Ethics. (LE, p. 5)

The "synonyms" he provides are these: Ethics is the inquiry "into what is valuable," or "into what is really important," or "into the meaning of life," or "into what makes life worth living," or "into the right way of living" (LE, p. 6). It is interesting to note that only the last of these phrases indicates a direct connection between ethics and conduct. As in the *Notebooks* and the *Tractatus,* Wittgenstein does not conceive ethics to be primarily concerned with problems of conduct; rather, the true center of ethical interest lies in discovering the permanent sense of human life so that life is then understood to be "worth living." In the *Notebooks* he said that it throws light on the nature of ethics to see that "suicide is, so to speak, the elementary sin" (NB, p. 91). In the same entry he wrote: "If suicide is allowed then everything is allowed." Suicide is the "elementary sin," that is, the ultimate ethical failure, because suicide represents an admission of failure to find the sense of life that renders it worth living. And if that sense is not found, then everything is allowed. That is to say, until the sense of life is established, issues of conduct (what is and is not "allowed") are moot. The fundamental task of ethics is, therefore, to discover the sense of life. The "synonyms" with which Wittgenstein glosses Moore's definition show that on this issue he had not significantly changed his mind since 1916.

It is also worthwhile to note that he believes this "wider" conception of ethics includes the central part of aesthetics (LE, p. 5). In the *Tractatus* he had said that ethics and aesthetics are one and the same (6.421), and in the *Notebooks* he explores one way in which the aesthetic point of view toward the art object is identical to the point of view of the happy man toward the world: both are looking "from outside," *sub specie aeternitatis* (NB, p. 83; see also p. 86). The preservation of the intrinsic connection between ethics and aesthetics marks another important continuity between the "Lecture on Ethics" and the earlier work.

Having specified the subject matter of ethics in this way, Wittgenstein immediately calls attention to a fundamental difference in the way the paradigmatic ethical expressions (e.g., 'good', 'valuable', 'important') are used from time to time. They are sometimes used in a "trivial" or "relative" sense:

> If for instance I say that this is a *good* chair this means that the chair serves a certain predetermined purpose and the word 'good' here has only meaning so far as this purpose has been previously fixed upon. In fact the word 'good' in the relative sense simply means coming up to a certain predetermined standard. (LE, p. 6)

The use of a value expression in a "relative" sense is quite common, and the logical form of such "relative" value judgments is easily revealed:

> Every judgment of relative value is a mere statement of facts and can therefore be put in such a form that it loses all the ap-

pearance of a judgment of value: Instead of saying "This is the right way to Granchester," I could equally well have said, "This is the right way you have to go if you want to get to Granchester in the shortest time"; "This man is a good runner" simply means that he runs a certain number of miles in a certain number of minutes, etc. (LE, p. 7)

If relative value judgments "don't present any difficulty or deep problems" to the philosopher (LE, p. 6), there is another use of value expressions that does. This Wittgenstein calls the use of such expressions in an "absolute" sense, and it is in *this* sense that such expressions properly belong to ethics. He introduces "absolute" judgments of value by contrasting two situations. In the first, one person, having observed another playing tennis, says "You play pretty badly." Suppose, says Wittgenstein, the tennis player replies. "Yes, I'm playing badly, but I don't want to play tennis any better." This is a perfectly intelligible response; we can without absurdity imagine the critic responding in turn, "Well, then, that's all right."

Consider, however, another situation, in some ways analogous to the first: A person observes another telling a preposterous lie and says, "You're behaving like a beast." What if the liar were to respond, "I know I'm behaving badly, but I don't want to behave any better"? Could the critic intelligibly reply, as he did in the tennis case, "Well, then, that's all right"? Certainly not, says Wittgenstein; he would instead say something like, "Well, you ought to want to behave better!"

Wittgenstein takes that last judgment to be an *absolute* judgment of value (LE, p. 6). The value expression ('ought' in this case) is being used in an absolute rather than a relative sense. And the difference between the two senses has to do with their differing connections to statements of fact:

Now what I wish to contend is that, although all judgments of relative value can be shown to be mere statements of facts, no statement of fact can ever be, or imply, a judgment of absolute value. (LE, p. 7)

Imagine, he suggests, an omniscient person keeping a complete record of everything that takes place in the world. In this record would be all movements of all bodies, all states of mind; in short, all *facts*. Would there be in this omniscient record any judgments of value? Certainly there would be *relative* judgments of value. For example, it would be recorded there that human beings of a certain time and culture tend to select and care for chairs of such-and-such dimensions, materials, shapes, etc.; and, since (*ex hypothesi*) chair C meets those specifications, it could therefore be recorded that C is a *good* chair. The relative value judgment would merely be a shorthand way of recording the facts about the preferences of a certain group of human beings.

But could there be recorded by the omniscient describer any *absolute* judgments of value? No, says Wittgenstein.

> [A]ll the facts described would, as it were, stand on the same level and in the same way all propositions stand on the same level. There are no propositions which are, in any absolute sense, sublime, important, or trivial. (LE, p. 7)

Propositions describe the facts, the way things are; so propositions can express value judgments only if those judgments are in some sense descriptions of facts. Relative value judgments *are* just descriptions of sociological facts, of course; so they are perfectly capable of being expressed in propositions. But absolute judgments of value go beyond the facts of a situation. When the critic says to the liar, "you *ought* to want to behave better," he is not (just) calling the liar's attention to a general preference of their society, or even to a preference of all rational beings everywhere. While it may be a fact that all rational beings prefer truth-telling to lying, the judgment does not describe that (alleged) fact.

Wittgenstein seems to think the key to seeing that absolute judgments of value are in no sense descriptions is their modality. Statements of facts are always contingent; they may be true or false, depending upon the circumstances. ' "Snow is white" ' is true if and only if snow is white. A relative judgment of value, since it is reducible to statements of fact, is likewise contingent: the truth of ' "This is the right road for you" ' depends upon (the fact of) some predetermined goal of mine (e.g., getting from Cambridge to Granchester). But an absolute judgment of value does not present itself as contingently true; rather, it is trying to express a *necessary* requirement or insight. As Wittgenstein says, if one could talk about the *absolutely* right road, it would be a road such that *anyone* would, *"with logical necessity,"* have to travel it, or be ashamed not to (LE, p. 8). Likewise, to speak of the *absolute* good is to speak of a state of affairs such that everyone, whatever his preferences, would be *necessarily* required to seek it, or feel guilty if he did not (LE, pp. 8–9). The hold upon me of a relative value judgment is contingent; it binds me only if some fact is true. But an absolute value judgment is just that—absolute; it binds one whether or not one has particular preferences or goals. It seems obvious that Wittgenstein is here reformulating the Kantian dictum that the Moral Law consists of categorical rather than hypothetical imperatives.

Having recognized the categorical necessity that attaches to judgments of absolute value, one can now easily see that ethics must be "supernatural" (LE, p. 8). The natural world consists of facts—contingent concatenations of objects. The truth and falsity of the propositions that describe these facts are likewise contingent. But absolute value judgments claim to present *necessary* truth; they seem to describe states of affairs that *necessarily* hold ("You *ought* to want to do better!"). And thus they show their own supernatural character:

No state of affairs has, in itself, what I would like to call the coercive power of an absolute judge. (LE, p. 9)

But should one not be hard-nosed and just call such "judgments" *nonsense* rather than supernatural? Yes, but at the same time one should not forget that there undoubtedly are situations in which we would use value expressions in an absolute sense. Wittgenstein gives two examples from his own experience:[7]

I believe that the best way of describing the first experience is to say that when I have it *I wonder at the existence of the world*. And I am then inclined to use such phrases as "how extra-ordinary that anything should exist" or "how extra-ordinary that the world should exist." I will mention another experience straight away which I also know and which others of you might be acquainted with: it is, what one might call, the experience of feeling absolutely safe. I mean the state of mind in which one is inclined to say "I am safe, nothing can injure me whatever happens." (LE, pp. 9–10)

Both these experiences—especially the first—have clear prototypes in the *Tractatus*. In the *Notebooks* (20 October 1916) he had written: "Aesthetically, the miracle is that the world exists. That what exists does exist" (NB, p. 86). In the *Tractatus* the "miracle" had become identified with the advent of *das Mystische:*

6.44   It is not *how* things are in the world that is mystical, but *that* it exists.

6.45   To view the world *sub specie aeterni* is to view it as a whole—a limited whole.
Feeling the world as limited whole—it is this that is mystical.

As was argued previously in chapter two, to become conscious of the world as a limited whole is necessarily at the same time to become aware of what limits that world, namely, the metaphysical self. The experience of *das Mystische* is thus essentially connected to a certain sort of godlike self-realization. To become aware of the miracle of the world's existence is also to become aware of the miracle of the self, the godhead of the independent I (NB, p. 74). One may speculate that it is this sense of self-realization that connects in Wittgenstein's sensibility the two experiences recounted in the "Lecture on Ethics." To have a heightened sense of the existence of the world, and thus of the self, could easily produce a sense of safety. To recognize that the world and self are coördinate is also (at least in the *Tractatus*) to recognize their ultimate independence; it is to recognize that—at least as regards the world—"nothing can injure me whatever happens" (LE, p. 10). It seems likely that the sense of the essential independence of self and world is still a part of Wittgenstein's perspective in 1929, though it is not clear that the distinction has the same metaphysical source at both periods.

Even if the experiences Wittgenstein recounts are connected to one another through the sense of godlike self-realization present in both, one may still wonder what connects them to *ethics*. Remembering that he considers the true center of ethical interest to be the discovery of the meaning of life may help make the feeling of absolute safety seem an ethical affection, since such a feeling of safety would seem to depend upon a secure conception of the sense of life; but what of the wonder at the existence of the world? Granting that there is such an experience, and even granting that it might be psychologically overwhelming at times, why should Wittgenstein have thought it had anything to do with the discovery of what is truly valuable?

The *Tractatus* is once again an aid in interpretation. There the key to the solution of life's problems lies in the "good exercise of the will" (6.43). Now, willing cannot alter the world itself—the world, after all, is independent of my will (6.373)—but it can change the limits of the world (6.43). It is, of course, the metaphysical self that limits the world (5.632); so good willing is a change within the self, a change which alters the whole meaning-aspect of the world to that self, and which makes the unhappy world a happy one (6.43). But what makes good willing possible for the self? Here, as we have seen, *das Mystische* is the crucial notion:

> 6.521 The solution of the problem of life is seen in the vanishing of the problem.
>
> . . .
>
> 6.522 There are, indeed, things that cannot be put into words. They *show* themselves. They are what is mystical.

And *das Mystische*, that which shows itself and makes good willing possible for a self, is intimately connected to the experience of wonder at viewing the world as a limited whole, *sub specie aeterni* (6.44 and 6.45).

So, since wonder at the existence of the world vouchsafes *das Mystische*, and since the showing of *das Mystische* is the key to the possibility of that good willing which causes the problem of life to vanish, there is in the *Tractatus* period a clear basis for connecting the experience of wonder at the world's existence to the ethical. It seems likely that in the "Lecture on Ethics" Wittgenstein was assuming a similar basis of connection.

In a conversation of 17 December 1930, F. Waismann explicitly queried Wittgenstein about the connection between experiencing wonder at the existence of the world and the ethical. He recorded Wittgenstein's reply as follows:

> Men have felt a connection here and have expressed it in this way: God the Father created the world, while God the Son (or the Word proceeding from God) is the ethical. That men have first divided the Godhead and then united it, points to there being a connection here. (wwk, p. 118)[8]

This remark is so obscure that a commentator could be excused (perhaps even praised) for ignoring it; but there may be an important link here to a slightly less obscure remark in the *Notebooks*. On 8 July 1916 he wrote:

"There are two godheads: the world and my independent I."
(NB, p. 74)

There are, of course, important differences between the two remarks, not the least of which is fourteen years; but there are intriguing similarities as well. It seems clear that Wittgenstein does not take talk about God the Father and God the Son as such talk is literally taken by the believing Christian. What then could he have meant by appealing to the Christian picture in this context?

One plausible answer is that in 1930 he is still working with the Tractarian notions of self and world. It has been shown above how seeing the world as a limited whole is necessarily to become acutely conscious of the metaphysical subject that limits it. One might be inclined to speak of this process as the self "proceeding" from the world, as the Son is said to proceed from the Father (cf. WWK, p. 118). In the *Tractatus* the metaphysical self that proceeds from the world viewed *sub specie aeterni* is the willing subject, i.e., the subject that takes to the world a certain attitude; and it is with the will that the issue of ethics arises: the will is the subject of ethical attributes (TLP 6.423). So there really are two "godheads": the world of facts (created by God the Father: WWK, p. 118); and the willing subject that infuses that world with an ethical aspect (God the Son who is the ethical: WWK, p. 118). And these godheads are, like the Persons of the Trinity, ultimately inseparable: the world is always *my* world; it is always limited by the metaphysical subject and always ethically charged by the happy or unhappy will of that subject. Since ethics has to do with finding the sense of life, and since that is a task for the willing subject, and since the experience of wondering at the existence of the (limited) world is a (perhaps *the*) way of calling that subject to the self-consciousness necessary for good willing, the wonder-experience, by revealing the connection between the two godheads of world (Father) and self (Son), has clear and significant ethical impact for Wittgenstein. His reply to Waismann seems to be using Christian theology as evidence for the presence of the *Tractatus* account of self and world in some of our fundamental patterns of moral-religious thinking, even if that account remains buried in symbols. He has not let go of his quasi-idealist metaphysics of the self.

Having presented two experiences as paradigm cases of occasions when he is likely to use value expressions in an absolute, rather than a relative, sense, Wittgenstein proceeds to discuss the logic of such absolute value judgments:

> And there the first thing I have to say is, that the verbal expression which we give to such experiences is nonsense! If I say "I wonder at the existence of the world" I am misusing language. (LE, p. 10)

The basis for making these judgments is, it seems, obviously Tractarian: any genuine proposition depicts a possible state of affairs; and, given the nature of depiction, any genuine proposition could turn out to be false. But to express one's wonder at the existence of the world is not to say something that could be false; thus, such an expression, whatever its grammatical form, is not a genuine proposition:

> To say "I wonder at such and such being the case" has sense only if I can imagine it not be the case. . . . But it is nonsense to say that I wonder at the existence of the world, because I cannot imagine it not existing. (LE, p. 10)

Wittgenstein seems to believe that propositions of the form "I wonder that . . ." are to be analyzed like propositions of the form "I believe that . . ." or "I say that . . ." His analysis of such "propositional attitudes" in the *Tractatus* (5.542–5.5422) demands that what follows the 'that' in such expressions must be a genuine proposition on its own, i.e., possibly true or possibly false.

> 5.5422 The correct explanation of the form of the proposition, '*A* makes the judgment *p*', must show that it is impossible for a judgment to be a piece of nonsense. (Russell's theory does not satisfy this requirement.)

What holds for judgments also holds for wonderings: one cannot wonder at a piece of nonsense. But it *is* nonsense to imagine that the world might not exist; the expression "Nothing exists" could never depict a possible state of affairs and could therefore never be a genuine proposition. So any verbal expression of the paradigmatic ethical experience of wondering at the existence of the world must be nonsense.

His treatment of the feeling of absolute safety seems different at first, but perhaps that is because what he says is very brief and inconclusive.[9] He maintains that it is a "misuse" of 'safe' to say that one is safe whatever happens (LE, p. 11).

> To be safe essentially means that it is physically impossible that certain things should happen to me and therefore it's nonsense to say that I am safe *whatever* happens. (LE, pp. 10–11)

Why *nonsense*? Presumably because my safety would have to consist in the existence of certain states of affairs (being in my room, safe from omnibusses in the street below; being already immune to whooping cough through previous exposure: LE, p. 10), and my *absolute* safety would demand that certain states of affairs *necessarily* exist (or necessarily do not). But the existence or nonexistence of states of affairs is, according to the *Tractatus,* always a contingent matter, never a necessary one; so absolute safety is nonsense. Again the Tractarian viewpoint seems to be presupposed in the Lecture.

It is no good to maintain, as one is tempted to do, that the expressions of absolute value judgments are *similes,* since any simile must be the simile for *something* (LE, p. 11). That is, one should be able to drop the simile and state the facts which lie behind it. But there are no facts which lie behind an experience of, for example, "absolute safety"; so talk about "absolute safety" is plain nonsense, not fancy simile.

So far the "Lecture on Ethics" is of a piece with the doctrines of the *Tractatus,* even if those doctrines remain largely unstated in the text itself. At this point, however, Wittgenstein recognizes a situation that pushes his thinking in the direction of the later work. He recognizes the powerful incongruity of attributing absolute value to an experience, like the experience of wonder at the existence of the world. After all, an experience is merely a fact, a part of the natural world; but absolute value is something "supernatural" (LE, p. 12). How could supernatural value attach to a perfectly natural fact? Is not the whole idea hopelessly confused?

He tries to get a handle on this question by considering the concept of a miracle. To wonder at the existence of the world is the experience of seeing the world as a miracle (LE, p. 13). A miracle, he says, is "simply an event the like of which we have never yet seen" (LE, p. 12). Suppose such an event were to occur—for example, suppose that a man listening to a lecture suddenly were to grow a lion's head and begin to roar. The lion-man would certainly seem to be a miracle. But what if, in reaction to this occurrence, the audience were to capture the lion-man and turn him over to scientists to be vivisected and studied? The miracle would then have disappeared. By their attitude the members of the audience would have shown that they consider the appearance of the lion-man to be just a fact that has yet to be comprehended in the present body of scientific knowledge; it is not *essentially* mysterious. If one calls it a "miracle," one is then using the term in a relative sense (LE, p. 12). To call something a *miracle*, in the absolute sense, is not just to say that it is scientifically uncomprehended; it is to say that it is scientifically incomprehensible.

> The truth is that the scientific way of looking at a fact is not the way to look at it as a miracle. (LE, p. 12)

To look at an event scientifically is a "way of looking" at it that is incommensurable with looking at it as a miracle.

It is this notion of a "way of looking" that makes it possible for a supernatural value to attach to natural fact. To see the existence of the world as a miracle is not to see some obscure nonnatural property (the property of being miraculous) there in the world; rather, it is just to see the purely natural facts available to be seen by everyone else and to look at those facts in a particular way. It is to take toward them a certain *attitude*. What makes the world a miracle is the self that views it; only certain of us are capable of that wondering perspective.

We see buried here in the Lecture the same problem of connecting thought and will that is so crucial in the *Tractatus*. How can what is available to be thought—contingent states of affairs—have any connection to the good willing that makes the world a happy one? And we can see too that in the late twenties Wittgenstein was trying to solve the problem as he did ten years earlier: by making will *attitude*, a mode of the metaphysical self's vision; and by leaving utterly mysterious the self's capacity to change the quality of its vision, moving from bad willing to good.

The interest of this brief discussion of miracles in the Lecture lies both in its intimation of past ways of thinking, just mentioned, and in its foreshadowing of some of his distinctive later themes, particularly the notion of a "way of looking." The incommensurability of different "ways of looking" is discussed in detail in section eleven of part two of the *Philosophical Investigations;* indeed, to work so that "our way of seeing is remodelled" (RFM, p. 122) is the central intention of his philosophy after 1933. Moreover, the notion of a "way of looking" at an experience seems intimately connected to his later conception of "forms of life." A particular "way of looking" at a given phenomenon (a man growing a lion's head or water becoming wine) may help to define one form of life over against another. (Indeed, the concept of a miracle helps to define that form of life distinctive to the later work. Chapter six will provide details.) And once the autonomy and incommensurability of forms of life are recognized, it is not so large a step to see that language itself is a part of such forms of life and may not function in all of them in the same way. None of these steps is taken in the "Lecture on Ethics" itself, of course, but it is interesting to note their foreshadowing. The movement away from the *Tractatus* was very gradual.

By the end of the Lecture Wittgenstein has presented considerations which, he believes, show the essential nonsensicality of any verbal expression of the paradigmatic ethical experiences:

> I see now that these nonsensical expressions were not nonsensical because I had not yet found the correct expressions, but that their nonsensicality was their very essence. For all I wanted to do with them was just *to go beyond* the world and that is to say beyond significant language. My whole tendency and I believe the tendency of all men who ever tried to talk Ethics or Religion was to run against the boundaries of language. This running against the walls of our cage is perfectly, absolutely hopeless. (LE, p. 13)

The same imagery is used in a conversation with Waismann in December of 1929:

> Man has the urge to thrust against the limits of language. Think for instance about one's astonishment that anything exists. . . . This thrust against the limits of language is *ethics*. (WWK, p. 68)

Because ethics has this nature, it can never be a science: "What it says does not add to our knowledge in any sense" (LE, p. 14). This very Tractarian conclusion is followed by another: the necessity of silence.

> I regard it as very important to put an end to all this chatter (*Geschwätz*) about ethics—whether there is knowledge in ethics, whether there are values, whether the Good can be defined, etc. In ethics, one constantly tries to say something that does not concern and can never concern the essence of the matter. (WWK, pp. 68–69)

But the nonsensicality of any ethical expression does not mean, of course, that the use of such expressions is silly or perverse:

> This running against the walls of our cage is perfectly, absolutely hopeless. . . . But it is a document of a tendency in the human mind which I personally cannot help respecting deeply and I would not for my life ridicule it. (LE, pp. 13–14)
>   Nevertheless we thrust against the limits of language. . . . But the tendency, the thrust, *points to something*. (WWK, pp. 68–69)

As in the *Tractatus,* the (necessarily) unwritten part of a lecture on ethics is by far the most important part.

III

THIS EXAMINATION of the "Lecture on Ethics" has so far shown how its main contentions rest upon foundations laid in the *Tractatus;* in some fundamental respects Wittgenstein's mind had changed very little in his ten-year absence from philosophy. In particular, one can see in the Lecture the continuing force of the picture of rationality-as-representation. In the Lecture there is, of course, still a very stringent distinction made between sense and nonsense; and there that distinction, which in some form occurs in all periods of Wittgenstein's thinking, yet reflects his Tractarian conviction that thought is thought only insofar as it describes reality. Language and thought continue to be seen as coextensive notions, and language continues to be "intellectualized" in his account. That is, he has not yet come to recognize the importance of seeing language as itself a specimen of human behavior; it still

seems to him purely passive and representational of reality, not itself
an active component of that reality. In the Lecture ethical expressions
are "mere nonsense" (LE, p. 12) because they are assumed to be attempts to represent (depict) something that cannot be a part of the natural world of contingent facts. Language is, in Wittgenstein's own image, a *cage* (LE, p. 13); our thought (and its medium, language) is
permanently immured within the confines of passive representation.
We may run against the walls of that cage, and that may be a noble
thing for a human being to do ("a tendency in the human mind which I
personally cannot help respecting deeply"); but there is absolutely no
hope that the walls will be breached. Judgments of absolute value will
always be nonsense. In the "Lecture on Ethics" the Tractarian picture
of rationality-as-representation still lives.

Another important continuity between the Lecture and the *Tractatus* is the subterranean persistence of a quasi-idealist metaphysics of
the self. It is, of course, only subterranean; in the Lecture there is no
explicit mention of solipsism, or the self as will, or the self as the limit
of the world. Nevertheless, as was shown above, some of the more
puzzling features of the Lecture—like the connection between the ethical and wonder at the existence of the world—become more understandable if the Tractarian conceptions of the self are assumed. These
conceptions go very deep in Wittgenstein's thinking, and they are connected in intricate ways with rationality-as-representation. It is no
wonder that it took a fundamental revolution in his thinking (and his
sensibility) to dislodge them.

It is extremely fascinating to recognize that this revolution was already taking shape at the time the Lecture was being composed and
delivered. The recorded conversations with Friedrich Waismann indicate that some substantial changes in Wittgenstein's thinking took
place between December of 1929 and December of 1930. (The "Lecture on Ethics" was written sometime between September 1929 and
December 1930; he had returned to Cambridge early in 1929, beginning in February the notebooks that became the *Philosophical Remarks*.)

In December of 1929, in a conversation at Moritz Schlick's house
in Vienna, Waismann records Wittgenstein as saying:

Man has the urge to thrust against the limits of language. . . .
This thrust against the limits of language is *ethics*. I regard it as
very important to put an end to all the chatter about ethics—

whether there is knowledge in ethics, whether there are values, whether the Good can be defined, etc. In ethics one constantly tries to say something that does not concern and can never concern the essence of the matter. . . . But the tendency, the thrust, *points to something*. (wwk, pp. 68–69)

This passage is clearly of a piece with the "Lecture on Ethics." Both emphasize the Tractarian theme of the limits of language (the Lecture calls it a *cage*), and both stress that ethical judgments are nonsensical attempts to push past those limits:

Anything we can say [about ethics] must, a priori, be only nonsense. Nevertheless we thrust against the limits of language. (wwk, p. 68)

In both, language is seen from the perspective of rationality-as-representation.

Thus it is startling to compare to these texts Waismann's record of a conversation that took place almost exactly a year later, on 17 December 1930. Three topics were discussed—Schlick's ethics, value, and religion—and on each Wittgenstein's thinking has pushed past its *Tractatus* conception.

In 1930 Moritz Schlick had published a book, *Fragen der Ethik*.[10] He claims there, according to Wittgenstein, that theological ethics contains two conceptions of the Good: a "superficial" one, in which the Good is good because God wills it; and a "deeper" one, in which God wills the Good because it is good (wwk, p. 115). But Wittgenstein believes that Schlick has his characterizations of the positions just backwards:

I think that the first conception is the deeper one: Good is what God orders. For this cuts off the path to any and every explanation why it is good, while the second conception is precisely the superficial, the rationalistic one, which proceeds as if what is good could still be given some foundation. (wwk, p. 115)

What is most interesting here is what is *not* said. In contrast to the almost contemporaneous "Lecture on Ethics," there is no mention in this conversation of the essential *nonsense* of Schlick's ethical position. Nowhere does Wittgenstein talk about the immutable limits of language, that "cage" against the walls of which ethical remarks helplessly yet nobly thrust. He does say in the next paragraph that the essence of the Good "has nothing to do with facts" (wwк, p. 115); but, rather than going on to ring familiar Tractarian changes, he glosses his remark by saying that therefore the Good "cannot be explained (*erklärt*) by any proposition" (wwк, p. 115). The problem with ethical propositions is not that such propositions are inherently nonsensical; there might, in fact, be an ethical proposition that did what was wanted:

> If any proposition expresses just what I mean, it is: Good is what God orders. (wwк, p. 115)

Rather, the problem with most ethical "chatter" (cf. wwк, p. 68) is that it attempts to *explain* the phenomena of the moral life. It is superficial, not nonsensical; it is narrowly rationalistic in its attempt to provide the good with some theoretical foundation.

This very significant condemnation of ethical theorizing is amplified in the next section of the conversation. It begins with Wittgenstein's distinction between sociology and ethics. Sociology describes the actions and valuations found among persons: "What I can describe is that people have preferences" (wwк, p. 116). Nowhere in sociology can there be first-order value judgments like "Such and such constitutes an advance in moral living" (le, p. 115); such judgments belong to ethics proper.

But if sociology is sometimes tempted to smuggle in living ethical judgments, ethics faces a correspondingly devastating temptation of its own. There one is tempted to try to delve beneath the living ethical judgments themselves to discover the rational foundations that explain them. Ethics is sorely tempted to offer a *theory* of ethical judgment. Having noted that some person (perhaps oneself) values (i.e., prefers) some things—e.g., truth-telling, or a Beethoven sonata—over others, one is tempted to try to explain what it is that makes those things valuable.

> Is value a particular state of mind? Or a form inhering in certain data of consciousness? My answer is: Whatever one

said to me, I would reject it; not indeed because the explanation is false but because it is an *explanation (Erklärung)*.

If anybody offers me a *theory,* I would say: No, no, that doesn't interest me. Even if the theory were true that would not interest me—it would not be *what* I seek. The ethical cannot be taught. If I needed a theory in order to explain to another the essence of the ethical, the ethical would have no value at all. (wwk, pp. 116–17)

Notice again how Tractarian themes are notable by their absence. Nowhere does Wittgenstein advert to the alleged nonsensicality of ethical judgments. In fact, by admitting that a theory of value is possible ("Even if the theory were true. . . ."), he seems to be denying that all value judgments are nonsense: how could there be a (true) theory of something which is nonsense? The problem is that a theory is profoundly *inappropriate* here; a theory is not what we (should) seek in ethical reflection. To explain the ethical is necessarily to dissipate its value.

> *For me* the theory has no value. A theory gives me nothing. (wwk, p. 117)

That this disavowal of ethical theory is not just a recapitulation of the "Lecture on Ethics" distinction between "relative" and "absolute" value judgments becomes clear in the third section of the conversation with Waismann. There the topic is religion, and Wittgenstein begins by asserting that speech is not essential to religion, since he can "quite well imagine a religion in which there are no doctrines, and hence nothing is said" (wwk, p. 117). Already one can see the differences here from the *Tractatus:* in the context of the earlier book the notion of religious *doctrine* could make no sense; yet here doctrine is not condemned—it is just noted to be nonessential to religion itself. The door is clearly left open to the possibility of doctrine's playing *some* role in religion:

> Obviously the essence of religion can have nothing to do with the fact that speech occurs—or rather: if speech does occur, this itself is a component of religious behavior and not a theory. Therefore nothing turns on whether the words are true, false, or nonsensical. (wwk, p. 117)

But in the *Tractatus everything* turns upon that! In the *Tractatus*, rationality-as-representation and its relative the picture theory are the fundamental notions, and philosophical analysis is pursued in their light: the primary task of philosophy is to draw the distinction between sense and nonsense. To admit that whether or not an expression is non-sense is beside the point: that is to leave the essence of the *Tractatus* behind.

Furthermore, this passage clearly moves beyond the *Tractatus* in another respect, since here religious language is characterized as a "component" of religious behavior. According to rationality-as-representation and the picture theory, language has one and only one function: the representation of facts. There is absolutely no hint that it might serve other purposes as well. But if language can be a component of religious behavior irrespective of that language's being true or false, sense or nonsense, then the grip of the Tractarian conceptions has been broken. The way is prepared for bringing into prominence "the fact that the *speaking* of language is part of an activity, or of a form of life" (PI, sec. 23). The limits of language have been breached; or, to put it better, the force of the "limits of language" picture has been sapped.

That Wittgenstein realizes this is made clear in the remarks that follow those quoted above:

> Neither are religious utterances *figurative,* for else they should be also expressible in prose. Thrusting against the limits of language? Language is not a cage. (WWK, p. 117)

"Not a cage": but that is exactly the image he used in the "Lecture on Ethics" (p. 13). The bars of that cage were held in place by rationality-as-representation and the picture theory. If the bars are now coming down, it is because their foundations are being eroded.

Finally, there is in this passage another slap at *theory*. The pejorative remarks about theory in this conversation are of great significance for anyone concerned to trace the development of Wittgenstein's thought. He connects theory, naturally enough, with the concept of explanation; and philosophical explanation he understands to be the attempt to provide *foundations* (WWK, p. 116). In his growing mistrust of explanation and theory in philosophy, one can see his dawning recognition of the deep connections between rationality-as-representation and foundationalism. When rationality-as-representation completely goes, as it soon will, the whole landscape of philosophical thinking is altered for Wittgenstein; nothing will remain in its former place.

IV

WHAT IS the significance of the "Lecture on Ethics" for understanding the path of Wittgenstein's thinking; in particular, what significance has it in the development and promulgation of his vision of the sound human life? First of all, the Lecture demonstrated that the fundamental doctrines of the *Tractatus* survived almost intact the ten-year sojourn away from philosophy. In the Lecture he is still thinking that language has necessary and rigid limits, limits imposed by the nature of thought itself. That is to say, the picture of rationality-as-representation is still central to his philosophical conceptions. He still believes that thought (and language, its medium) can do no more than depict, truly or falsely, the existence of facts; for him, language and thought are still purely representational. Since that is the case, and since "absolute" ethical judgments cannot be analyzed as statements of fact, then such judgments are just examples of a human tendency "to run against the boundaries of language" (LE, p. 13). Therefore, as in the *Tractatus,* ethics has essentially nothing to do with thinking. Morality and religion have to do with considerations that are past thought, just as they do for Kierkegaard (mentioned with approval in a 1929 conversation with Waismann). And since ethics and language-thought cannot interpenetrate, the philosopher must resist the tendency to try to *say* something about the ethical: "I regard it as very important to put an end to all the chatter about ethics. . . ." (WWK, pp. 68–69). As in the *Tractatus,* silence becomes a part of the paradigmatic ethical deed and life.

In addition to the persistence of rationality-as-representation, there is even some evidence that important parts of the *Tractatus* metaphysics of the self have survived into the "Lecture on Ethics." This evidence, indirect to be sure, is deployed in section two in this chapter. If the argument there for its existence is correct, this shows that the quasi-idealist metaphysics derived from Schopenhauer was a vital part of the form of his early ethical vision, not just a youthful enthusiasm.

Finally, the Lecture and its contemporaneous conversations show that for Wittgenstein the importance of the ethical had in no way diminished. In the Lecture, after having argued that ethical judgments are nonsense produced by trying to penetrate the limits of language, he adds that such judgments spring from "a tendency in the human mind which I personally cannot help respecting deeply and I would not for my life ridicule it" (LE, p. 14). In the conversation of 30 December 1929 with Waismann he insisted that the tendency to make ethical remarks *"points to something"* (WWK, p. 69), and in December of 1930 he said:

> I can only say: I don't belittle this human tendency; I take my hat off to it. And here it is essential that this is not a sociological description but that I speak *for myself.*
>
> For me the facts are unimportant. But what men mean when they say that *"The world is there"* lies close to my heart. (WWK, p. 118)

The ethical intensity of the *Tractatus* is undiminished in the "Lecture on Ethics" and in the conversation with Waismann. To do philosophy is still an ethical deed for Wittgenstein.

So, this examination of the "Lecture on Ethics" does not reveal any great change in the form or the content of Wittgenstein's ethical vision. The years between 1919 and 1929—filled with some joy, some bitterness, and constant internal turmoil—did not in themselves shake his faith in the ethical perspective of the *Tractatus*. When he returned to Cambridge he was still thinking in essentially the same terms. But the conversation of 17 December 1930 with Waismann and the writings collected in *Philosophical Remarks* show that those terms were quickly criticized and eventually abandoned. Starting in 1930, the whole focus of Wittgenstein's philosophical thinking was to shift; and in that shift the ground of his ethical vision was also to alter in fundamental ways. It is to that shift that the argument of this book must now turn.

CHAPTER 4

Showing and saying in the later work

S O FAR we have examined Wittgenstein's ethical vision in two periods of his thinking: the time of the composition and publication of
the *Tractatus;* and the time of his return to philosophy in 1929. We turn
now to examine his work beginning early in the 1930s and continuing
until his death in 1951—all this commonly known as the "later" Wittgenstein. Lying beneath this later work is the same question that an-
chors the earlier: where and how is the sense of life to be found? Both
the early work and the late are fundamentally ethical in intention; both
are Wittgenstein's responses to the Socratic question of human being.

In the *Tractatus,* as we have seen, the standard Western philosophical answer achieves its apotheosis: because rationality, the distinctive
human excellence, is representation, the ethical task for a human being

103

is the heroic intellectual ascent to the representation of things *sub specie aeternitatis*. As a result of the Tractarian analysis of the conditions of representation, an analysis which brings to self-awareness the godhead of the independent I, the locus of the sense of life is discovered to be in the *will* of the heroic self; and the upshot is a thoroughgoing narcissism. Both in language and in life the Tractarian self is the maker of meaning.

In the later work, however, one finds a radically different response. Absent from the texts are any conclusions about ethics, the good, the sense of life, and so forth; he seems exclusively concerned with topics in logic, epistemology, philosophy of mathematics, and philosophy of mind. There is even the loss of the Socratic question itself, since to raise the "question" of the sense of life starts one down the path of rationality-as-representation and the will to power. The heroic attempt to raise and to answer (even if only by "showing") philosophical questions is replaced by a kind of writing much more diffuse and humble. Wittgenstein's later writing shows his unsayable answer to an unutterable question: Here, in a life exemplified by this sort of writing, by this kind of attention to things, is found "the sense of life."

But what sort of writing is it? What are its characteristic methods and intentions? To answer these questions by providing a hermeneutic for Wittgenstein's later work is the burden of this chapter. In the chapters that follow, this hermeneutic is put to work to give us a reading of the later Wittgenstein as a thinker possessed of an ethical vision of the very deepest sort.

I

However tempting the prospect, it is useless to try to summarize Wittgenstein's later work. He himself recognized that a systematic exposition of his thoughts was not possible to achieve. Recall these frank statements from the preface to the *Philosophical Investigations*:

> I have written down all these thoughts as *remarks,* short paragraphs, of which there is sometimes a fairly long chain about the same subject, while I sometimes make a sudden change, jumping from one topic to another. —It was my intention at first to bring all this together in a book whose form I pictured differently at different times. But the essential thing was that

the thoughts should proceed from one subject to another in a natural order and without breaks.

After several unsuccessful attempts to weld my results together into such a whole, I realized that I should never succeed. The best I could write would never be more than philosophical remarks; my thoughts were soon crippled if I tried to force them on in any single direction against their natural inclination. (PI, p. ix)

A philosopher's inability to write traditional philosophical prose might well strike one as merely an unfortunate quirk, and at the outset it must have appeared so to Wittgenstein himself; but he eventually came to see that his unusual style was not accidental:

—And this [style of writing] was, of course, connected to the very nature of the investigation. For this compels us to travel over a wide field of thought criss-cross in every direction. — The philosophical remarks in this book are, as it were, a number of sketches of landscapes which were made in the course of these long and involved journeyings. (PI, p. ix)

In view of this authoritative denial of the possibility of systematic presentation, how then does one make entry into his thoughts? Following his own suggestion that the later thoughts can be seen in "the right light only by contrast with and against the background of my old way of thinking" (PI, p. x), in this chapter we will attempt to open up his later thinking by tracing there the recapitulation of a distinction between what can be said and what must be shown, a distinction that has already been shown to be at the heart of the *Tractatus*.

To claim that a distinction between showing and saying is present in Wittgenstein's later work may seem silly on its face, since chapter two demonstrated that the distinction arose in the *Tractatus* because of the dominating presence there of rationality-as-representation and the picture theory of the proposition; and, however real the continuities, it is clear that the author of the *Investigations* does *not* follow the author of the *Tractatus* in believing this early theory to reveal "the incomparable essence of language" (PI, sec. 97). Obviously, the very same distinction between showing and saying could not survive such a sea change. After the middle thirties a distinction between what can be said and what must be shown is still fundamental in Wittgenstein's thinking, but it has its source in his peculiar conceptions of philosophy and human life, not in any particular philosophical doctrine like the picture theory. The distinction springs directly from his profound and intense vision of the sound human understanding and the sound human life. The limit of language that the later distinction between showing and saying marks is, to put it crudely, a limit of philosophical language.

All this will ultimately need a great deal of explanation; so let us begin by examining the notion of *nonsense,* a term of philosophical criticism central to both incarnations of Wittgenstein's thinking. As we have already seen, in the *Tractatus* the rigorous demarcation of sense from nonsense is the philosopher's fundamental aim (TLP, p. 3). Since most nonsense results from our "failure to understand the logic of our language" (TLP 4.003)—as is the case with the traditional problems of philosophy—to speak nonsense or to ask a nonsensical question is usually a very bad thing. It is to do something ridiculous, like to ask "whether the good is more or less identical than the beautiful" (4.003). But since, according to the doctrines of the *Tractatus,* ethics, logic, and Tractarian philosophy all lie outside the boundaries of sense, 'nonsense' is not always a derogatory characterization in Wittgenstein's early vocabulary. Sometimes there is something that cannot be conveyed except by uttering something that is, strictly speaking, nonsense. This is the case for the propositions of logic: they show the formal structure of language and world; but they are themselves literally senseless. They do not represent the existence of contingent states of affairs. It is also the case for Wittgenstein's philosophy itself. Witness the *Tractatus:* it says nothing, but it intends to show everything important.

Even these few remarks remind us of the intimate connection in the *Tractatus* between nonsense and the doctrine of showing. The realm of sense is the realm of what can be said; it is that which squares with rationality-as-representation and the picture theory. But something is necessary to avoid a positivist *reductio* of this philosophy, and the doctrine of showing is Wittgenstein's answer. Some nonsense—the benign variety—*shows* something that cannot be said.

> 6.522 There are, indeed, things that cannot be put into words. They *show themselves*. They are what is mystical. (TLP)

So the Tractarian use of 'nonsense' as a term of criticism goes hand in hand with the doctrine of showing. Without the latter, the former is severely incapacitated by the threat of a *reductio*. All this has been argued in detail in chapter two.

In the *Investigations* 'nonsense' is still the fundamental term of philosophical criticism, but there it seems always to condemn:

> 464.　　My aim is: to teach you to pass from a piece of disguised nonsense to something that is patent nonsense.

Again:

> 246.　　In what sense are my sensations *private?* —Well, only I can know whether I am really in pain: another person can only surmise it. —In one way this is false, and in another nonsense.

And again:

> "I believe that he is suffering." —Do I also *believe* that he isn't an automaton?
> It would go against the grain to use the word in both connections.
> (Or is it like this: I believe that he is suffering, but am certain that he is not an automaton? Nonsense!) (PI, p. 178)

The most incisive statement in the *Investigations* concerning philosophical sense and nonsense occurs at section 119:

> 119.　　The results of philosophy are the uncovering of one or another piece of plain nonsense and of bumps that the understanding has got by running its head up against the limits of language. These bumps make us see the value of the discovery.

A curious feature of Wittgenstein's thinking is that sometimes the *Investigations* and the *Tractatus* look *less* alike than they really are, and sometimes they look *more*. In section 119 the latter is the case. Here are familiar, apparently Tractarian, themes: the limits of language; and metaphysical philosophy as the "plain nonsense" produced when those limits are ignored. But where and how do these powerful images function in the later work? In the *Tractatus* nonsense is specified against an explicit theory of meaningfulness-within-a-language. The limits of language are drawn there by the picture theory of the proposition, the essence of language and thought; and nonsense is just what fails to meet the requirements of that theory. Against what is nonsense specified in the *Philosophical Investigations?* Surely that work contains no (tacit or explicit) theory of meaningfulness-within-a-language. What serves, then, as the baseline against which "the limits of language" can be circumscribed? And unless some such baseline can be drawn, what kind of philosophical weight is carried by calling something nonsense? These questions are extraordinarily deep, and our search for adequate answers will occupy this entire chapter, necessitating an apparently circuitous path.

Wittgenstein's own most direct approach to our questions is found at sections 499–500 of the *Philosophical Investigations:*

499.   To say "This combination of words makes no sense" excludes it from the sphere of language and thereby bounds the domain of language. But when one draws a boundary it may be for various kinds of reason. If I surround an area with a fence or a line or otherwise, the purpose may be to prevent someone from getting in or out; but it may also be part of a game and the players supposed, say, to jump over the boundary; or it may be to show where the property of one man ends and that of another begins, and so on. So if I draw a boundary line that is not yet to say what I am drawing it for.

500.   When a sentence is called senseless, it is not as it were its sense that is senseless. But a combination of words is being excluded from the language, withdrawn from circulation.

These puzzling remarks are, if true, very important, for they indicate we are most often misled when thinking philosophically about sense and nonsense. Consider the statement, "I, James C. Edwards, am feeling pain in Jones's body" (cf. PI, pp. 221–22). Is this statement a specimen of nonsense? Most philosophers—especially those influenced by the tradition culminating in the *Tractatus*—are disposed to try to answer the question by focusing attention on *the statement itself* in order to see whether it makes sense. The underlying picture operating here is that there are objective canons of sense; some uttered combinations of words meet these canons and others do not. The task of philosophy is to acquaint one with the standards of sense; and then, holding them up to these standards, one may judge various utterances to be either sense or nonsense. Such judgments can be perfectly objective, it is claimed, since the canons of sense are objectively given in the nature of thought and language. When, for example, one judges a particular philosophical position to be nonsensical, one means by this that any full statement of that position inevitably violates the canons of sense comprised in thought and language.

In the *Tractatus,* of course, these standards of sense in thought and language are those of rationality-as-representation and the picture theory. The nature of thought demands that passive representation of reality is thought's only possible function, and the picture theory of language purports to give one a technique for determining whether a putative proposition really is a thought or is only masquerading as one.

But this picture of sense and nonsense certainly does not survive into the *Philosophical Investigations.* Wittgenstein came to see how dangerous a picture is involved in believing that standards of sense are somehow "out there," somehow given once and for all in thought and language themselves. In sections 499–500 he is suggesting another picture as more appropriate: judging some utterance to be nonsense is much like saying "I cannot go along with you there." It is to heed or to erect a boundary; and, as he reminds us, boundaries are drawn *by us,* and for quite different reasons. The canons of sense are not given once and for all; they vary at different times, for different persons, and for many reasons. To see judgments of sense and nonsense in this light tends to diminish their apparent "objectivity" and to make philosophical criticism that depends upon such judgments seem much less "scientific," since to make such a judgment is just to call attention to a boundary that someone, perhaps only oneself, has drawn in language for a particular purpose. It is a grammatical remark: "We don't talk like that." We don't cross that boundary.

In the *Tractatus* the boundary between sense and nonsense is totally impersonal. The limits of language and thought are given in the essences of language and thought themselves, and the individual speaker and thinker is completely powerless to alter those limits. The structure of thought assumes a daunting, inhuman aspect.

> 97.   Thought is surrounded by a halo. —Its essence, logic, presents an order, in fact the a priori order of the world: that is, the order of *possibilities,* which must be common to world and thought. But this order, it seems, must be *utterly simple.* It is prior to all experience, must run through all experience; no empirical cloudiness or uncertainty must be allowed to affect it. —It must rather be of the purest crystal. But this crystal does not appear as an abstraction; but as something concrete, indeed, as the most concrete, as it were the *hardest* thing there is (*Tractatus Logico-Philosophicus* No. 5.5563). (PI, sec. 97)

Wittgenstein took such pictures seriously, since they represent our deepest philosophical intuitions and since their presence may shape our perceptions in hidden but fundamental ways. This picture of the structure of thought as fixed a priori—as utterly simple, nonexperiential, "crystalline"—has great charm, as the history of Western philosophy illustrates; but in the *Investigations* it is marked as a dangerous illusion. There the distinction between sense and nonsense acquires human size and features. No longer is the structure of thought an alien, rigid, determined system; sense is something *we* make (or fail to). (For a comparison, think here of Kierkegaard's revulsion for Hegel's impersonal, deterministic System.) To judge something to be nonsense is to draw attention to a boundary, a very human thing, and boundaries have significances that are not given once and for all by the "essence" of a boundary:

> If I surround an area with a fence or a line or otherwise, the purpose may be to prevent someone from getting in or out; but it may also be part of a game and the players supposed, say, to jump over the boundary; or it may show where the property of one man ends and that of another begins, and so on. So if I draw a boundary line that is not yet to say what I am drawing it for. (PI, sec. 499)

Boundaries are drawn by me (or by us). These lines are not inhumanly rigid; they may be redrawn or ignored (perhaps with certain penalties). A certain kind of freedom is possible: what can be excluded from language also could be included; what can be withdrawn from circulation could later be reintroduced (see PI, sec. 500).

II

THESE REMARKS are, to say the least, obscure; but before the puzzling features of sections 499 – 500 can be understood it will be necessary to approach the notion of philosophical nonsense from another direction. It is crucial for us to recognize the unusual and special significance of the use of 'nonsense' as Wittgenstein's fundamental term of criticism.

For most contemporary philosophers the epithet 'nonsense' functions merely as an index of the intensity of criticism. When such a philosopher judges a given philosophical theory or argument to be nonsense, he just means to indicate that it is obviously faulty for one reason or another, or that its faults are *silly* and *uninteresting* once revealed. Perhaps most philosophical constructions are finally inadequate to their tasks; but most are not, according to this conception, *nonsense,* since their flaws are far from being obvious or silly. A natural scientist could use the notion of nonsense in precisely the same way. To characterize a particular scientific theory (e.g., the flat-earth hypothesis) as nonsense is just to say that it is *obviously* and *uninterestingly* faulty, at least to scientists. Thus in its ordinary scientific and philosophical usage, 'nonsense' merely intensifies a judgment that a given theory or argument is inadequate to its task. The really fundamental terms of criticism on this conception are ones like *true/false, plausible/implausible,* etc.; the use of 'nonsense' just indicates the intensity with which a term of criticism like 'false' or 'implausible' is being pressed in a given instance. It is not a term with a special and autonomous sense of its own.

For Wittgenstein, however, the notion of nonsense is fundamental and autonomous; nonsense is something special to philosophy. And this autonomy is intimately connected to his peculiar and untraditional conception of philosophy itself. Traditional philosophy has never doubted that there are objective and eternal philosophical truths to be expounded, no matter how difficult they may be to find and to state. Philosophical truths are, of course, a priori; they do not deal with mere matters of fact. But they are still statable truths: there are conceptual truths to be discovered as well as truths of fact. Philosophers who see their discipline in this traditional way operate with a particular model of philosophy, one that may be called the "scientific" model of philosophy. Calling it that draws attention to some of its distinctive features, features it shares with the physical and social sciences: it aims for philosophy to be an objective and impersonal discipline collecting data impartially and constructing theories ("analyses") that can, ideally, be accepted and built upon in the way that scientific theories are.

The sentences that make up the corpus of natural science are, if true at all, true because they accurately state facts: they (correctly) describe and explain the world. Science intends to bring out into the open the order hidden behind the veil of the phenomena. In like manner, the accomplishments of philosophy are traditionally considered to be explanatory and descriptive. But rather than describing contingent facts, they accurately describe and explain concepts and conceptual relations. The "scientific" model of philosophy exclusively emphasizes these descriptive and explanatory aims for philosophical work. Like natural science, "scientific" philosophy is considered to solve its problems by bringing out into the open what once was hidden. (The "analysis of concepts" is supposed to be a primary means to this end.) The assumption throughout is that philosophical problems are no less pressing and genuine than scientific ones, although they are not straightforward empirical problems. They are *logical* problems, and they are solved by the discovery of objective and eternal philosophical (logical, conceptual) truths.

Three features of this "scientific" model deserve close attention. The first has to do with the connection between explanation and generality. The "scientific" model stresses the explanatory aim of philosophy, and our standard conception of adequate explanation involves the notion of generality. We typically explain the puzzling behavior of some phenomenon by showing that there is some general law of which this behavior is just an instance. The particular case loses its peculiarity when it is seen as the outcome of some general (usually hidden) pattern or regularity. Thus science aims at solving the puzzles that give rise to it by constructing explanatory theories of greater and greater scope. "Scientific" philosophy also typically attempts to explain particular facts or problems by the construction of general theories or analyses. As an example, think of the picture theory of the *Tractatus* as a general theory used to explain how a proposition is able to communicate a new sense to us (4.027). The particular case or puzzle is explained when set against the general philosophical theory; thus it is the general theory that really answers our philosophical needs. A second feature to be noted is the role of discursive argument in such philosophy. On the "scientific" model it is by way of argument that philosophical truths are discovered and made known. A philosophical truth is, ideally, open to proof by means of such argument. A third feature has to do with the terms of appraisal of philosophy done on the "scientific" model. Not surprisingly, the model evaluates philosophical claims, arguments, positions, and ideologies in (the scientific, descriptive) terms of truth and falsity, plausibility and implausibility, correctness and error.

In his own practice Wittgenstein rejects this model of philosophy in its entirety.

109. It was true to say that our considerations could not be scientific ones. . . . And we may not advance any kind of theory. There must not be anything hypothetical in our considerations. We must do away with all *explanation,* and description alone must take its place. . . . The problems are solved, not by giving new information, but by arranging what we have always known. Philosophy is a battle against the bewitchment of our intelligence by means of language.

124. Philosophy may in no way interfere with the actual use of language; it can in the end only describe it.
      For it cannot give it any foundation either.
      It leaves everything as it is.

126. Philosophy simply puts everything before us, and neither explains nor deduces anything. —Since everything lies open to view there is nothing to explain. For what is hidden, for example, is of no interest to us.
      One might also give the name "philosophy" to what is possible *before* all new discoveries and inventions.

128. If one tried to advance *theses* in philosphy, it would never be possible to question them, because everyone would agree to them.

133.　　　For the clarity we are aiming at is indeed *complete*
clarity. But this simply means that the philosophical
problems should *completely* disappear.

The real discovery is the one that makes me capable
of stopping doing philosophy when I want to. —The
one which gives philosophy peace, so that it is no longer
tormented by questions which bring *itself* in question.
—Instead we now demonstrate a method, by examples;
and the series of examples can be broken off. —Problems are solved (difficulties eliminated), not a *single*
problem.

There is not *a* philosophical method, though there are
indeed methods, like different therapies.

The most clear-cut textual evidence of Wittgenstein's rejection of
the "scientific" model occurs in the *Blue Book* (1933–34):

[P]hilosophers constantly see the method of science before
their eyes, and are irresistibly tempted to ask and answer questions in the way science does. This tendency is the real source
of metaphysics, and leads the philosopher into complete darkness. I want to say here that it can never be our job to reduce
anything to anything, or to explain anything. Philosophy really
is 'purely descriptive.' (BB, p. 18)

These passages demonstrate how very far away from science Wittgenstein considered his own philosophical work to be. "It was true to
say that our considerations could not be scientific ones. . . . And we
may not advance any kind of theory." (PI, sec. 109). This attitude is in
direct contrast to the one with which one approaches the problems of
science (and of philosophy on the "scientific" model), for there the
problems *are* solved "by giving new information." Philosophy, in
Wittgenstein's view, is precisely nonscientific in being possible "*before* all new discoveries and inventions," even discoveries about concepts (PI, sec. 126). It is "non-scientific" as well in that it dispenses
with philosophical evaluations in terms of right/wrong and true/false.

It is useful to emphasize three of Wittgenstein's most specific di-
vergences from the "scientific" model of philosophy. The first is his
adamant refusal to advance any philosophical theories or theses. The

second divergence is connected with this rejection of philosophical theorizing; it is Wittgenstein's hatred of explanation-as-generalization. Science aims at such explanation; and Wittgenstein was sure that philosophy had succumbed to its influence:

> Our craving for generality has another main source: our preoccupation with the method of science. I mean the method of reducing the explanation of natural phenomena to the smallest possible number of primitive natural laws; and, in mathematics, of unifying the treatment of different topics by using a generalization. (BB, p. 18)

He rejected this "contemptuous attitude towards the particular case" BB, p. 18), and his rejection runs through all his philosophical interests. It is very clear in his notes on Frazer, for instance, that Wittgenstein believes many of the anthropologist's excesses in *The Golden Bough* are due to his believing that all magic and myth *must* be accounted for by some small set of general principles.

The third divergence from the "scientific" model is Wittgenstein's curious description of how philosophical difficulties come to an end. In contrast to science, which is never complete and which proceeds by the constant accumulation and replacement of theory and knowledge, good philosophy (according to Wittgenstein) aims at complete clarity. ("For the clarity we are aiming at is indeed *complete* clarity. But this simply means that the philosophical problems should *completely* disappear.") This clarity, it should be noted, comes all at once, not piece by piece. Science proceeds toward the correct description of the world part by part, theory by theory. But in his philosophy, says Wittgenstein, correct understanding comes all at once. ("—Problems are solved (difficulties eliminated), not a *single* problem.") This is one of the most striking differences between Wittgensteinian and "scientific" philosophy, and it is one of the most difficult to understand. What sort of understanding is it that comes all at once, and for what sort of problem is such understanding the appropriate remedy?

These questions bring us back to the fundamental importance of the notion of nonsense. Since on Wittgenstein's conception the constructions of metaphysical philosophy itself are literally nonsense, since all traditional philosophical problems, issues, arguments, and theories fail to make any real sense, it is not surprising that enlightened

philosophical understanding must be so "unscientific" on his account
and that his own philosophical techniques, designed to show forth that
nonsense, look so queer to the traditional philosopher. But having said
all that, we are still left puzzled by the substantial force of the term
'nonsense'. If it is not drawn against a theory of language like that of
the *Tractatus,* and if it is not functioning as an intensifier in a "scientific" conception of philosophy, then what is it doing?

One may begin with the obvious and remind oneself that for the
later Wittgenstein nonsense and language are still intimately connected; the philosopher is beset with nonsense because something has
gone wrong with his language, or rather, something has gone wrong in
the philosopher's relation to his language.

> Philosophy [i.e., Wittgensteinian philosophy] is a battle
> against the bewitchment of our intelligence by means of lan-
> guage. (PI, sec. 109)

But if our intelligence has been bewitched by language, thus producing
nonsense, what is the nature of the spell? After all, language is ours;
we use it to our purposes, in our own ways. How does our servant so
enchant us? The notion of a grammatical picture is crucial here:

> 115.   A *picture* held us captive. And we could not get out-
>   side it, for it lay in our language and language seemed to
>   repeat it to us inexorably. (PI)

What is a grammatical picture? Here are some examples culled
from the later work.

> 1.   The picture one associates with the question "Are
>   there three consecutive sevens in the expansion of pi?":
>   Here the picture is something like an infinitely long line
>   of numbers, reaching to the horizon. One can see only a
>   small part of the numbers, but there is another (God?)
>   who has better eyes or a telescope, and he can see far-
>   ther. In fact, he can see as far as the numbers reach. One
>   wonders whether at any spot along the line of numbers
>   there occur three consecutive sevens. One can imagine a
>   drawing of this picture. (See PI, sec. 352)

2.   The picture that men have souls: in a drawn picture, the soul might be represented by a spot of light or a dove. (See PI, sec. 422)

3.   The picture of blindness as a darkness in the head or in the soul of the blind man. (See PI, sec. 424)

4.   The picture that thinking goes on in the head, that when one would like to know what John is thinking one wants to be able to see what is going on in John's head: this sort of picture occurs frequently in cartoons. It is related to the picture that thinking goes on in a ghostly medium, represented by the illuminated lightbulb in the "thought-balloon" over Pogo's head. (See PI, sec. 427)

5.   The picture of the carbon atoms of benzene lying at the corners of a hexagon: a familiar representation in textbooks of chemistry. (See PI, p. 184e and sec. 422)

6.   The picture of the awakening of consciousness at some point in the evolutionary process: "The picture is something like this: Though the ether is filled with vibrations the earth is dark. But one day man opens his eyes and there is light." (See PI, p. 184e)

7.   The picture of the earth as a very old planet, existing for eons before our birth: this is contrasted with the picture of one who believes it came into being just fifty years ago. (See z, sec. 462)

8.   The religious picture of the all-seeing eye of God. (See LC, p. 71)

From this sampling, one can see that under the rubric 'picture' Wittgenstein has collected a variety of things. Compare and contrast, for example, pictures 1, 4, 5, 7, and 8. There are great differences here, but there are similarities as well. The crucial similarity lies in the relationship of pictures to language. Pictures inhere in our language, and they determine our perception of our language in some basic ways.

In the first place, a grammatical picture seems to give us a definitive account of the way we should speak. That is, under the influence of such a picture we seem to know in a flash the way in which certain words and expressions are to be used; we seem immediately to intuit their grammars. Under the spell of such intuition we may easily forget or fail to see other uses of the words and expressions in question, uses that do not accord with the paradigm given in the picture. The picture then holds us captive; all the uses of the words that come to mind are those the picture suggests. The others get forgotten or ignored. The specification of our grammar that is given by a grammatical picture is usually incomplete, and therefore misleading.

But grammatical pictures do more than furnish the philosopher with a (misleading, partial) picture of his grammar. They seem also to give a direct insight into the facts on which that grammar rests. A picture is ordinarily intended to be an iconic representation of some facts, as when a blueprint represents the structure of a certain machine; and grammatical pictures likewise seem to be attempts to represent iconically the facts that determine the forms of our language. Grammatical pictures seem to show forth the way things are at the very deepest level; they seem to represent the metaphysical facts on which the grammatical forms of our language ultimately rest. When, for example, persons talk about the soul, or about the impossibility of hiding anything from God, they are easily led by the pictures inherent in the grammar of their talk (and their connection with talk about other sorts of things) to conceive of what they are saying in certain ways, e.g., to conceive of the soul as an entity—the seat of consciousness—within the body, or to conceive anthropomorphically of God as a superperson who can in some way literally see everything.

> When we look into ourselves when we do philosophy, we often get to see such a picture. A full-blown representation of our grammar. Not facts; but as it were illustrated turns of speech. (PI, sec. 295)

The examples of pictures given three paragraphs back are in some sense an illustration of our grammar, seeming representations of metaphysical facts.

Now ordinarily these grammatical pictures are both inevitable and perfectly harmless. Having some sort of pictures associated with, say, our talk about God is inescapable. For Wittgenstein 'picture' was not necessarily a term of reproach.

> "God's eye sees everything" —I want to say of this that it uses a picture. I don't want to belittle the person who says it. . . .

If I say he used a picture, I don't want to say anything he himself wouldn't say. . . . When I say he's using a picture, I'm
merely making a grammatical remark. . . . (LC, p. 71)

Usually these grammatical pictures are quite harmless. When one is
puzzled about friend Sharon's reaction to a proposal of marriage and
says, "I wish I knew what was going on in her head" (or "what she
feels in her heart," or "what is going on in her mind"), the (incipiently
Cartesian) pictures present in one's speech are not in the least troublesome. The troubles begin when one starts to think *philosophically*
about, say, human beings, or about God. Then these inevitable grammatical illustrations begin to do their dirty work, forcing one's thinking
into certain paths, the servant bewitching his master.

We predicate of the thing what lies in the method of representing it. Impressed by the possibility of a comparison, we
think we are perceiving a state of affairs of the highest generality. (PI, sec. 104)

One thinks that one is tracing the outline of the thing's nature over and over again, and one is merely tracing round the
frame through which we look at it. (PI, sec. 114)

Why should this be the case? What *is* philosophical thinking, such
that it promotes the enchantment by language that leads to talking nonsense? It is impossible to believe that mere *inattention* habitually
causes us to lose sight of the application of a picture (cf. PI, sec. 349,
374, 422) or to "cross" pictures belonging to different grammars (PI,
sec. 191). No, some real and deep compulsion is involved; we are,
Wittgenstein says, *bewitched* by language when doing philosophy.

The problems arising through a misinterpretation of our
forms of language have the character of *depth*. They are deep
disquietudes; their roots are as deep in us as the forms of our
language and their significance is as great as the importance of
our language. (PI, sec. 111)

Wittgenstein concludes section 111 with this remark:

—Let us ask ourselves: why do we feel a grammatical joke to be *deep*? (And that is what the depth of philosophy is.)

Grammatical jokes do present a certain kind of nonsense; perhaps the deep and pernicious nonsense of philosophy can be illuminated by the comparison. Lewis Carroll's books and poems are full of such jokes; since he is mentioned twice in the *Philosophical Investigations* (sec. 13 and p. 198), perhaps it is appropriate to use one of his whimsies as an example.[1] In chapter seven of *Through the Looking-Glass,* the White King, searching about for his messengers, tells Alice,

"Just look along the road, and tell me if you can see either of them."
"I see nobody on the road," said Alice.
"I only wish *I* had such eyes," the King remarked in a fretful tone. "To be able to see Nobody! And at that distance too! Why, it's as much as *I* can do to see real people, by this light."

Later the Messenger appears, and the following dialogue ensues:

"Who did you pass on the road?" the King went on, holding out his hand to the Messenger for some more hay.
"Nobody," said the Messenger.
"Quite right," said the King: "this young lady saw him too. So of course Nobody walks slower than you."
"I do my best," the Messenger said in a sullen tone. "I'm sure nobody walks much faster than I do!"
"He can't do that," said the King, "or else he'd have been here first."[2]

Why is this funny? And why does its humor seem to be deeper than that built, like slapstick, on mere physical incongruity or surprise? The incongruity that produces the humor in Carroll's dialogue is rooted in the grammar of our language. It is the grammar that gets us leaning in one direction and then, just at the crucial moment, pulls the carpet in another, spilling us onto the floor. For example, replying to the King, Alice innocently says, "I see nobody on the road." 'To see' is here a transitive verb; it takes a direct object. The grammar of 'to see', what some have called the intentionality of sensation, leads one to expect that whenever one sees, one sees *something*. There must be something—something real?—that is the object of one's seeing; so when Alice tells the King she sees nobody, he assumes that 'nobody' is the name of the object that she must see. (He also assumes that this "object" is some sort of person.) So he compliments the visual acuity that allows her to see (the person) "Nobody" at great distance and in bad light. One is given a certain picture by the grammar of 'to see'; the King takes this picture literally, and inspired nonsense is the result. A picture produced by the grammar of our language holds the King captive, and we laugh at his royal bewitchment. The depth of the humor lies in the fact that we recognize that his comical predicament is not entirely fortuitous; there is some basis for the nonsense he is talking. We are tempted to call the joke a "philosophical" one because we sense it has its roots in something more than just chance circumstance, namely, in language (and hence *thought*) itself.

Wittgenstein says that the depth of philosophy has the same source. Lest one think it utterly implausible that a self-conscious philosopher could make a mistake comparable to the King's, consider this section from the *Investigations:*

518.   Socrates to Theaetetus: "And if someone thinks mustn't he think something?" —Th. "Yes, he must." — Soc. "And if he thinks something, mustn't it be something real?" —Th. "Apparently."

And mustn't someone who is painting be painting something—and someone who is painting something be painting something real! —Well, tell me what the object of the painting is: the picture of a man (e.g.), or the man that the picture portrays?

Like the King and his grammar of seeing, Socrates (or at least Theaetetus) is led by the grammar of his language to assert that thought must always be about something real, an assertion that quickly leads him into dark labyrinths of philosophy, for if all thought is of the real, how then is false judgment about the existence of particulars possible? We appear to need a philosophical theory, ultimately a whole philosophy of language, to account for the phenomenon; philosophy-as-explanation (i.e., metaphysics) seems a requirement of intellectual integrity. Like the King of Wonderland, says Wittgenstein, the philosophers are captivated by a grammatical picture. All are talking nonsense.

A grammatical picture is a conceptual reality; it is there in our language. As a "picture" it seems to represent to us the metaphysical facts upon which some part of our grammar rests and to which it necessarily conforms. We *read* it as a picture, in this literal, representational sense. Metaphysical philosophy, taking as its task the explication and systematization of these grammatical pictures, thus presents itself as a kind of superscience, revealing the superfacts on which ordinary facts depend. Philosophy thus becomes the queen of the sciences, since its subject matter is absolutely fundamental to all others. On what does this powerful conception ultimately rest? It rests first of all upon the assumption that grammatical pictures are really pictures, i.e., that they (are intended to) represent facts (or superfacts). But whence that assumption? There is no denying that the grammar of a language is filled with images, metaphors, tropes; it is arguable that language could not fail to be "pictorial" in this sense. The question is: why do we begin to read these grammatical pictures as literal ones? Why do we take them to be literal representations of the superfacts on which our grammar rests and to which it conforms?

Another way to raise this same question, using an important Wittgensteinian distinction which has remained somewhat murky, is to ask why it is that the *images* naturally inherent in our grammar are constantly being turned by us into *pictures*. Wittgenstein himself makes the distinction between image (*Vorstellung*) and picture (*Bild*) at sections 300–301 of the *Investigations*. There he is discussing the language-game we play with 'pain'; in particular he is remarking upon the behaviorist tendency to focus attention only upon the overt behavior constitutive of the language-game, thereby being tempted to identify someone's being in pain with his exhibiting a certain sort of behavior.

300.   It is—we should like to say—not merely the picture of the behavior that plays a part in the language-game with the words "he is in pain," but also the picture of the pain. Or, not merely the paradigm of the behavior, but also that of the pain. —It is a misunderstanding to say "The picture of pain enters into the language-game with the word 'pain'." The image of pain is not a picture and *this* image is not replaceable in the language-game by anything we should call a picture. —The image of pain certainly enters into the language-game in a sense; only not as a picture.

301.   An image is not a picture, but a picture can correspond to it.

What does it mean, that an image is not a picture? Wittgenstein's answer is clear: "Images tell us nothing, either right or wrong, about the eternal world. (Images are not hallucinations, nor yet fancies.)" (z, sec. 621). Pictures, of whatever sort, *do* purport to tell us something about the world. Because they are pictures, they model (represent), truly or falsely, some state of affairs. But an image, says Wittgenstein, does not represent, as does a picture. It does not reach out to model some reality. Images are thus not hallucinations, for they are not delusory pictures; nor are they fancies, for they are neither under our control, as are our fancies, nor are they intended as fantastic representations of reality. An image may indeed be a constituent part of a language-game, but this image is not as such functioning as a *representation*.

But if an image is not a representation, what is it? Reflection upon Wittgenstein's examples of grammatical pictures affords us a rudimentary understanding, sufficient to our present purposes. Grammatical pictures, hence grammatical images, are just that: *grammatical*. They are present in (in a certain sense, they *are*) the grammar of our language. Take, for example, the image of pain. Because we (truthfully) say things like "The first pain was in the chest; it started about two o'clock and lasted about an hour," we have the image of pain as an awful *inner event:* inner, because we say "*in* the chest"; event, because we can tell when it started and when it stopped. The image of pain is given there in the grammar: a pain is a thing, an event, spatially and temporally locatable.

An image, then, is just a particular grammatical pattern in our speech. It is the way we talk about something. While an image can certainly strongly incline us toward certain pictures, pictures which naturally seem "right" (a drawing of a red, pulsating glow, centered in the chest: the pain of heart attack), these "natural" pictures only *correspond to* (PI, sec. 301) our image; they are not the image itself. (A person unfamiliar with our culture's pictorial conventions might not understand the drawing at all, even if he had had a heart attack and was a speaker of English. There are no truly "natural" representations.) A drawing of the sort just mentioned is, of course, not intended as a literal representaion of the pain of heart attack. We would grossly and comically misunderstand its sense if we expected the chests of heart attack victims literally to glow; we would be literalizing an image into a physical picture. A more subtle (and much more common) literalization occurs when we use the grammatical image of pain as awful inner event as a *metaphysical* picture: then we do not look for red glows; but we think of the pain as an intangible "something" occurring in the literal, though mysterious, territory of consciousness. We thereby erect a metaphysical account on the literalization of an image.

Using Wittgenstein's terminology, we might now make a distinction between grammatical images and grammatical pictures. (I am not claiming that Wittgenstein himself consistently did so; only that he *could* have.) Images are naturally and inevitably present in our grammar; they become grammatical pictures—and thus lead to the convolutions of metaphysical philosophy—when they are literalized into representations of the superfacts upon which our language-games rest. But why does this literalization take place?

Rationality-as-representation assumes that the fundamental and definitive task of thought is the representation of facts; language, the medium of thought's expression, must therefore have representation as its fundamental intention too. Since grammatical images are everywhere embedded in language, one who is under the spell of rationality-as-representation is certain to read them as real pictures, as literal representations of superfacts. Since they are deep (perhaps inescapable) features of our language, hence of our thought as well, and since the sole task of thought is representation of reality, these grammatical images *must,* it seems, represent reality too. What else could they be doing? Thus rationality-as-representation is the crucial factor here; it is that powerful and honored conception that turns grammatical images into representations and thus, according to Wittgenstein, leads us into the toils of philosophy. Grammatical images enchant us when we conjoin them with rationality-as-representation and thus try to read them as representations of metaphysical superfacts. Rationality-as-representation is a literalization of mind itself; it is a reduction of *mind* to *intellect.* The literalization of images into pictures is the consequence of a prior literalization of thought into representation, person into seeing eye.

But now the question arises: whence rationality-as-representation? A full discussion of this must wait on a fuller understanding of Wittgenstein's later distinction between showing and saying, but it is perhaps worthwhile to insist here that rationality-as-representation is not some sort of *mistake*. What has gone wrong is something very deep and untouched by traditional philosophy. One is reminded of some words of Kierkegaard's:

> It is from this side, in the first instance, that objection must be made to modern philosophy; not that it has a mistaken presupposition, but that it has a comical presupposition, occasioned by its having forgotten, in a sort of world-historical absent-mindedness, what it means to be a human being. Not indeed, what it means to be a human being in general; for this is the sort of thing that one might even induce a speculative philosopher to agree to; but what it means that you and I and he are human beings, each one for himself.[3]

But, to return to our earlier comparison, there is still a great difference between Lewis Carroll's White King and Plato's Theaetetus: we actually laugh at the King, but Theaetetus is no figure of fun. The exchange between Alice and the King is a joke; but the dialogue between Socrates and Theaetetus is philosophy, serious business indeed. If Kierkegaard is right in thinking that modern philosophy rests upon a comical presupposition, why don't we get the joke? If, according to Wittgenstein, the depth of philosophy is the depth of a grammatical joke, and if philosophy is nonsense, why aren't we laughing?

III

LET US pause here to take stock of where we have come. In this chapter we are trying to demonstrate the existence in Wittgenstein's later work of a distinction between what can be said and what must be shown; and, as in the *Tractatus,* we have assumed that the distinction in the later work is intimately bound up with the use of 'nonsense' as the fundamental term of philosophical criticism. Of course, the category of nonsense in the later work is not an easy one to understand, especially since the conceptions that gave that category some bite in the *Tractatus*—the picture theory, for example—are conspicuously absent after the middle thirties. How then can the distinction between sense and nonsense be drawn? Wittgenstein's remarks in sections 499–500 of the *Investigations,* gesturing at a conception of nonsense rooted in human activity rather than in the crystalline structure of thought itself, are puzzling, even when seen in the light of his disavowal of the traditional "scientific" model of philosophy. Even to take note of the role of language in the generation of philosophical nonsense, seeing there the bewitching power of grammatical pictures when taken literally, in accordance with rationality-as-representation, leaves mysterious some crucial features of his conception of nonsense. In particular it still leaves unexplained both the particular and autonomous force of nonsense as a category of criticism in Wittgenstein's hands and the power of rationality-as-representation to bewitch us into nonsense by seeing grammatical pictures as metaphysical representations of superfacts.

To make another start at illuminating the first of these mysteries, it will be necessary to return to the topic of Wittgenstein's radical conception of his philosophical methodology. To grasp what 'nonsense' means for Wittgenstein we must observe its use in his actual philosophical criticism, and so must understand the way in which that criticism is pursued. If it is correct that he disavowed the "scientific" model of philosophy, what did he put in its place? The notion of a *language-game* offers an important clue to his alternative model.

Language-games are crucial to Wittgenstein's philosophy, since the source of disguised philosophical nonsense lies in the grammatical pictures inherent in a natural language and since the critical use of language-games is somehow supposed to break the hold of such pictures and to free us from the nonsense they create. But how exactly are language-games supposed to accomplish this task? Are they functioning merely as heuristic devices, dramatically illustrating substantive philosophical theses and thus serving as ways of pressing philosophical arguments independent of the language-games themselves? (The language-game Wittgenstein invents at section 8 of the *Investigations* seems to fit this heuristic model: he there seems to be accusing Augustine of a hasty generalization in his account of language, illustrating the hastiness by means of the language-game of section 8, which does not easily fit the Augustinian model.) But not all of his uses of language-games can be accommodated to the heuristic model. Sometimes it seems that, rather than illustrating independent philosophical theses, language-games function as final standards of sense; they determine what it makes sense to say and do.

654.   Our mistake is to look for an explanation where we ought to look at what happens as a "proto-phenome-

non." That is, where we ought to have said: *this language-game is played.*

655.   The question is not one of explaining a language-game by means of our experiences, but of noting a language-game. (PI, sec. 654–55)

Here he seems to assume that language-games, the ones we actually do or possibly could play, are immune to philosophical questioning or support. Particular moves within a language-game may be questioned, justified, explained. The language-game as a whole, however, cannot be. Language-games are "proto-phenomena." They provide the final standards of sense.

What, then, is the true role of language-games in Wittgenstein's philosophy? Are they heuristic devices, or are they standards of sense? His most explicit remark about his use of language-games occurs in section 130 of the *Philosophical Investigations:*

> Our clear and simple language-games are not preparatory studies for a future regularization of language—as it were first approximations, ignoring friction and air-resistance. The language-games are rather set up as *objects of comparison* which are meant to throw light on the facts of our language by way not only of similarities, but also of dissimilarities.

This remark is quite similar to one from a notebook of Wittgenstein's probably written about 1934, and quoted by Rush Rhees.[4]

> When I describe certain simple language games, this is not in order to construct from them gradually the processes of our developed language—or of thinking—which only leads to injustice (Nicod and Russell). I simply set forth the games as what they are, and let them shed their light on the particular problems.

It is easy to see how these warnings are superficially applicable to the use of language-games like the language-game in section 2 of the *Investigations*. Looking at that language-game, one might believe that it was intended to be a "first approximation" to a "future regularization of language"; so it is useful to be told explicitly that this is not

Wittgenstein's intention. The real difficulty presented by section 130 is the notion of "objects of comparison."

The notion of an "object of comparison" can only be understood when set against Wittgenstein's radically nontraditional conception of his own philosophical practice. It is worthwhile to remind ourselves that Wittgenstein himself claimed that his practice of philosophy was *revolutionary*. In his Cambridge lecture of 1932–33 (recorded by G. E. Moore and published in Moore's *Philosophical Papers*) Wittgenstein said that what he was doing was a "new subject" and not a stage in a "continuous development." (All excerpts from the lectures are from ML, p. 278.) According to Wittgenstein (via Moore), there was now, in philosophy, "a 'kink' in the 'development of human thought,' comparable to that which occurred when Galileo and his contemporaries invented dynamics. . . ." This revolutionary development was the discovery of a "new method" like that when "chemistry was developed out of alchemy."

In these lectures Wittgenstein did not offer much detail about this new method. He did say that philosophy begins when we get "in a muddle about things" and that the "new subject" consisted "in something like putting in order our notions as to what can be said about the world." But it should be noticed that the "new method" of philosophy does not consist in or depend upon the discovery of any new facts; it deals with "trivial" things—"things we all know already." Philosophy can remove our "intellectual discomfort" only by a "synopsis" of these trivialities. Moore adds, "As regards to his own work, [Wittgenstein] said it did not matter whether his results were true or not; what mattered was that a 'method had been found'."

These remarks are cryptic indeed. They can be fully understood only against the backdrop of all the later work; but we must begin to build that clarifying backdrop somewhere, and we may fruitfully start with a suggestive, if puzzling, remark in the same 1932–33 lectures. At one point there Wittgenstein touched on the kind of reasoning properly used in settling aesthetic disputes. Moore reports Wittgenstein's lecture:

> What Aesthetics tries to do, he said, is to give *reasons*.
> . . . *Reasons,* he said, in Aesthetics, are "of the nature of further descriptions," e.g., you can make a person see what Brahms was driving at by showing him lots of pieces by

Brahms, or by comparing him to a contemporary author; and all that Aesthetics does is "to draw your attention to a thing," to "place things side by side." He said that if, by giving "reasons" of this sort, you make the other person "see what you see" but it "still doesn't appeal to him," that is "an end" of the discussion; and that what he, Wittgenstein, had "at the back of his mind" was "the idea that aesthetic discussions were like discussions in a court of law," where you try to "clear up the circumstances" of the action which is being tried, hoping that in the end what you say will "appeal to the judge." And he said that the same sort of "reasons" were given, not only in Ethics, but also in Philosophy. (ML, p. 278)

The last sentence of the quoted paragraph is our touchstone, but let us look first at the development of the passage. Aesthetic arguments arise, of course, out of disputes over works of art. For example, there could arise a dispute over whether Brahms was right to reject Joachim's suggestion that his Fourth Symphony should be opened by two chords. (This is Wittgenstein's own example.) Now, what sort of reasons (i.e., what sort of reasoning) would be appropriate to use in the defense of Brahms's rejection of the suggestion? What Wittgenstein says is very curious. Moore reports: *"Reasons,* he said, in Aesthetics, are 'of the nature of further descriptions.'" All that argument in aesthetics does "is to draw your attention to a thing, to 'place things side by side.'" One could defend Brahms's rejection by trying to show one's disputant that Joachim's suggestion does not "fit" with (to use Moore's phrase) "what Brahms was driving at." And how could one do this? Well, perhaps one would play for one's disputant lots of works by Brahms and try to get him to "hear" against this background the incongruity of the Joachim-revised Fourth Symphony. Or perhaps one could make the point by comparing Brahms to a contemporary composer, so as to indicate to the disputant something of the spirit and mood of Brahms's work, the tradition from which it came, or the audience for which it was intended. Or perhaps all that one could do (and, perhaps, all that would be required) is to play *seriatim* both the revised and unrevised versions of the symphony and say, "Don't you hear that the first way is wrong, that it sounds better (that it sounds *right*) the second way?"

Given their characteristic form and intention, it is possible and proper that aesthetic arguments not end in agreement; in such matters (in contrast to other sorts of disputes) there is no proper way for either party rationally to *compel* the agreement of the other. All that reasoning in such disputes can do is to try to "make the other person 'see what you see'." If, after all your efforts at illumination, what he sees in the work of art " 'doesn't appeal to him'," then that is " 'an end' " of the discussion. Moore has recorded that

> what he, Wittgenstein, had at "the back of his mind" was "the idea that aesthetic discussions were like discussions in a court of law," where you try to "clear up the circumstances" of the action which is being tried, hoping that in the end what you say will "appeal to the judge." And he said that the same sort of "reasons" were given, not only in Ethics, but also in Philosophy.

It is easy to see that on Wittgenstein's account of aesthetic reasoning the notion of an "object of comparison" plays a fundamental role. A critic frequently will try to make his point about a certain work, or style, or artist by comparing it to some other. This technique occurs implicitly in Wittgenstein's own example of the dispute over Brahms's Fourth Symphony, but a more explicit example is perhaps useful to examine. Imagine that someone is impressed with Eudora Welty's writing and decides that she is *the* great writer of the American South. One who disagreed with this judgment might try to change the person's mind by getting him to read a Welty story in close conjunction with a Faulkner story of similar theme, the assumption being that alongside the Faulkner piece Miss Welty's work will appear facile and lightweight. The rationale behind this familiar critical technique is that the "object of comparison" makes it possible to see the Welty story perspicuously, in its proper relationship to other things. What was once appealing, now no longer is. (Or perhaps it is appealing—but nothing more.) Of course, the procedure can be used in the opposite way too. An "object of comparison" can lead one to see value where one never saw it before, as when in an art education class the teacher compares one of Picasso's works to a classic painting in order to give the student some idea of what each artist was after.

All that reasoning in aesthetics can do is "to draw your attention to a thing" by "plac[ing] things side by side." These things that are placed "side by side" serve as "objects of comparison." All aesthetic reasons are "of the nature of further descriptions," descriptions which aim at getting one's disputant to see the controversial aesthetic object in a certain way. Wittgenstein took this to mean that there is no proper way to force agreement in aesthetic argument. If, after a course of discussion, one is unable to alter the perceptions of one's disputant so that they correspond with yours, that may be a proper end of the discussion. (It *may be* a proper end: perhaps with more effort one would succeed, but perhaps one would only bully the recalcitrant disputant into agreement or silence. There may be no easy way to decide when a genuine impasse has been reached.) If the discussion ends in disagreement, one may think (and say) that the judgments of one's disputant are (e.g.) *perverse;* but that is a different charge from one of irrationality or bad logic. For Wittgenstein, standards of aesthetic taste or value are recognized to be personal in a way that the basic principles of logic and rationality do not seem to be. One pays a certain price, perhaps, for saying at the end of a long discussion, "Well, in spite of all you've said, I still believe Harold Robbins's novels are great art"; but it is not the same sort of price one would pay for saying, "Yes, I believe that p entails q and that q entails r, but I don't believe that p entails r."

When Wittgenstein rejected for his own practice the "scientific" model of philosophy, he substituted what can be characterized as the "aesthetic" model, "aesthetic" because some of its central features can best be understood by considering the account of aesthetic reasoning recorded in the Moore lectures and by taking with utmost seriousness Wittgenstein's claim that the same sorts of reasons given in aesthetics are also given in philosophy (ML, p. 278). This is not to say, of course, that for him all philosophy *is* aesthetics; it is just that for him there are fundamental similarities between the kind of reasoning he thought to be characteristic of aesthetic disputes and the kind of reasoning he thought proper to philosophy in general.

What, then, is this "aesthetic" model of philosophy we find in his practice? At the outset, one can best say what it clearly is *not*. It is *not* the "scientific" model. It does *not* see philosophical problems as genuine problems calling for fruitful solution. It does *not* aim at the construction ("discovery") and substantiation ("proof") of philosophical theories of great generality and explanatory power. It does *not* hold that discursive argument is the way to philosophical enlightenment. And most important of all, it does *not* postulate a realm of statable philosophical truths which it is the task of the philosopher to find, state, and defend. Clearly these denials, like the *via negativa* to God, leave a great deal yet to be said.

The process of elucidating the "aesthetic" model and the process of arguing its presence in Wittgenstein's work are one and the same. One good way to connect the account of aesthetic reasoning to general philosophical considerations is to look closely at the way aesthetic and philosophical disputes *end* for Wittgenstein. His criterion for having found the solution of philosophical problems is intensely personal:

> For the clarity we are aiming at is indeed *complete* clarity. But this simply means that the philosophical problems should *completely* disappear.
>
> The real discovery is the one that makes me capable of stopping doing philosophy when I want to. —The one that gives philosophy peace, so that it is no longer tormented by questions which bring itself in question. (PI, sec. 133)

These remarks, along with

> There is not a philosophical method, though there are indeed methods, like different therapies. (PI, sec. 133)

and

> The philosopher's treatment of a question is like the treatment of an illness. (PI, sec. 255)

have given to Wittgenstein's work a *therapeutic* air which many philosophers find distasteful.

These philosophers have rightly deplored the excesses to which a simpleminded identification of philosophy and therapy can lead. One may, however, deplore the excesses without having at the same time to deny that the comparison can illuminate Wittgenstein's philosophical methods and goals. The comparison is illuminating in this way: illness (including mental illness; the emphasis on psychoanalytic therapy in these comparisons is both common and important) is, by definition, a destructive state of the affected organism; it is something to be avoided, or remedied, if possible. In the same way, Wittgenstein sees philosoph-

ical perplexity as a destructive state of the person who is thus per-
plexed. Here we find another difference between Wittgenstein's practice and science: in science, perplexity is most often healthy, i.e., it
leads to progress; in philosophy, according to Wittgenstein, it is never
healthy. It is always a symptom of pernicious confusion. Scientific
questions ("What causes the peculiar behavior of this gas at high tem-
peratures?") ought to be asked. Philosophical questions ("Can I ever
know whether another person is in pain?") ought not to be. Therapy is
the cure of disease, the restoration of the organism to its normal functioning (so far as this is possible). The techniques of Wittgensteinian
philosophy aim at a similar goal: the removal of confusion and philosophical perplexity, thus enabling the person to resume a normal way
of life, no longer tormented by his earlier confusions and scruples.
"For the clarity we are aiming at is indeed *complete* clarity. But this
simply means that the philosophical problems should *completely* disappear." In science, one makes a problem disappear by gaining clarity. In
philosophy, one gains (i.e., *re*gains) clarity by making the problems
disappear. This is a nontrivial difference.

Some therapy aims only at returning the organism to the state existing before the onslaught of the disease. When a physician treats the
infected throat of a patient, his aim is to remove the infection. He does
not expect the treatment of the throat with antibiotics also to mend the
patient's broken arm. Neither does he expect the infection and its cure
to leave the patient impervious to reinfection. Some other kinds of
therapy (e.g., psychoanalysis, on some accounts) change the organism
in deeper ways; they change what counts as "normal functioning."
Philosophy seems to resemble psychoanalytic therapy in this regard.

> The real discovery is the one that makes me capable of stop-
> ping doing philosophy when I want to. —The one that gives
> philosophy peace, so that it is no longer tormented by ques-
> tions which bring *itself* in question. (PI, sec. 133)

This discovery and capability is the result of a fundamental change in
the philosopher.

Here one can begin to see an important connection between therapy and Wittgenstein's account of aesthetic reasoning. Certain types of
therapy—including psychoanalysis and Wittgensteinian philosophical
therapy—result, if successful, in a deep-seated change in the person
treated. In psychoanalysis and in philosophy this change is of a partic-

ular sort: both therapies (if successful) effect what might be called a "change in sensibility" in the patient; they alter some of those deep perspectives in terms of which experience is appropriated, ordered, understood. For an example of such change, consider what happens in a course of analytic psychotherapy. When a person undergoes analytic treatment for, say, compulsive handwashing, the object of the therapist cannot felicitously be described as returning the patient to *his* "normal functioning." In a very real sense, *for this patient* compulsive hand-washing is his "normal functioning." For a person of his sensibilities and with his past, some pathological behavior is inevitable. What is needed now, of course, is not just the extinction of the pathological behavior: that might be done with electric shocks. What is needed is a change in what counts as the patient's "normal functioning," so that the pathological symptoms will truly disappear and thus will not return in another form. Since life's inevitable traumas cannot be removed, what is needed is a change in (what might be called) the *sensibility* of the patient. He needs to be equipped to weather these traumas (and their recurrence in fantasy) with limited impairment, and this can only be accomplished if he becomes a different sort of person. He needs to come to a new way of appropriating his experience; he needs a different set of psychic patterns, another set of images through which his realities can be organized. Therefore, a change in sensibility is what psychotherapy (at least in some forms) aims for.

This sort of change seems rather far removed from discrete cognitive acquisitions. One might express this distance by saying (as does Stanley Cavell) that the acquisition of self-knowledge (culminating in a change in sensibility) is not the acquisition of *facts about oneself,* or by saying that when one acquires facts about oneself, "acquiring facts" has a different grammar from when one says that the physicist "acquires facts" about the structure of subatomic particles. Cavell is illuminating on this point:

> The more one learns, so to speak, the hang of oneself, and mounts one's problems, the less one is able to *say* what one has learned; not because you have *forgotten* what it was, but because nothing you said would seem like an answer or a solution: there is no longer any question or problem which your words would match. You have reached conviction, but not about a proposition; and consistency, but not in a theory. You

are different, what you recognize as problems are different, your world is different. ("The world of the happy man is different from that of the unhappy man" (*Tractatus,* 6.43).)[5]

It is because certain paradigms of therapy do their work by effecting such a change in sensibility that the therapeutic air of Wittgenstein's later work connects up with his account of aesthetic reasoning, since in aesthetic reasoning it is also a change in sensibility that resolves disagreement. It is that sort of change that (e.g.) alters one's perception of Eudora Welty's stories, making them seem lightweight in comparison to Faulkner's. To come to believe that Welty is not a great writer, when before one was passionately convinced of her unsurpassed genius, is not like coming to believe that yesterday's temperature report in the newspaper was incorrect; it is comparable to the sort of deep alteration effected in therapy, changing in a significant way some basic feature of one's view of the world. The change in belief about the temperature might well leave every other belief unaltered; the aesthetic reversal could not but bring other differences in its train: hence calling it an alteration in *sensibility.*

There is direct textual evidence that Wittgenstein believed that an "alteration of perception/sensibility" of the sort we have discussed is the final goal of good philosophical practice. Consider section 144 of the *Philosophical Investigations.* In the preceding sections, Wittgenstein has been concerned with the complexities inherent in our notion of a rule. Something of value can be learned about rules, he says, by considering the teaching and learning of a rule. Sometimes, as it happens, a pupil will not understand his teacher; he will get the rule wrong. And sometimes (perhaps most of the time) it will be possible for the teacher to correct the student's faulty understanding of the rule and teach him to apply the rule correctly. There will be times, however, when the teacher will be stumped; he will not be able to get the student to grasp the rule correctly. "—And here too our pupil's capacity to learn may come to an end" (PI, sec. 143).

"What," asks Wittgenstein, "do I mean when I say 'the pupil's capacity to learn *may* come to an end here'?" (PI, sec. 144). He rejects the idea that he says this from his own experience, even granting the hypothesis that he has had the experience in question. "Then what am I doing with that proposition?" He answers his own question in a characteristically indirect manner:

Well, I should like you to say: 'Yes, it's true, one can imagine that too, that might happen too!' —But was I trying to draw someone's attention to the fact that he is capable of imagining that? —I wanted to put that picture before him, and his *acceptance* of the picture consists in his now being inclined to regard a given case differently: that is, to compare it with *this* rather than *that* set of pictures. I have changed his *way of looking at things*. (Indian mathematicians: "Look at this.") (PI, sec. 144)

The mysterious reference to Indian mathematicians is clarified by the following passage from the *Zettel*.

I should like you to say: 'Yes, that's true, that can be imagined; that might even have happened!' But was I trying to draw your attention to the fact that you are able to imagine this? I wanted to put this picture before your eyes, and your *acceptance* of this picture consists in your being inclined to regard a given case differently; that is, to compare it with *this* series of pictures. I have changed your *way of seeing*. (I once read somewhere that a geometrical figure, with the words "Look at this," serves as a proof for certain Indian mathematicians. This too effects an alteration in one's way of seeing.) (Z, sec. 461)

These are interesting and important passages, having special importance for the correct understanding of Wittgenstein's practice of philosophy. Notice what he is doing. He takes a statement that seems to be just the description of a fact— "The pupil's capacity to learn may come to an end here"—and uses it in a particular way. How do statements of fact traditionally enter philosophical argument? They enter as premises in arguments—ideally, valid deductive arguments. (For example, "We are sometimes mistaken in our claims about what we perceive. When I see a tomato there is much that I can doubt.") But it is clear that Wittgenstein's statement about the pupil's capacity to learn does not fit in this way; it is not the premise of an argument to some philosophical thesis. Rather, he intends that a certain possibility in the statement *strike* one and thus *change one's way of looking at* the topic under consideration. "—I wanted to put that picture before him, and his acceptance of that picture consists in his now being inclined to regard a given case differently: that is to compare it with *this* rather than *that* set of pictures. I have changed his *way of looking at things*" (PI, sec. 144). The statement does not serve as part of an argument, as a factual premise does; one might say, however, that it is the whole of an "argument" of a very special sort. The object of this sort of "argument" is not to prove the truth of some philosophical proposition; rather, its object is the determination of a "new way of looking at things."

The sort of thing that Wittgenstein claims in *Philosophical Investigations,* section 144, and *Zettel,* section 461, to be doing in his philosophical criticism is, we can see, the same sort of thing that he described as the goal of aesthetic reasoning in the Moore lectures. In aesthetics, according to Wittgenstein, one also tries to "change [a] way of looking at things" by "plac[ing] things side by side." You try to get another person to " 'see what you see' " and to accept (cf. PI, sec. 144) your "way of looking at things." In both cases, the aesthetic and the philosophical, one is not so much learning a truth ("Faulkner is a better writer than Eudora Welty" or "Here a pupil's capacity to learn may come to an end") as one is getting a new perspective on a writer or a phenomenon. And this new perspective may not be adequately expressible in terms of truths learned (cf. therapy). What is wanted is not *belief,* but understanding. What is wanted is an alteration of the image in terms of which experience is ordered.

The comparison of Wittgenstein's accounts of philosophical and aesthetic reasoning can help us to understand in a deeper way the role played by grammatical pictures in philosophical perplexity. We have already seen how the notion of a grammatical picture is fundamental to explaining the connection between language and the bewitchment of our intelligences that results in the nonsense of philosophy. The presence of such "illustrated turns of speech" enchants us when we begin to think philosophically, and Wittgensteinian philosophers must concern themselves with dispelling the bewitching power of these grammatical pictures. The major way of breaking this authority is just to realize that one is confronted with a grammatical picture, i.e., to see such pictures *as* grammatical pictures, as pictures which "correspond to" (PI, sec. 301) grammatical images, not as literal representations of reality. Then one is not likely to be forced into nonsense and obscurity while being led by "crossed" pictures (PI, sec. 191), and neither is one likely to confuse grammatical pictures with superfacts.

But what does recognizing a grammatical picture as a grammatical picture, and as nothing more than a grammatical picture, come to? How is that to be accomplished?

> I wanted to put this picture before your eyes, and your *acceptance* of this picture consists in your being inclined to regard a given case differently; that is, to compare it with this series of pictures. I have changed your *way of seeing*. (z, sec. 461)

Here we have Wittgenstein explicitly connecting the notion of a (grammatical) picture to the "aesthetic" philosopical goal of changing one's way of seeing. Notice that Wittgenstein does not assert that a "changed way of seeing" removes all pictures. Rather, here he is identifying the influence of a grammatical picture with a way of seeing something: to see something differently is just to see it in terms of a *different* picture or set of pictures. The first pictures have lost their bewitching grip; no longer are they taken literally.

But the second pictures are not taken literally either. That would be just to swap one servitude for another. The "acceptance" of a grammatical picture of which Wittgenstein speaks does not mean *literal* acceptance; it does not mean taking a different set of grammatical images as literal representations. Grammatical pictures need to be deliteralized, not (*per impossibile*) removed. This notion is introduced in section 122 of the *Investigations*.

> A main source of our failure to understand is that we do not *command a clear view* of the use of our words. —Our grammar is lacking in this sort of perspicuity. A perspicuous presentation produces just that understanding which consists in "seeing connections." Hence the importance of finding and inventing *intermediate cases*.
>
> The concept of a perspicuous presentation is of fundamental significance for us. It earmarks the form of account we give, the way we look at things. (Is this a "Weltanschauung"?)

Incidentally, section 122 is a recapitulation of some remarks Wittgenstein made on Frazer and *The Golden Bough* in 1931.

> 'And so the chorus indicates a hidden law' is what we feel like saying of Frazer's collection of facts. I *can* set out this law in an hypothesis of development, or again, in analogy with the

schema of a plant I can give it in the schema of a religious ceremony, but I can also do it just by arranging the factual material
so we can easily pass from one part to another and have a clear
view of it—showing it in a "perspicuous" way.

For us the conception of a perspicuous presentation is fundamental. It indicates the form in which we write of things, the
way in which we see things. (A kind of *"Weltanschauung"* that
seems to be typical of our times. Spengler.)

This perspicuous presentation makes possible that understanding which consists just in the fact that we "see the connections." Hence the importance of finding *intermediate links*.

But in our case an hypothetical link is not meant to do anything except draw attention to the similarity, the connection,
between the *facts*. As one might illustrate the internal relation
of a circle to an ellipse by gradually transforming an ellipse
into a circle; *but not in order to assert that a given ellipse in
fact, historically, came from a circle* (hypothesis of development) but only to sharpen our eye for a formal connection. (F,
pp. 34–35)

One of Wittgenstein's sharpest complaints about Frazer's treatment
of his data in *The Golden Bough* is that he is constantly forcing the
material into a preconceived and rigid pattern. He wants to explain
magical and ritual action as resting upon the adoption by the "primitive" people of a small set of erroneous "causal" principles; and he
looks so hard for this pattern that he always finds it, even when in order
to do so he must outrageously underestimate the intellectual powers of
"primitive" people and distort the clear sense of their behavior. Frazer
is so much in the grip of his "picture" that ostensibly contrary data
make no impact at all. His is a clear case of a common philosophical
pathology: a limitless "craving for generality."

Wittgenstein admits that Frazer (or anyone) *can* set out ("present") the anthropological data to make them conform to certain patterns, e.g., a hypothesis of development; but it must always be remem-
bered that there are alternative methods of presentation:

I *can* set out the law in a hypothesis of development, or again,
in analogy with the schema of a plant I can give it in the
schema of a religious ceremony, but I can also do it just by arranging the factual materials so that we can easily pass from

one part to another and have a clear view of it—showing it in a "perspicuous" way. (F, p. 34)

It is this sort of perspicuous presentation that Wittgenstein considers fundamental "for us" (PI, sec. 122), i.e., for enlightened philosophers. As Rush Rhees points out, the word translated "perspicuous" is *"übersichtlich,"* and it is constantly used by Wittgenstein in writing about logical notation and mathematical proof. In order to guard against succumbing to the destructive method of generalizing in philosophical contexts, one must set out the troublesome data "so that we can easily pass from one part to another." Thus,

> A perspicuous presentation produces just that understanding which consists in "seeing connections." Hence the importance of finding and inventing intermediate cases. (PI, sec. 122)

Once the data are presented perspicuously one is able to see the connections between them, ideally *all* the connections. Once one has found or invented an appropriate "intermediate case," one's view of a particular phenomenon may substantially alter. The phenomenon may lose its puzzling aspect, or it may now no longer seem so clearly to conform to a particular pattern. For example, an anthropologist who sees a person in a "primitive" society pierce a picture of his enemy with a knife, may draw the conclusion that the person believes the ritual of piercing has some "causal" efficacy in harming the enemy. The anthropologist sees the ritual action in the light of other actions which he understands, like the actual stabbing of an enemy; and thus he "understands" it. Through the image of an actual stabbing, he "reads" the ritual as a primitive attempt at murder. But with *another* comparison in mind, he might understand it differently.

> Burning in effigy. Kissing the picture of a loved one. This is obviously *not* based on a belief that it will have a definite effect on the object which the picture represents. It aims at some satisfaction and it achieves it. Or rather, it does not *aim* at anything; we act in this way and then feel satisfied. (F, p. 31)

Here an "intermediate case" has been found, and it can change one's perception, one's "way of looking at," the ritual action. One has discovered a "formal connection" (F, p. 35) that removes some of one's puzzlement about the ceremony.

More understanding of the fundamental notion of a "perspicuous presentation" can be gained by noticing the function of such a notion in aesthetic disputes. Wittgenstein's account of the proper resolution of an aesthetic dispute consists in gaining a "perspicuous presentation" that leads to "seeing connections." Recall our case of the dispute over whether Eudora Welty is a great writer. Person A believes she is merely a delightful and skillful entertainer; B considers her a literary genius of great depth and power. A might press his position by getting B to compare Miss Welty's works with other works on both ends of the scale that has been drawn in the argument. That is, A gets B to read works that B himself admits are merely competent entertainment (e.g., a popular historical novel like Gore Vidal's *Burr*) and also to read some works that he admits are undoubtedly great (e.g., Thomas Pynchon's *Gravity's Rainbow*), all the time thinking of Miss Welty's works and their value. Let us imagine that after this reading B does want to withdraw his earlier judgment. (Of course, he *might* still persevere.) What has happened to B? He has undergone what we have called an "alteration of perception" or an "alteration of sensibility." He has a "new way of looking at things." And it is also true to say that he was brought to his new sensibility by seeing a connection he had never properly seen before, namely, the connection between Miss Welty's work and that of some of her contemporaries. The word in section 122 that Miss Anscombe translates 'connection' (*Zusammenhang*) can also be translated as 'relation'. Thus one might say that B is now conscious of a *relation* between Miss Welty's work and others' of which he was ignorant. A perspicuous presentation of Miss Welty's work has led B to a certain valuation of it. What A has done for B is to alter his perception and understanding of Welty's work by presenting him with various "objects of comparison." Some of these "objects of comparison" are "intermediate cases" he has found, i.e., works of fiction which pull one way, toward light entertainment, and works of fiction which pull the other, toward depth and revelation. Once these other cases are presented to B and his attention is drawn to relevant features shared by them all, he is able to see in a new way some of the connections (relations) between them, and he is led to a new judgment about the case initially in dispute. Like the anthropologist who now sees ritual killing in a new way, B has a new perspective on Eudora Welty's fiction. He has been given a perspicuous presentation of this work in its widest context.

There is a crucial difference, however, between the strictly aesthetic case and the philosophical one. The "acceptance" of a new perspective on a writer is "literal" in a way that the Wittgensteinian "acceptance" of another grammatical picture emphatically is not. The aesthetic alteration we have imagined has not led to the abandonment of aesthetic judgment itself; the altered sensibility is properly still an aesthetic one: it still judges in aesthetic categories. The alteration of philosophical sensibility envisioned by Wittgenstein is much more radical; it aims at the end of philosophical judgment itself, at the deliteralization of mind. It seeks, not to substitute one judgment or perspective for another, as in aesthetic argument; but instead to free one from the captivity to *any* grammatical picture. It wants *no* "way of looking at things" to assume a literal status. Mind must be able to range freely over all the "formal connections" (F, p. 35) among things, getting a clear view of them all, sticking at none as a literal representation. The change in sensibility affording the mind this freedom must be deep indeed. The mind's freedom from literalization, because it is intimately connected to the use of 'nonsense' as the fundamental term of philosophical criticism, will become an increasingly important theme in the rest of this chapter.

Having deployed the comparison with aesthetic reasoning, it is now time to return to the issue that provided our entry into Wittgenstein's nontraditional conception of philosophy, namely, the role of language-games. It can now be seen why the two most familiar conceptions of that role are inadequate. Language-games can neither be heuristic devices used to illustrate substantive philosophical theses arguable on other grounds, nor can they be the final philosophical standards of sense; both these conceptions fail because they presuppose a "scientific" model of philosophical reasoning. If language-games are heuristic devices, there must actually be philosophical truths to be argued and illustrated; but the whole tenor of Wittgenstein's later work is to disavow such a "scientific" (metaphysical) conception of philosophy. And language-games cannot be the final standards of sense, most obviously because language-games can be invented as well as discovered: they can be fantastic as well as realistic (think of the *Brown Book*). Furthermore, some remarks in the *Investigations* explicitly undercut the standards-of-sense conception.

131.　　　For we can avoid ineptness or emptiness in our assertions only by presenting the model [i.e., the language-
game] as what it is, as an object of comparison—as, so
to speak, a measuring-rod; not as a preconceived idea to
which reality *must* correspond. (The dogmatism into
which we fall so easily in doing philosophy.)

Objects of comparison are not standards of sense.

The "aesthetic" model of philosophy sketched above gives one a
way of seeing how language-games are quite literally functioning as
objects of comparison. If the toils of philosophy are spun out of the
literal appropriation of the grammatical pictures inherent in language,
and if what is wanted to free one from these toils is the acceptance of
another picture, an alteration of perception-sensibility like that aimed
at in aesthetic disputes, then language-games, by presenting an illuminating context for the grammatical picture at issue, can help to
work the alteration that liberates the understanding. A "perspicuous
presentation" of the grammar that surrounds the troublesome picture—a presentation that, by finding and inventing intermediate cases,
reveals the whole set of possible connections and relationships of that
picture with other pictures—is a way of drawing its poison; it is a way
to free the understanding from the grip of that picture, interpreted literally. Instead of one picture or pattern, a perspicuous presentation of
various actual and made-up language-games furnishes the mind with a
multitude of grammatical images, each having its own power and
claim on our attention. No one can seize our exclusive allegiance. Just
as in an aesthetic context objects of comparison, successfully chosen
and perspicuously deployed, can change one's view of the value of a
given work or artist, so too can objects of comparison like language-
games alter one's perception of a given grammatical picture. In both
cases what is wanted is a particular sort of resolution: an alteration of
perception-sensibility.

The notion of an alteration of perception-sensibility is crucial for
understanding the deepest features of Wittgenstein's later thinking, especially his use of 'nonsense' as a fundamental term of criticism. His
description of aesthetic reasoning in the Moore lectures shows that in
such contexts the point of reasoning is not best understood as an alteration in belief. The person who has, under the conviction of aesthetic
reasoning, come to revise some conception of value is not someone

who has merely replaced one set of beliefs with another, as an accountant, looking again at a firm's books, might replace his belief in the firm's solvency with a belief that it is bankrupt. That sort of change, important as it is, is neither as deep nor as personal as that which typically occurs in aesthetic contexts. The change in the accountant's belief does not, in ordinary circumstances, change *him;* he is essentially the same person as before the bankruptcy was found. But a change in aesthetic contexts is a change in the person himself, a change in his individuating sensibilities; such an alteration is a change in the very way in which experience is appropriated. It alters some of the basic images and ideals that order our experience and give it a particular character and value. After the change many (perhaps all) things are experienced differently. Furthermore, the kind of change that occurs in the aesthetic context is *individual* in a way that the accountant's change in belief is not. Any competent accountant, we may suppose, will draw the conclusion that the firm in question is bankrupt, but the aesthetic change, as Wittgenstein pointed out, is not "objective" in that way. Recall Moore's report of the Cambridge lectures:

> what he, Wittgenstein, had at "the back of his mind" was "the idea that aesthetic discussions were like discussions in a court of law," where you try to "clear up the circumstances" of the action which is being tried, hoping in the end what you say will "appeal to the judge." (ML, p. 278)

It is perfectly possible that it will not appeal, of course, and that may be an end of the discussion. The anticipated change in sensibility may not occur; experience may continue to be appropriated just as before. There is no proper way to coerce agreement in aesthetic contexts, as there (sometimes) is in accountancy.

Because the aesthetic changes are so deep and so individual, we found it illuminating to characterize them as alterations of perception-sensibility, rather than as changes in belief. And if Wittgenstein was right in asserting that the same kind of reasons are given in philosophy as in aesthetics (ML, p. 278), then the proper end of philosophy is likewise an alteration of perception-sensibility, not a change in belief. Here, at long last, we come to face directly Wittgenstein's use of 'nonsense' as his favored term of philosophical criticism. Because a sensibility is constituted by those basic images and ideals that order experience and give it sense, including the sense of being either true or false, it is improper to judge a sensibility itself as either true or false; it is out of a particular sensibility that judgments of truth or falsity proceed.[6] Any judgment of truth or falsity is made in terms of some basic assumptions about the nature of adequate evidence, proper modes of investigation, and so forth; and these images and ideals of truth are not, of course, universally shared. In some cultures oracles are consulted; in others, psychoanalysts and sociologists. This recognition gives us the key to the notion of philosophical nonsense: to judge something to be nonsense is to judge it to be neither true nor false; nonsensical utterances, although grammatically they appear to be assertions, do not reach to the level of truth or falsity. We cannot appropriate them in these categories. In the later Wittgenstein's terms, a nonsensical utterance fails to reach the level of truth and falsity because it proceeds from a sensibility radically different from his own—and perhaps radically defective, too. The utterances are nonsense because he does not find himself in the sensibility from which those utterances proceed.

> We also say of some people that they are transparent to us. It is, however, important as regards this observation that one human being can be a complete enigma to another. We learn this when we come into a strange country with entirely strange traditions; and, what is more, even given a mastery of the country's language. We do not *understand* the people. (And not because of not knowing what they are saying to themselves.) We cannot find our feet with them. (PI, p. 223)

The last sentence literally reads: "We cannot find ourselves in them."[7]

To judge some apparently assertive utterance to be philosophical nonsense is a judgment *of* a sensibility, made *out of* another sensibility, and aimed at an *alteration* in that first sensibility. The Wittgensteinian philosopher confronted with the utterances of traditional metaphysical philosophy is something like the traveler confronted with a radically foreign culture: he sees; he hears; he is even able to understand the sentences that are being uttered. But in a deep sense he does not understand the *people* who utter those sentences: he does not find himself in those men and women; his sensibility is utterly different. As long as this is the case (and, of course, sensibilities can alter in fundamental

ways, as Evans-Prichard discovered when he lived among the Azande)
he will find the life of those people a deep mystery. Their culture will
make no real sense to him; he might even use the word 'nonsense' to
characterize that culture.

The Wittgensteinian philosopher is thus something like a traveler
in a strange land, but he is also like someone closer to home: the person confronted with a new artistic paradigm. This comparison comes
out in sections 398–401 of the *Investigations*, where Wittgenstein is
considering the philosophical notion of the "visual room." The notion
of a "visual room" is the result of accepting certain familiar philosophical arguments about the privacy of experience, the reality of sense
data, and the like. The "visual room," says the philosopher, is the
room I alone can see; it is the private "content" of *my* visual experience. This notion is not, as some might claim, utterly incoherent; Wittgenstein says to the philosopher: "I understand you" (PI, sec. 398).
Here is his conclusion:

400.   The "visual room" seemed like a discovery, but what
        its discoverer really found was a new way of speaking; it
        might even be called a new sensation.

401.   You have a new conception and interpret it as seeing
        a new object. You interpret a grammatical movement
        made by yourself as a quasi-physical phenomenon which
        you are observing. (Think for example of the question:
        "Are sense-data the material of which the universe is
        made?")

        But there is an objection to my saying that you have
        made a "grammatical" movement. What you have pri-
        marily discovered is a new way of looking at things. As
        if you had invented a new way of painting; or, again, a
        new metre, or a new kind of song.—

Notice the attitude he takes to the philosophical notion of the "visual room": he does not evaluate the conception in terms of truth or
falsity, correctness or error, plausibility or implausibility. Instead of
these "scientific" terms of criticism, he uses "aesthetic" objects of
comparison: the philosopher has invented a new way of painting, a
new kind of song. Ways of painting and singing are neither true nor
false. It *is* true, of course, that one may be irresistibly attracted or re-

pelled by a kind of song or a style of painting, and this attraction or repulsion may express itself in such a remark as *"That's* not singing!" (cf. atonal music). (The epistemological counterpart of such a remark is "All we ever *really* see are sense data.") But it is impossible to prove that such remarks are false (or true), and to try to do so is not the enlightened philosopher's task. Sometimes, of course, one can be led to see that atonal music *is* music after all, or that a sense datum theory of perception is not something one wants to (or has to) accept; but these are particular processes of education, processes not amenable to a "scientific" model of reasoning and learning. These processes have to do with altering the sensibility of one's disputant, getting him to see sense where before he saw only gibberish, or getting him to see the lack of sense in what heretofore had held him captive.

These sections of the *Investigations* show quite well something of the relationship of the Wittgensteinian philosopher to the metaphysical philosopher of the tradition. The metaphysician is an enigma to him. He understands that the metaphysician has a great attraction to a certain way of looking at the world, and he may understand to some extent what this way of looking at the world is like. (One can easily understand what it would be like to "believe" in sense data.) But the Wittgensteinian philosopher himself has no attraction to the metaphysician's *Weltanschauung;* in fact, it repels him. In a very real sense, he does not find himself in the metaphysician; rather, he is a person of a different (perhaps changed) sensibility. These considerations show an important feature that the Wittgensteinian philosopher doesn't share with the traveler in a strange land: while the traveler may be tolerant of the different sensibilities he finds—indeed, he may actively court such tolerance—the Wittgensteinian philosopher strenuously opposes the fundamental sensibility of the metaphysician. He sees it as something to be altered, not as a sensibility acceptably different from his own. The point is not to understand the "sense" of the metaphysician's life, but to alter the sensibility that produces that life and its attraction. Philosophy, says Wittgenstein, is a battle against bewitchment; it aims at the conquest of an enemy, not the imaginative participation in different sensibilities.

It is just here that Wittgenstein is not the vulgar "conceptual relativist" one sometimes encounters in the literature. While it is certainly true that no one sensibility is global, and that there is genuine, perhaps irremediable, conflict among various sensibilities, this is in no way to say that one of these is just as good as another. It may be the case that there is no purely discursive and argumentative way for the Azande and the nuclear physicist to resolve their differences, in which case their forms of life and thought may really be "incommensurable," as the jargon has it; but this alleged fact of incommensurability certainly does not mean that they must equally honor one another's predilections. Indeed, *both* may feel that they have good reasons for trying to convert the other. Thus, the fact of incommensurability may show the disputants the real nature of their conflict; but it will not show that there *is* no conflict, nor does it (alone) show that it's not a conflict worth pursuing.

Our discussion in section two of the role of grammatical pictures in generating philosophical perplexity revealed that the fundamental constituent in the metaphysical sensibility is rationality-as-representation. Without that literalizing impulse, without the powerful image of thought (and thinker) as seeing eye, we would not become enchanted by the pictures inherent in our grammar; we would not identify our conceptions with the reality for which they are metaphors. The fundamental task of philosophy, therefore, is to liberate one from the literalizing intellect, to free one from the bonds of rationality-as-representation and thus to restore one to a proper relationship with one's language. And that means, ultimately, freeing one from philosophy itself.

IV

THIS CHAPTER has of necessity followed a meandering course. Our intention has been to show a transmuted distinction between showing and saying in Wittgenstein's later work, and the notion of nonsense—a term of criticism fundamental to both the *Tractatus* and the *Investigations*—seemed to be a key. But to understand the peculiar and autonomous sense of 'nonsense' it has been necessary to investigate Wittgenstein's radically nontraditional model of philosphy—"aesthetic," not "scientific"—and to see how notions like language-games and perspicuous presentations function within it. These necessary excursions seem to have drawn us far afield. Let us return to those sections of the *Philosophical Investigations* with which we began and see whether their puzzling aspects may have been clarified by our tortuous journey. The remarks in question are these:

> 499.   To say "This combination of words makes no sense" excludes it from the sphere of language and thereby

bounds the domain of language. But when one draws a boundary it may be for various kinds of reason. If I surround an area with a fence or a line or otherwise, the purpose may be to prevent someone from getting in or out; but it may also be part of a game and the players supposed, say, to jump over the boundary; or it may be to show where the property of one man ends and that of another begins, and so on. So if I draw a boundary line that is not yet to say what I am drawing it for.

500.   When a sentence is called senseless, it is not as it were its sense that is senseless. But a combination of words is being excluded from the language, withdrawn from circulation.

As we noted in section one of this chapter, these remarks paint a very different picture from the *Tractatus*. There the distinction between sense and nonsense is totally impersonal. The limits of language and thought are given in the essence of language-thought itself, and the individual is completely powerless to alter those limits: "Thought is surrounded by a halo" (PI, sec. 97). But in the images of the *Investigations* to judge something to be nonsense is to erect a boundary, to draw a line; and these lines are not inhumanly rigid. Thus, 'nonsense' as a term of philosophical criticism assumes a new weight. In the *Tractatus* the term functions finally and impersonally. If something is nonsense, then it is nonsense for everyone, now and forever. The limits of thought are permanently fixed, and given by the nature of thought itself. But in the *Investigations*, 'nonsense' is a term addressed to an individual, a particular individual, wrestling with a philosophical problem. It is an attempt to point out or to draw a certain boundary in his language but the individual is not bound by the "essence of language" to heed the warning.

In the later work the whole significance of the notion of "the limits of language" has altered. For the author of the *Tractatus*, the limits of sense are quite literal; that is, the image that language has such limits is itself taken literally, in accordance with rationality-as-representation. It is as if there really is a sphere of sense bounded by nonsense, with the discovery of the nature of language (thought, representation) giving one a way to plot the eternal boundaries of that sphere. For the later Wittgenstein, however, the notion of language's limits has lost its literal aspect. He does not any more look for such limits out there, given by the nature of things. The remarks in sections 499–500 are attempts to deliteralize the image of the inexorable limits of sense by deploying as an alternative the images of the alterable boundary and the words withdrawn from circulation. The point is to show the traditional image for what it is: an image, not the literal truth.

> I wanted to put this picture before your eyes, and your *acceptance* of this picture consists in your being inclined to regard a different case differently; that is, to compare it with this series of pictures. I have changed your *way of seeing*. (z, sec. 461)

For the later Wittgenstein, as we have seen, philosophical argument models aesthetic reasoning in fundamental respects. Philosophical judgments like the paradigmatic "Nonsense!" are aimed at some particular individual, some subject; and they aim at the alteration of his most fundamental philosophical sensibilities. In this emphasis on the personal, "subjective" character of philosophical enlightenment there is a deep connection between the later Wittgenstein and Kierkegaard. (We have already noted Kierkegaard's influence on the author of the *Tractatus.*) Neither has any confidence in the worth of large-scale, impersonal, "objective" philosophizing. Both see their task as the engagement of the reader *as an individual* in the common search for sound understanding and life. Both want to address their readers as particular persons, as subjects; and the nontraditional literary forms in which they cast their work are attempts to guarantee that they not be read "objectively," as presenting conclusions (theses) to be considered. In capsule, both Wittgenstein and Kierkegaard aim at getting the individual reader to *recognize himself* in the process of philosophizing—to "come to his senses"—and then to make a certain movement in relation to this philosophizing.

This formula needs some explaining. Both Wittgenstein and Kierkegaard see their readers as victims of *illusions* of one sort or another. For Wittgenstein the fundamental illusion is philosophy itself; that is, that philosophy—considered as a rational, impersonal, "objective" endeavor which collects data and constructs theories ("analyses") to be argued about, modified, accepted, and built upon—is a proper ideal of thinking and living. On the contrary, philosophy conceived in this way is a sham, an illusion.

Philosophers constantly see the method of science before their eyes, and are irresistibly tempted to ask and answer questions in the way science does. This tendency is the real source of metaphysics, and leads the philosopher into complete darkness. (BB, p. 18)

The philosopher subject to the illusions of philosophy is *ill*.

The philosopher is the man who must cure himself of many sicknesses of the understanding before he can arrive at the notion of the sound human understanding.

If in the midst of life we are in death, so in sanity we are surrounded by madness. (RFM, p. 157)

Again:

The sickness of a time is cured by an alteration in the mode of life of human beings, and it was possible for the sickness of philosophical problems to get cured only through a changed mode of thought and of life, not through a medicine invented by an individual. (RFM, p. 57)

And most bluntly:

Philosophizing is an illness and we are trying to describe minutely its symptoms. Clinical appearance.[8]

This illness manifests itself first of all, as we have seen, in a faulty relationship between an individual and his language, the "bewitchment of our intelligence by means of language" (PI, sec. 109); and the primary vehicles for this bewitchment are the grammatical pictures inherent in any language. The illness of philosophy is not the presence of these pictures; the sickness is our captivity to them. We do not recognize them *as* pictures; hence we feel ourselves powerless before them and the confusions they bring when taken literally. This feeling of powerlessness is an important phenomenological feature of the philosopher's captivity to his pictures. In the grip of a grammatical picture we feel things *must* be a certain way; and when that conception leads to absurd consequences, we try bravely to swallow them down. After all, we think, what choice do we have? Here Wittgenstein wants the individual to *recognize himself* in the process of thinking. Bewitched by a picture, the individual forgets himself; he loses consciousness of himself and becomes merely an invisible and impotent observer of "the way things are." He becomes the powerless seeing eye of the *Tractatus*. He may become confused, even recognize his confusion; but he is so far powerless to remove it. He is the fly buzzing in the fly bottle, powerless to escape suffocation.

The object of philosophical criticism is to bring the individual to a certain kind of self-consciousness in the midst of the process of philosophizing, and hence to a certain kind of freedom within it and from it. To recognize a picture as a picture—and, even more helpfully, to recognize alternative pictures to a common one—is to free oneself from captivity to that picture and from the philosophical perplexity (or clarity) it brings. One no longer feels that things *must* be a certain way. Essentially, one is brought to a kind of self-consciousness about the process of philosophizing itself: whereas before one felt oneself inexorably compelled to certain ways of thinking about a thing—and, thus, as an individual played no visible role in the process of thinking itself—now one recognizes that one is free to adopt other conceptions, that one's thinking here is not compelled by "the facts"; and to the extent that this freedom is acquired, the individual *recognizes himself* (*his* pictures, *his* grammar's pictures) in the process of philosophizing. He recognizes himself, and thus he is freed; he is freed, and thus he recognizes himself. When one comes to see that some conception is a *picture,* and not the thing itself, then suddenly *one* (powerful, free) reënters the knowing relationship.

So long as I am bound to one way of looking at something, then I am not conscious of myself in the process of looking; my full attention is directed toward the thing, as perceived through the one picture. So long as a picture is taken literally, it is not seen as a "subjective" construction; and the individual is—I am—lost. To come to see a picture *as* a picture—as one image among others—is, however, necessarily to be brought to self-consciousness, if only because one is then aware of one's own choice between this image or that. And such a choice makes one self-conscious; it is, after all, *my* choice. Once the self is aware of its own inescapable presence in the process of philosophizing, once the pictures have been deliteralized into the self's own images, the process itself will lose its enchanting power. No longer will it seem sensible to seek the necessary and objective view of things *sub specie aeternitatis*.

Wittgenstein says that his aim is to show the fly the way out of the fly bottle, a metaphor of moving from captivity to freedom, and from death to life. One is freed when one comes to see a picture *as* a picture, when one is directly faced with alternative ways of thinking about something.

> I wanted to put that picture before him and his *acceptance* of the picture consists in his now being inclined to regard a given case differently: that is, to compare it with *this* rather than *that* set of pictures. I have changed his *way of looking at things*. (PI, sec. 144)

Such an alteration of sensibility, culminating in a particular kind of self-consciousness and freedom, is the object of all proper philosophical criticism.

For the later Wittgenstein, of course, the fundamental philosophical illusion is philosophy itself. In any course of philosophical therapy—like that of the *Investigations*—two movements can be identified. First, there is the attempt to free the individual from captivity to particular grammatical pictures which have led to confused and perplexing philosophical theorizing. Second, and this is the final hope of Wittgenstein's work, there is the attempt to free the individual from his captivity to philosophy itself. We have already seen him characterize philosophy as an illness; philosophy itself is the deadly trap within which the fly buzzes. David Pears puts it nicely: Wittgenstein had "the idea that philosophy is not one of the normal activities of the human spirit."[9] The proper job of the philosopher is to put an end to philosophy.

> For the clarity we are seeking is indeed *complete* clarity. But this simply means that the philosophical problems should *completely* disappear.
>
> The real discovery is the one that makes me capable of stopping doing philosophy when I want to. —The one that gives philosophy peace, so that it is no longer tormented by questions which bring itself into question. (PI, sec. 133)

Of course, it is a particular picture of philosophy that Wittgenstein abhors; indeed, the traditional picture, which portrays philosophy as the "queen of the sciences," as a branch of exact knowledge. Philosophy, finally pursued, can reveal to us the hidden nature of the world; it can present to us an account, a general picture, of the way things are. This is philosophy-as-metaphysics, an endeavor to give ultimate explanations and final justifications.

> The aim of philosophy, abstractly formulated, is to understand how things in the broadest possible sense of the term hang together in the broadest possible sense of the term.[10]

This extraordinary hope entangles us in particular grammatical pictures; without it, without the overwhelming impulse to philosophize about our lives, our pictures would serve us quietly and well. And this hope Wittgenstein sees as pernicious *illusion* from which we must—on pain of a kind of death—get free. Such freedom is the final aim of the Wittgensteinian philosopher. It may not be possible to escape using grammatical images that have the capacity to mislead, but it is possible not to be misled; and in the final instance this means stopping our prideful impulse to metaphysics.

Just here—because philosophy itself must end: the whole rigamarole of thesis/counterthesis, argument/counterargument, ideology/counterideology—we finally approach the notion of *showing* in the later work. How can philosophy-as-metaphysics be brought down? It cannot be *argued* to death, for argument—rational discourse—is its meat and drink. How silly and self-destructive to propound the thesis (the *philosophical* thesis, no less) that philosophy is illusion! No, philosophy must end in *silence,* in a silence of theses, arguments, and ideologies. Showing, not saying.

But what is shown? Wittgenstein's vision of the sound human understanding: "The philosopher is the man who must cure himself of many sicknesses of the understanding before he can arrive at the notion of the sound human understanding" (RFM, p. 157). And what is that? Wittgenstein himself very properly refrains from any attempt either to explicate or to argue his vision; in chapter six I will attempt an account of its major themes. The most important feature for us to notice here is the twofold absence of metaphysical philosophy from this vision. That is, the envisioned human life is not a philosophical one, since the sound person will have foregone the prideful desire to know his life rather than to live it; and, moreover, the vision itself is not a philosophical one, since it does not present itself to the intellect as a philosophical thesis or ideology. It is shown; and it does its work of altering our sensibilities, or it fails. Either way, we don't properly argue about it.

Wittgenstein believed in the sound human understanding, but not as one may believe in the truth of some thesis; rather, he believed in it as the practicing physician believes in the physical soundness toward which his efforts for his patient are directed. The state of health is not the "methodological presupposition" of the physician's activity; it is the real possibility which he and others have known and recognized to be a good. He holds no thesis about health; he is *acquainted* with what a healthy human life is like—and an unhealthy one as well. Wittgenstein was privy to a physician's vision of the healthy human understanding, and his work in philosophy was a continuing effort to realize that vision for himself and others. Central to Wittgenstein's vision of the whole person was that "changed mode of thought and of life" in which the sickness of philosophical problems was cured (RFM, p. 57), and to recognize this is to understand some of his personal intensity. He was not coolly considering various philosophical theses; he was seeking to win permanently for himself and others some sanity, a sanity that is now threatened by madness even as our lives are threatened by death (RFM, p. 157).

Once we are shown the central place of this vision of the sound human understanding, we can understand the deepest source of philosophical criticism of philosophy in the later works. In the *Tractatus* that source is a philosophical theory: a philosophical position or question is nonsense if it doesn't meet the standards of the picture theory. In the *Investigations* the fundamental term of criticism is still 'nonsense' but now the limits of language are not specified by a philosophical theory, but by the vision of the sound human understanding. In the final analysis, to pronounce some philosophical utterance to be nonsense is to assert it to be maintaining and strengthening the activity of philosophizing itself. It is a criticism aimed at changing the sensibility from which the utterance naturally proceeds. The boundary beyond which the nonsensical utterance strays (see PI, sec. 499–500) is a boundary established and recognized by the sound human understanding; it is not a boundary given by the essence of thought or language itself (whatever that might mean). As Wittgenstein points out, boundaries may be established for any number of reasons: protection, information, fun. This boundary we establish because we have seen through the philosopher's utterances to the sensibility that generates them, and we do not find ourselves in that sensibility. It appalls us, in fact. We have no use for the combinations of words that proceed from that sensibility; so we exclude them from the domain of our language and our life. If the bewitched philosopher doesn't heed the boundary we point out, his error is not so much an intellectual one, as if he had failed to recognize the truth of some *thesis* we have been propounding. Rather, he has failed to understand or heed a *gesture,* toward a different sensibility and a different life. He has neglected to respond to a *moral* admonition, an *Äußerung* warning him away from a way of thinking and living we find to be diseased and deadly.

The comparison of "good" philosophical therapy to gestures returns us to the necessity for silence as the proper end of philosophy. Why does not Wittgenstein *say* what has just been said? Why does he not explicate his vision of the sound human understanding and then say directly what role it plays in his work? Because to *say* this would be self-defeating. As philosophers we are trained to be abnormally sensitive to all wavelengths of discourse; and whenever anything is said, we go to work on it, separating "factual statements" from "evaluation," "necessary truths" from "contingent propositions," and the like. This professional sensibility of ours is especially attuned to search for "philosophical theses," and it is inevitable that we would hear Wittgenstein's vision as a philosophical *thesis* about philosophy and life. And then out would come the shiny knives, and we'd go to work. Our professional deformation would, by presenting us with another philosophical thesis, effectively distance the vision and draw out its power to alter our sensibilities, as if the medicine supposed to restore us were to have its energies coöpted by the disease. (We all know the infinite capacities philosophers have for taking and making painful arguments.) Wittgenstein, recognizing this fact, refuses to present his vision directly. It must sneak by our usual habits of thinking in order to stun us and to alter our sensibilities in the proper way.

> As one can sometimes reproduce music only in the inner ear, and cannot whistle it, because the whistling drowns out the inner voice, so sometimes the voice of a philosophical thought is so soft that the noise of the spoken words is enough to drown it and prevent it from being heard, if one is questioned and has to speak. (z, sec. 453)

To *say* anything to philosophers about the sound human understanding would drown out its real sense. Thus all of Wittgenstein's books are gestures; they are showings, not sayings.

In this connection it is important to reflect upon the fact that Wittgenstein is engaged in calling the philosopher away from one comprehensive and engrossing form of life to another. Rather than the movement from one philosophical thesis to another, he wants to provoke a severance from the very impulse to think and live within the medium of philosophical theses. He is, in other words, aiming to convert the philosopher to a new and incommensurable sensibility, and for this task discursive argument would be both pointless and positively dangerous.

How, then, is such conversion effected? To answer that question one must first recognize that what is at stake here is a *practice,* a form of life, and in this context—as, indeed, in every other—instances of theoretical reasoning are secondary to reasoning of a practical sort. One must also recognize that there is no way to subsume the new practice at issue under a *telos* already accepted by the philosopher. Wittgenstein aims for the philosopher to begin to live a radically new sort of life, one in which the very standards of human excellence—especially the excellence of philosophy—are significantly altered; and necessary to accomplish such a transition between incommensurables is experience of the new life itself. To get agreement in such situations one must first get one's opponent actually to play one's own game, so to speak; by playing it to understand its *telos* from within; to feel for himself its attractions; and thus to recognize the game's internal standards of excellence. Here it is crucial that for the opponent there must be some actual mode of participation, some sustained activity within the new way of life, before the conversion can be accomplished. The new form of life must, that is, be *shown,* not just talked about; somehow the vision must be actually vouchsafed, at least partially and provisionally. Then, and only then, can one's opponent see the point of what one might *say* in the course of playing one's game, or in defense of it.[11]

So Wittgenstein must, in the process of the *Philosophical Investigations* itself, initiate the philosopher into the new form of life and thought he covets for him. He must get the philosopher playing the new game, so that its standards become—at least provisionally—the operative ones. Then the particular remarks he makes will have their proper force and significance; then, perhaps, the particular terms of criticism he employs will assume their proper weight, not being assimilated to the traditional "scientific" model of philosophy. Therefore the real point of the *Philosophical Investigations* is the way it's written, the kind of activity it produces in the attentive reader (and thus the kind it also prevents).

The showing of the vision of the sound human understanding is in the *activity* of reading Wittgenstein's book. One thing that Wittgenstein offers us in his own silence and indirection is the possibility of an intelligible narrative of the philosophical tradition. In his remarks he is providing us a story, the moral of which is the bankruptcy of the tradition his work completes. The point of the story is that we get free of the illusion that we can and must represent the world *sub specie aeternitatis*, that to try to do this is an ideal of rationality itself. But—and this is his genius—he gives us in his remarks only the *elements* of this cleansing narrative. *We* must make the *Philosophical Investigations* into a book; we must, in effect, *write* the book by constructing a narrative for the disembodied and unidentified voices that speak from the pages. We must imagine a context for all those voices, thus making them parts of our own myth, our own narrative. Thus we embody and identify them within, and against, ourselves.

So the style of the *Philosophical Investigations* is the mode of its showing; it aims to initiate the reader into the new sensibility which is its source and object. Because the book is full of jokes, irony, incompatible images (language as game, as tool, as music; philosophy as therapy, as art criticism, as anthropology), and also full of "philosophical positions" which evaporate upon scrutiny, to be able to read it requires that one lose the representational sensibility of the philosopher; otherwise it is not a *book* at all, but a jumble. This is crucial: philosophers *must*, it seems, read as if rationality-as-representation were true. They must, that is, hear every philosophical remark as an attempt to represent how things stand *sub specie aeternitatis*. But in his later work Wittgenstein intends to defeat that sensibility by overwhelming it with recalcitrant but irrepressible material. No perceptive philosopher can ignore the voices of the *Investigations*, but neither can the responsible critic convert the book into a metaphysical treatise. (Many have tried, I know.) The book, considered as philosophical representation, is self-destructive; it cannot contain itself in its own critical categories. It refutes our every attempt to read it representationally, yet this capacity heightens rather than diminishes our compulsion to come to terms with it.

To read the book *as a book* forces one to think in a new way, to instantiate the sensibility Wittgenstein wants, thus making possible permanent conversion to the sound human understanding. The book intends that no reader be able to read it as traditional philosophy. By forcing its reader also to be its writer, the book aims to reconstruct its reader in the process of reading; it intends to initiate the reader, at least for a time, into the desired sensibility, thus making it possible for him to hear the story Wittgenstein wants to tell, to see the true source of the nonsense of philosophy and its life.

CHAPTER 5

Wittgenstein and Descartes

B OTH THE *Tractatus* and the *Investigations* essentially depend upon distinctions between what can be said and what must be shown. While not complete by any means, the hermeneutic for Wittgenstein's later work developed in the previous chapter gives us a sense of how the *Philosophical Investigations* and the other later works must be read in light of what he is trying to show, not say, there. We can now see that fundamental to Wittgenstein's later philosophical criticism is not a philosophical thesis of his own but his abhorrence of the form of life characterized by metaphysical philosophy itself. Thus the later work is grounded in a moral vision—a conviction about where and how the sense of life is to be found—in just the same way as is the earlier. The sense of life is to be found, not in philosophy, but in that form of life which the later remarks exemplify: the sound human understanding.

But what is that form of life which stands over against metaphysical philosophy and from which his remarks proceed? The remainder of this book will pursue an answer to this question. In this chapter Descartes is deployed as an illuminating object of comparison, and in the next a more direct exposition of the sound human understanding is attempted.

I

AN ANSWER to our question must have something to do with what we have been calling *rationality-as-representation,* since the destruction of that conception, so ambivalently embraced in the *Tractatus,* is the central endeavor of Wittgenstein's later work. In the philosophy of Descartes—or, perhaps, in the way in which that philosophy subsequently appeared to the tradition it created—rationality-as-representation is given its paradigmatic expression.

Genuine revolutions in philosophical thinking are rare, but Descartes produced one when he made epistemological questions basic to all other philosophical concerns. In the scholastic tradition immediately preceding him, questions of how one knows such-and-such were not yet seen as absolutely fundamental (think, for example, of the relative insignificance of epistemological issues in the *Summa*). But for Descartes *all* questions had to take a back seat to questions about how and to what extent we can know the world. It would be easy to underestimate the significance of this shift in perspective. It was not just that Descartes was suggesting that we substitute one set of philosophical questions for another, as a natural scientist might suggest that we defer investigating one set of phenomena until we have gotten clear about some other set that promises to help us with explaining the one we deferred. What Descartes did was to alter the philosopher's entire conception of his task; he reconstituted the nature of philosophy itself. (Indeed, it could be said that Descartes *created* philosophy as a particular and autonomous mode of thought.) And with that he reconstituted Western culture.

What are the salient features of the Cartesian revolution? What did it mean to make epistemological questions basic to philosophy and to Western culture? Let us distinguish first, by way of contrast, what we may call a "religious" attitude of a person to reality, an attitude that was once dominant in the cultures from which we descend. From this "religious" perspective, the fundamental, normative relationship between the person and reality is, in its most general description, *harmony*. The person naturally desires to live in harmony with the realities which create and support him; true harmony with them is the basic aim of human life; and its achievement is human virtue. The specification of what counts as such harmony varied from culture to culture, of course; but in almost all cases, from Hebrew to Greek, the harmony was thought to be gained by some kind of immediate personal (including community) encounter with the realities. This personal relationship was facilitated and evidenced by certain forms of life adopted by the culture, forms of life designed to propitiate, to honor, to worship, to attend to, the various realities underlying human life. The realities to be encountered, and thus acknowledged, are the natural element within which the person lives and dies. Person and element are made for one another; there is no necessary distance, no barrier to be bridged. To live in harmony is to dwell in the world as the trout in the stream, supported by the elements of one's life as the water supports the fish, bringing air and nourishment as a matter of course. Or not. It is to dwell within, not without.

A crucial point to be noted is the immediacy of that relationship. In the "religious" attitude, the realities with which persons must live in harmony are apprehended *concretely and immediately*. That is, those realities must be apprehended in those ways if harmony with them is to be achieved. These realities need not themselves be conceived as persons, but they are understood to be the sorts of things that persons can themselves encounter in concrete and immediate instances. Think here, for example, of the story in Genesis 32 of how Jacob got the name 'Israel': all night long by the ford of the Jabbok he wrestled a divine being to a draw, suffering only the dislocation of his hip, refusing to let the angel go until a blessing had been conferred. His new name—his new self—was contingent upon that quite immediate encounter with the numinous. And in the Greek tradition there is a corresponding emphasis upon the need for immediate contact: think of Plato's myth in the *Symposium* of how the preëxistent soul can encounter the impersonal and eternal Forms, thus making possible their remembrance in the life of virtue.

So, given this "religious" attitude, salvation or virtue depends upon the person's possibility for concrete and immediate encounter with the realities underlying his life, encounters that in one way or another make it possible for him to live in harmony with those realities. Harmony is achieved when the person's life mirrors realities that are themselves active, if not actually alive and personal.

But with Descartes all this has changed. The "religious" attitude just sketched is replaced by what we may properly call a "scientific" one. With the Cartesian revolution, reality becomes "the external world," that which lies outside the mind and is to be viewed, represented, *known*. Man, formerly a being seeking—with fear and trembling, to be sure—to encounter the fundamental realities, now becomes the self-conscious, self-enclosed *knower* who wants to represent them. Whereas formerly human virtue consisted in a life lived in harmony with concretely encountered realities, for Descartes salvation ("truth") consists in *accurate, justified representation* of a world essentially external and passive. Religion, considered as the attempt for human virtue, becomes metaphysics—the attempt "to understand how things in the broadest possible sense of the term hang together in the broadest possible sense of the term." [1]

The Cartesian exaltation of epistemology is intimately connected with an extraordinary extension of the mind's powers of abstraction. In the *Meditations* the mind is seen in a constant process of greater and greater abstraction, stepping back first from the world, then from its representations of the world, then back even from itself, attempting to represent the justification of its own powers of representation. The mind, the vehicle of representation, becomes the self. (That is the real point of Cartesian mind-body dualism.) "What am I?" asks Descartes. And he answers, "A thinking thing." Even the body—my body—becomes just a set of representations produced in sense experience; luckily, that set of representations is finally found by Descartes to be justifiably affirmable.

The person, that concrete reality capable of encountering other concrete realities, has itself now become an abstraction. He has become an extensionless point, the ever-restless, continuously representing mind, trying desperately to justify his representations. And just as the person has become a fantastic entity, so too has "the world." Reality inevitably has become the Kantian *Ding-an-sich*, the thing-in-itself that will always frustrate our claims to have represented it. Concrete encounter with the sustaining realities becomes impossible. Cartesian "scientific" knowledge is mediation; there is always a barrier, the representation, between the mind-self and the finally unknowable world.

The burden of Western philosophy after Descartes has been to try to live with the consequences of his epistemological revolution; that is, to try to secure some "knowledge" of the world, in lieu of being able to secure the world itself: the grace of our (lost) possibility of harmony. Locke's empiricism becomes Berkeley's idealism, which (via Hume) becomes Kant's transcendental realism. All human issues seen through philosophical lenses become issues of knowledge: "Is it true?" is the post-Cartesian question. The world, formerly our natural element, has retreated behind the representing screen of the mind, and the question now becomes whether or not we can be confident that any of our representations mirror the realities beyond them. Not surprisingly, most post-Cartesian philosophers have argued that we can be confident of some truths. With remarkable integrity and ingenuity they have taken up the Cartesian challenge and tried to furnish justified representations of the world. Philosophy in the West after the seventeenth century is the attempt to exorcise the specter of Descartes' Evil Genius.

It is worthwhile to reflect upon an important feature of Cartesian philosophy already noted, namely, its extraordinary movement from the concrete to the abstract. In the ancient conception, person, reality, and their contact with each other were all concrete entities or events. When Jacob wrestled with the angel of Yahweh, it was an unmediated, flesh-and-blood encounter between concrete entities (you can't wrestle a representation); when the preëxistent soul encounters the Forms in the *Symposium* myth, both soul and Form directly interact. After Descartes, however, the person becomes the mind, the vehicle and vessel of representations; reality becomes the hidden source of such representations; and their contact just is the process of representation itself. Note the abstraction in each case: the concrete person of body and consciousness is reduced to pure consciousness; historical and physical identity is lost in favor of the abstract and the impersonal. Under the Cartesian conception I here and now become a set of representations, abstractly describable, set within an indescribable (because utterly unspecified) abstract consciousness. Where has the person James C. Edwards gone in that description? Literally nowhere. Also gone is the study in which I write, that quite concrete place of paneling, Klimt prints, and windows full of trees; in its place is "the external world," the abstract and ungraspable cause of my representations of wood, pa-

per, color, and light. Suddenly my study has lost its charm; it has become alien.

Intimately connected to this overblown abstraction is another feature of the Cartesian revolution in philosophy, namely, the self-forgetfulness that it (initially) encourages. Formerly, many (perhaps most)
fundamental issues facing human beings explicitly were set in terms
that accented decision, not inquiry. "Will you serve God or mam-
mon?" Such expressions had the virtue of calling the individual to attention: they forced the person to self-consciousness by confronting
him with an issue in the form of a decision. The conversion of all important human issues into epistemological ones allows the individual
to slip into a kind of absentmindedness. For the Cartesian, every relationship to reality is a representational relation; direct and unmediated
contact with the real is impossible. So my task as a representer is to
represent accurately; correct action will follow (only) from correct
representation. But correct representation involves only a relationship
between the representing belief-idea-proposition and the reality to be
represented; the individual who frames the belief has no essential role
in that relationship. It is accidental that I, James C. Edwards, represented that such-and-such is the case; what matters is whether the representation in question accurately mirrors the state of affairs.

Thus an insidious kind of self-forgetfulness is encouraged, even required. Consciousness of self is liable to inhibit framing beliefs that
accurately represent what is there; all attention ought to be directed
to the relationship between the belief (that abstract entity) and "the
world" (equally abstract). The individual becomes irrelevant; he becomes the seeing eye, nothing more. (Think of the image of the metaphysical self in the *Tractatus*.) Objectivity in representation, when it
becomes the final end for a person, transforms him into a nonentity, a
spectral observer. ("But really you do *not* see the eye" [TLP 5.633]).
The Cartesian revolution in philosophy promotes that sort of absentmindedness; I become consciousness, and consciousness becomes a
ghost. Kierkegaard might well have been thinking of Descartes when
he wrote with such scorn of "the objective tendency, which proposes to
make everyone an observer, and in its maximum to transform him into
so objective an observer that he becomes almost a ghost." [2]

But it is a paradoxical feature of such Cartesian self-forgetfulness
that it must eventually become narcissistic self-enchantment. Metaphysical thinking of the Cartesian sort is essentially representational; it
sets the world up before the subject. This movement, which initially

directs attention away from the subject and toward the objective world, must at some point double back upon itself. If in representation the objective world is thrown into sharp relief, then at the same time so is the seeing eye of the subject; and sooner or later that subject will notice its own fascinating presence. (This is precisely the progress of the *Tractatus*.) Narcissus, gazing about, must sooner or later look into the still pool and be charmed by what he sees. And once representation is recognized necessarily to involve a representing subject, it loses its naïve assurance and must more and more study itself so as to safeguard the process of "objective" representation itself from unwarranted and distorting intrusion. The self-forgetful "ghost" produced by the "objective tendency" Kierkegaard derides all too quickly becomes the self-enchanted Kantian (or Tractarian) subject; narcissism is the necessary second moment of the Cartesian revolution. So in philosophical thinking there is a constant dialectic between self-abandonment and self-enclosure; an overweening subjectivity is the correlate and consequence of the movement to Cartesian objectivity.

The two Cartesian tendencies just sketched, the movement from the concrete to the abstract and the required self-forgetfulness of objectivity, a self-forgetfulness in constant dialectic with self-enchantment, are defining marks of our culture. They are not only found in contemporary conceptions of religious faith; they are definitive for our conceptions of natural science, education, and politics as well. Our culture has accepted, almost without demur, the attitude toward reality exemplified in Cartesianism. We now *are* Cartesian minds, abstracting and representing and then worrying about the consequences of our inevitable alienation; we are not any more just *in* the world, encountering (for good or for ill) the various realities there. We *view* the world; we constantly step back and observe it. And then we step back and observe ourselves observing it. And so on. One cannot stop that just by trying. Indeed, it must be asked whether one can stop at all.

It should be clear that the Cartesian impetus toward world view is a paradigmatic expression of rationality-as-representation; the metaphysicalizing of the person, the literalization of mind into intellect—both are avatars of the conception that identifies the essence of thought to be the representation of reality. One can now see how this traditional conception of rationality is not an isolated and negligible philosopher's doctrine; rather, it determines a whole culture, a form of life. It is, in the deepest sense, a moral vision, determining good and evil by posing the ultimate terms in which we think and live; and it is the moral vision of rationality-as-representation that Wittgenstein abhors and to which he opposes his own.

II

HOW THEN does Wittgenstein oppose Descartes? He does not battle Descartes as do the rest of the tradition, for they accept the terms of the Cartesian challenge. His is an attempt to undercut the challenge itself, to remove the philosophical attraction of Descartes' fundamental viewpoint. But since that Cartesian conception is so familiar and so powerful (since it is likely that even opposition to it will be seen in its own most basic terms) it is imperative that Wittgenstein find a vantage outside the Cartesian world itself. Only from there can he speak so as to avoid being coöpted. And since philosophy itself is now so deeply imbued with Cartesian notions (we expect there to be "clashing views," and the like), Wittgenstein's search is ultimately for a kind of thinking and speaking that is not philosophical.

Two consequences of Cartesian thinking have been most visible in the philosophical tradition and in the culture shaped by that tradition: first, the notion that knowledge (and thus life generally) needs to be established on some unshakable foundation; and second, the conception of the person as (contingently) embodied mind. Not surprisingly, these two philosophical contentions are given a great deal of attention in Wittgenstein's later work and so provide good examples of his opposition to Descartes.

Both foundationalism and mind-body dualism have, of course, close connections to skepticism. It is the skeptical challenge to our common representations of the world, a challenge exemplified in the first two paragraphs of Meditation I, that leads Descartes to the search for solid foundations:

It is now several years since I first became aware how many false opinions I had from my childhood been admitting as true, and how doubtful was everything I have subsequently based on them. Accordingly I have ever since been convinced that if I am to establish anything firm and lasting in the sciences, I must once for all, and by a deliberate effort, rid myself of all those opinions to which I have hitherto given credence, starting entirely anew, and building from the foundations up.[3]

The only way to ensure that our representations of the world can withstand the attack of the skeptic is to rest those representations firmly on a foundation itself impervious to skeptical undermining. Thus we have the Cartesian search for certainty, the attempt rationally to justify our most fundamental beliefs about reality.

Mind-body dualism is related to philosophical skepticism in another way. Descartes' own espousal of dualism was the result of his attempt to find a certain foundation for knowledge; in particular it was the result of his coming to rest upon the certainty of his own existence as a thinking thing. But if mind-body dualism is a Cartesian result of attempting to vanquish a wholesale skepticism, it has in turn spawned a skepticism of its own, most notably the nest of issues known collectively among philosophers as "the problem of other minds."

It will be useful for us to probe Wittgenstein's responses to foundationalism and mind-body dualism. In both cases he is confronting a paradigmatic response to philosophical skepticism, a response validated by the basic Cartesian assumption that our relationship to reality is in essence literally representational and thus that our representations of that reality stand in need of philosophical justification. As we see Wittgenstein struggling against that assumption, and as we see more clearly the particular ways in which he struggles, some important features of his radically non-Cartesian vision (and hence *world*) will be illuminated. In this chapter's analysis my aim is certainly not to present a complete account of Wittgenstein's responses to Descartes: that would require a book in itself. But even this brief exposition of their encounter will provide, not only an illustration of the hermeneutic described in chapter four, but also a bridge into the more direct discussion of the sound human understanding to be attempted in chapter six. We will begin with foundationalism.

A lucid exemplification of Wittgenstein's radically nontraditional attitude toward the Cartesian roots of philosophical skepticism is found in *On Certainty*. This material, similar in style and structure to the *Philosophical Investigations,* was written in the last year and a half of Wittgenstein's life. Goaded by Norman Malcolm's interest in the topic, Wittgenstein began to concern himself with G. E. Moore's famous "defence of common sense." In his classic papers "A Defence of Common Sense" and "Proof of an External World," Moore intends to demonstrate by argument that the skeptic is wrong in making his skeptical claims. The claim that no one can really know of the existence of an "external world" (i.e., a "world" that exists independently of one's experiences) has been especially traumatic to philosophers. Moore quotes Kant in this connection:

> It still remains a scandal to philosophy . . . that the existence of things outside of us . . . must be accepted merely on *faith,* and that, if anyone thinks good to doubt their existence, we are unable to counter his doubts by any satisfactory proof.[4]

Because of the peculiar importance of this sort of philosophical doubt, Moore sets out to show that it is mistaken. He wants to provide Kant with the "satisfactory proof" that will counter the doubts of the skeptic. It should be quite clear that, although Kant is the philosopher most prominently mentioned, the ultimate grounds of Moore's enterprise are Cartesian. Moore is trying to answer in his own way the doubts raised by Descartes in Meditation I, doubts which, given the Cartesian centrality of epistemology, seem philosophically inescapable. Thus it is perfectly fair to say that in his papers Moore is trying to defeat the *Cartesian* skeptic, i.e., the skeptic licensed—demanded—by the Cartesian quest for epistemological justification.

It is instructive to note how Moore begins his "defence of common sense" against the Cartesian skeptic.

> I am going to begin by enunciating . . . a whole long list of propositions, which may seem, at first sight, such obvious truisms as not to be worth stating: they are, in fact, a set of propositions, every one of which (in my opinion) I *know,* with certainty, to be true. . . . The propositions to be included in this list are the following:
>
> There exists at present a living human body, which is my body. This body was born at a certain time in the past and has existed continuously ever since, though not without undergoing changes; it was, for instance, much smaller when it was born, and for some time afterwards, than it is now. Ever since it was born, it has either been in contact with or not far from the surface of the earth; and, at every moment since it was born, there have also existed many other things, having shape and size in three dimensions (in the same familiar sense in which it has), from which it has been *at various distances* (in the famil-

iar sense in which it is now at a distance both from that mantelpiece and from that bookcase, and at a greater distance from the bookcase than it is from the mantelpiece); also there have (very often, at all events) existed some other things of this kind with which it has been *in contact* (in the familiar sense in which it is now in contact with the pen that I am holding in my right hand and with some of the clothes I am wearing). Among the things which have, in this sense, formed part of its environment . . . there have, at every moment since its birth, been large numbers of other living human bodies, each of which has, like it, (a) at some time been born, (b) continued to exist for some time after birth, (c) been, at every moment of its life after birth, either in contact with or not very far from the surface of the earth; and many of these bodies have already died and ceased to exist. But the earth had existed also for many years before my body was born, and for many of these years, also, large numbers of humans had, at every moment, been alive upon it; and many of these bodies had died and ceased to exist before it was born. Finally (to come to a different class of propositions) I am a human being, and I have, at different times since my body was born, had many different experiences, of each of many different kinds: [Here there follows a list of such experiences, including perceptions of one's own body and the bodies of other human beings, thoughts of imaginary beings and events, dreams, expectations of the future, and the like.] And, just as my body has been the body of a human being, namely myself, who has, during his lifetime, had many experiences of each of these (and other) different kinds; so, in the case of very many of the other human bodies who have lived upon the earth, each has been the body of a different human being, who has, during the lifetime of that body, had many different experiences of each of these (and other) different kinds.[5]

For Moore, it seems, a thoroughgoing skepticism of the reality of the external world consists in negative answers to two questions:

(1) Are there physical (or, material) objects?
(2) Do we know that there are physical (material) objects?

A less thoroughgoing, but still quite disturbing, sort of skepticism would consist in a negative answer to the second question and an agnostic attitude toward the first. (The second question, and the second sort of skepticism, remind one of the quote from Kant in Moore's second essay: Kant cannot *know* of the existence of physical objects; hence their existence, if affirmed at all, must be accepted on *faith*.)

Moore accepts (1) and (2) as genuine (philosophical) questions which beg genuine (philosophical) answers. Like Descartes, he does not consider the questions to be in any important way peculiar or out of place. (Indeed, to ask them is a mark of critical intelligence.) He wants to answer the questions affirmatively and thus show that the skeptic is wrong in the answer he gives. In responding to the skeptic's incorrect reply, Moore approaches question (1) by way of question (2). He reasons, correctly, that an affirmative answer to question (2) entails an affirmative answer to question (1). If one can truly *know* that there are physical (material) objects, then physical objects must exist. (Moore is assuming, of course, an account of knowledge in which for one to know that *p,* where '*p*' is the name of a proposition-sentence, it must be true that *p.*) The aim of Moore's work in "Proof of an External World" and "A Defence of Common Sense" is to show that one does know propositions that entail the existence of physical objects (this is the point of the long list of propositions quoted above that Moore claims he knows: they are propositions which, if true, entail the existence of physical objects); hence, the thoroughgoing skeptic of the reality of the external world is vanquished.

Wittgenstein is not convinced by Moore's "proof." *On Certainty* begins with a series of animadversions on particular aspects of Moore's arguments; we seem at once to be in familiar philosophical territory: argument and counterargument.[6] Understood in this way, however, these initial thrusts and parries distort the character of Wittgenstein's later work. They fail to show its radical novelty; they fail to indicate the great distance between Wittgenstein and Moore. Their dispute over the proper response to the philosophical skeptic runs much deeper than mere unhappiness on Wittgenstein's part with particular features of Moore's argument. Rather, the dispute turns upon fundamentally differing relationships to philosophical argument itself. Moore is happy inside the philosophy created by the Cartesian revolution; he wants to restore order to the room, to set things in their proper places and fix them there, safe from skeptical hooliganism. Wittgenstein, on the other hand, sees the Cartesian enclosure as a trap, not a living room; he wants to escape, not straighten up his cell.

Moore takes for granted the terms within which the skeptical challenge is set. He never doubts that the Cartesian demand for the rational justification of one's most basic beliefs is a legitimate one; he never, that is, questions the metaphysical intellect's demands for primacy. But Wittgenstein challenges the Cartesian context of philosophical puzzle and argument itself, refusing to accept the philosophical skeptic's problems in the way they are put to him. The skeptical problems must be "answered," according to Wittgenstein, by showing that for the sound human understanding they cannot and ought not be answered at all. In this sense they are not genuine problems. Their genesis presupposes some sort of disorientation, not ignorance. Wittgenstein answers the skeptic, not by entering the skeptic's world and revealing its hidden order, but by creating a new world, a new way of seeing, and by persuading the skeptic to live with him there.

For Moore the notion of representational philosophical truth is unproblematic. Philosophical truth will consist in those representational propositions which are the correct answers to the philosophical questions asked. Thus for Moore his proof of the external world is taken to demonstrate that there really are in truth objects that exist independently of our sensory awareness of them, i.e., that a realist philosophical ideology is metaphysically true. As we have seen, however, Wittgenstein rejects this notion of philosophical truth. To conceive of philosophical truth in this way is already to enter the Cartesian world created by the literalization of mind into intellect. It is to accede to rationality-as-representation: to assume that the ultimate demand of thought is metaphysical truth, truth understood as the passive representation *sub specie aeternitatis* of an antecedently given reality. To accept the challenge to demonstrate the truth of some metaphysical ideology or other is, for Wittgenstein, to give the game away; it is in the final instance to surrender to a moral vision of self and world antithetical to the sound human life.

It is interesting and instructive to trace how in *On Certainty* Wittgenstein refuses to play the skeptic's game while at the same time responding to his challenge. He wants in his remarks to sketch an alternative way of looking at the things that provoke the skeptic without—of course—constructing a literal *Weltanschauung* of his own. This alternative can then serve as an "object of comparison" parallel in function to those discussed in chapter four. As always, Wittgenstein's intention in *On Certainty* is to free us from captivity to a certain way of looking at something by confronting us with other powerful images, other persuasive ways of seeing. Rather than attempting our conversion to his own philosophical ideology, he wants in this way to make possible the loss of ideology altogether. Then the fly is out of *all* the fly bottles.

What is the image, the picture, assumed by the Cartesian skeptic? It is a familiar picture of both the *nature* and the *structure* of knowledge. First of all, knowledge is assumed to be a mode of representation. To know that something is the case is to be in proper possession of an accurate representation of a state of affairs; to know, for example, that the cat is on the mat is to be in a proper position to give assent to the proposition that models (pictures, re-presents) the cat's being on the mat. The Cartesian, whether Moore or the skeptic, never questions the conception that knowledge is accurate representation; the question for the philosopher is whether one is ever in a position justifiably to assert that his representations of reality are accurate. The skeptic against whom Moore is arguing, for instance, holds that we are never in a position to have confidence in our representations of an "external world": perhaps it is not, in spite of our representations, "external" after all. Moore, on the other hand, is trying to demonstrate that our representations of an external world *do* picture the way things stand. This characteristic Cartesian obsession with epistemological justification rests unabashedly on the notion that knowledge is accurate representation of reality.

Moreover, the Cartesian picture accepted by the skeptic and by Moore also assumes that knowledge is an edifice with particular foundations. As a way of illuminating his program of philosophical doubt, in the first Meditation Descartes himself explicitly uses the image of removing a building's foundations. The Cartesian assumption is that some representations of reality are more fundamental than others; these are the stones upon which the whole of our dwelling depends. If they are compromised, then the entire structure will crumble and fall. If we are to establish anything "firm and lasting in the sciences" (Descartes), we must satisfy ourselves that we are building upon a base strong enough to carry the weight. Are our most fundamental representations really true *sub specie aeternitatis?* That question provokes the Cartesian quest for certainty, raising, among other things, the Kantian "scandal" that Moore is trying to settle.

In summary, the Cartesian picture holds that knowledge is representational in nature and foundational in structure. The task for a human being, still the Socratic essentially rational creature, is to make sure that his life—theory and practice—rests upon representations of reality that are accurate and comprehensive. The only alternative to such representations true *sub specie aeternitatis* is a house built upon sand rather than stone: theoretical skepticism and practical despair.

How does Wittgenstein build an alternative image to the familiar Cartesian one? He first remarks that certain of our "beliefs"—indeed, those common "beliefs" most intriguing to the skeptic—seem to have a special, systematic character. He calls such a system of "beliefs" a "picture of the world" (*Weltbild*).

146.   We form *the picture* of the earth as a ball floating free in space and not altering essentially in a hundred years. I said ' "We form the picture etc." ' and this picture now helps us in the judgment of various situations.

    I may indeed calculate the dimensions of a bridge, sometimes calculate that here things are more in favor of a bridge than a ferry, etc. etc., —but somewhere I must begin with an assumption or a decision.

147.   The picture of the earth as a ball is a *good* picture, it proves itself everywhere, it is also a simple picture—in short, we work with it without doubting it. (OC, sec. 146–47)

The sentences that express a *Weltbild* (such as "The earth is a spherical body floating free in space" or "The existence of physical objects is continuous in space and time") seem to be ordinary representational propositions, claims as to the facts, and therefore subject to testing. But to see such propositions in this way is radically to misunderstand their role in our thinking.

213.   Our "empirical propositions" do not form a homogeneous mass. (OC, sec. 213)

167.   It is clear that our empirical propositions do not all have the same status, since one can lay down such a proposition and turn it from an empirical proposition into a norm of description.

    Think of chemical investigations. Lavoisier makes

experiments with substances in his laboratory and now
he concludes that this and that takes place when there is
burning. He does not say that it might happen otherwise
another time. He has got hold of a definite world-picture—not of course one that he invented: he learned it
as a child. I say world-picture and not hypothesis, because it is the matter-of-fact foundation for his research
and as such goes unmentioned. (OC, sec. 167)

Wittgenstein has noticed that what seems on its surface to be an
empirical proposition—the representation of a fact—may actually be
playing another role altogether. He uses the image of a *mythology* here:

95. The propositions describing this world-picture might
be part of a kind of mythology. And their role is like that
of rules of a game; and the game can be learned purely
practically, without learning any explicit rules. (OC,
sec. 95)

The sentences describing the mythology of a culture are *taken for
granted* by that culture; they guide the thinking of that culture, impart-
ing significance here, withdrawing it there. Representation, or fact-
stating, is dependent upon this mythological context, for without our
first giving significance to some things rather than to others, naming
and stating could not occur. Without the mythology, all would be ungraspable flux:

96. It might be imagined that some propositions, of the
form of empirical propositions, were hardened and
functioned as channels for such empirical propositions
as were not hardened but fluid; and that this relation altered with time, in that fluid propositions hardened, and
hard ones became fluid.

97. The mythology may change back to a state of flux,
the river-bed of thought may shift. But I distinguish between the movement of the waters on the river-bed and
the shift of the bed itself; though there is not a sharp division of the one from the other. (OC, sec. 96–97)

At any given time and place, certain ways of behaving, imaging, and speaking are given final and unthinking sanction; they form the mythology of that culture. It is the river-bed of the mythology within which the particular life of the culture flows: naming, stating, arguing, playing, worshipping.

However much the descriptions of a culture's mythology may appear to be representational, i.e., to be testable empirical propositions, they are not. This is well brought out in this remark:

> 204.   Giving grounds, however, justifying the evidence, comes to an end; —but the end is not certain propositions striking us immediately as true, i.e., it is not a kind of *seeing* on our part; it is our *acting* which lies at the bottom of the language-game.
>
> 205.   If the true is what is grounded, then the ground is not *true*, nor yet false. (OC, sec. 204–5)

At the bottom of a language-game—at the bottom of human life—is not seeing, but doing; not representation, but action.

The mythology of a culture exercises a regulative role in its thinking. The mythology is systematic, and this systematic character is essentially connected with the notions of testing, falsification, and confirmation.

> 141.   When we first begin to *believe* anything, what we believe is not a single proposition, it is a whole system of propositions. (Light dawns gradually over the whole.)
>
> 142.   It is not single axioms that strike me as obvious, it is a system in which consequences and premises give one another *mutual* support.
>
> 143.   I am told, for example, that someone climbed this mountain many years ago. Do I always inquire into the reliability of the teller of this story, and whether this mountain did exist years ago? A child learns there are reliable and unreliable informants much later than it learns facts which are told it. It doesn't learn *at all* that the mountain has existed a long time: that is, the question whether it is so doesn't arise at all. It swallows this

consequence down, so to speak, together with what it learns.

144.   The child learns to believe a host of things. I.e., it learns to act according to these beliefs. Bit by bit there forms a system of what is believed, and in that system some things stand unshakeably fast and some are more or less liable to shift. What stands fast does so, not because it is intrinsically obvious or convincing; it is rather held fast by what lies around it. (OC, sec. 141–44)

Also:

102.   Might I not believe that once, without knowing it, perhaps in a state of unconsciousness, I was taken far away from the earth—that other people even know this but do not mention it to me? But this would not fit into the rest of my convictions at all. Not that I could describe the system of these convictions. Yet my convictions do form a system, a structure.

103.   And now if I were to say 'It is my unshakeable conviction that etc.', this means in the present case too I have not consciously arrived at the conviction by following a particular line of thought, but that it is anchored in all my *questions and answers,* so anchored that I cannot touch it.

104.   I am for example also convinced that the sun is not a hole in the vault of heaven.

105.   All testing, all confirmation and disconfirmation of a hypothesis takes place already within a system. And this system is not a more or less arbitrary and doubtful point of departure for all our arguments: no, it belongs to the essence of what we call an argument. The system is not so much the point of departure, as the element in which the arguments have their life. (OC, sec. 102–5)

The acquisition and maintenance of a *Weltbild* is not a matter of the conscious activity of the representational intellect. This point has already come out implicitly in the comparison of a *Weltbild* with a mythology, and in the suggestions that the sentences in a *Weltbild* exercise a normative role for the persons who hold it. It is evident as well in sections 143–44, quoted earlier. The child "swallows down" great parts of his culture's *Weltbild*. He does not *consciously* accept them; indeed, he may never become explicitly conscious of them at all. Remember: at the bottom of all is doing, not seeing; trust, not justification by intellection.

Wittgenstein's implicit recipe for discovering the *Weltbild* of a particular person or culture is connected with the possibility of doubt. Those *Grundanschauungen* (oc, sec. 238) which are not, in the course of nonphilosophical thinking, open to doubt and investigation constitute a *Weltbild*. As Wittgenstein expresses himself, certain things "stand fast" (*Feststehen*) for a person or for a culture. This characterization better enables one to see what Moore is really doing in "Proof of an External World" and "A Defence of Common Sense," and it also makes clear why Moore's work is insufficient to its stated goals.

> 151.   I should like to say: Moore does not *know* what he
>   asserts he knows, but it stands fast for him, as also for
>   me; regarding it as absolutely solid is part of our *method*
>   of doubt and inquiry. (oc, sec. 151)

In enumerating those propositions which he claims to know to be true, Moore has merely listed some of the propositions that, by "standing fast" for him, make up his *Weltbild*. But of course what Moore wants to do in his essays is to *secure,* to *establish,* that *Weltbild.*

What sense, if any, does it make for a philosopher to try to establish a *Weltbild?* Could there be, as the Cartesian skeptic demands, a rational justification of one's "fundamental attitudes" (oc, sec. 238)? We have seen that the sort of justification Moore offers is *proof*—he wants to secure, to establish by knockdown argument, his philosophical ideology; he tries to show that our most fundamental representations are true. But Wittgenstein is very different here. For him, a *Weltbild* is not open to proof; it cannot be established or overturned by discursive argument.

Consider the following passages:

> 91.   If Moore says he knows the earth existed etc., most of
>   us will grant him that it has existed all that time, and

also believe him when he says he is convinced of it. But has he also got the right *ground* for his conviction? For if not, then after all he doesn't know (Russell).

92.　　However, we can ask: May someone have telling grounds for believing that the earth has only existed for a short time, say since his own birth? —Suppose he had always been told that, —would he have any good reason to doubt it? Men have believed that they could make rain; why should not a king be brought up in the belief that the world began with him? And if Moore and this king were to meet and discuss, could Moore really prove his belief to be the right one? I do not say that Moore could not convert the king to his view, but it would be a conversion of a special kind; the king would be brought to look at the world in a different way.

　　Remember that one is sometimes convinced of the *correctness* of a view by its *simplicity* or *symmetry,* i.e., these are what induce one to go over to this point of view. One then simply says something like: "That's how it must be." (oc, sec. 91–92)

Wittgenstein is suggesting that this imagined conflict of world-pictures cannot be settled by means of a proof of the correctness of one over the other. The resolution of the conflict will be a kind of conversion from one *Weltbild* to another. Wittgenstein says: "The king would be brought to look at the world in a different way." The same point is made in the following passage.

262.　　I can imagine a man who had grown up in quite spe-cial circumstances and been taught that the earth came into being 50 years ago, and therefore believed this. We might instruct him: the earth has long . . . etc. —We should be trying to give him our picture of the world.

　　This would happen through a kind of *persuasion.* (oc, sec. 262)

　　Again in some later passages of *On Certainty* there is a rejection of Moore's "proof" and a corresponding reliance on persuasion for re-solving a conflict between world-pictures.

608.   Is it wrong for me to be guided in my actions by the propositions of physics? Am I to say I have no good ground for doing so? Isn't this precisely what we call a 'good ground'?

609.   Supposing we met people who did not regard that as a telling reason. Now, how do we imagine this? Instead of the physicist, they consult an oracle. (And for that we consider them primitive.) Is it wrong for them to consult an oracle and be guided by it? —If we call this "wrong" aren't we using our language-game as a base from which to *combat* theirs?

610.   And are we right or wrong to combat it? Of course there are all sorts of slogans which will be used to support our proceedings.

611.   When two principles really do meet which cannot be reconciled with one another, then each man declares the other a fool and heretic.

612.   I said I would 'combat' the other man, —but wouldn't I give him *reasons?* Certainly; but how far do they go? At the end of reasons comes *persuasion.* (Think what happens when missionaries convert natives.) (OC, sec. 608–12)

Given the mythological character of a *Weltbild*, it is not surprising that Wittgenstein should reject rational argument in favor of persuasion. The use of argument makes sense only within the context created by a particular mythology.

105.   All testing, all confirmation and disconfirmation of a hypothesis takes place already within a system. And this system is not the more or less arbitrary and doubtful point of departure for all our arguments: no, it belongs to the essence of what we call an argument. The system is not so much the point of departure, as the element within which the arguments have their life.

It would make no sense to try to confirm the basic paradigms of confirmation. Furthermore, notions like *test, confirmation,* and *argument*— because for us they are already conceptually linked to representational notions of *truth* and *falsity*—cannot be applied to basic descriptions of world-pictures. Such descriptions are not representational. While they may have "the form of empirical propositions" (OC, sec. 96), in reality they are "part of a kind of a mythology," with a role "like that of rules of a game" (OC, sec. 95). They channel our representations of reality—they are, indeed, the element within which such representations have their life—but they themselves do not represent. They are neither true, nor yet false. They are the ungrounded ground of our lives (OC, sec. 204, 205). Thus, to try to argue about them, to try rationally to justify them (Moore's "proof"), is nonsense; it is to accede to the Cartesian conception of rationality-as-representation.

That Wittgenstein did not so accede is beautifully brought out in the following remarks from *On Certainty:* he beards the Cartesian lion in his den.

508. What can I rely on?

509. I really want to say that a language-game is only possible if one trusts something (I did not say "can trust something").

510. If I say "Of course I know that's a towel" I am making an *utterance (Äußerung)*. I have no thought of a verification. For me it is an immediate utterance.

I don't think of past or future. (And, of course, it's the same for Moore, too.)

It's just like directly taking hold of something, as I take hold of my towel without having doubts.

"What can I rely on?" is *the* Cartesian question, of course; and the Cartesian answer is: representations of reality themselves rationally demonstrated to be trustworthy; representations of nature in nature's own language. For Descartes, at the bottom of human life is *thought;* thought understood as intellection, as the (justified) literal representation of reality. For Wittgenstein, at the bottom of human life is *trust,* a particular mode of action (cf. OC, sec. 204).

This mode of acting is not, of course, *mindless;* but it is *thoughtless,* when (as with Descartes) thought and intellection are identified. That it is not mindless is clear from the fact that it is the ground of *human* life, and from the fact that it may naturally express itself in speech. That it is nevertheless thoughtless (in the sense of rationality-as-representation) is clear from its directness, from its immediacy. The action does not rest upon some prior process of justification. Indeed, it does not rest upon anything at all; it is blind, in the way that the infant's trust in the mother is blind. Wittgenstein characterizes the linguistic expression of such trust as an *Äußerung,* an utterance. He means to indicate that such a use of language is not representational; it is not a picture of some reality, nor does it rest upon such a picture. A picture always is intermediate; it mediates the person and the reality confronting him. But an *Äußerung* is not language-as-mediation; as Wittgenstein says, "It's just like directly taking hold of something, as I take hold of my towel without having doubts" (oc, sec. 510). The utterance is not the abstract representation of some reality; rather, it is natural *expression* (not representation) of the action whereby one takes hold of a particular form of human life. It is the natural expression of trust, not the representation of trustworthiness. To be able to make such an expression of trust is itself an expression of human intelligence. Someone who could not take some things for granted would not be recognizable as a human being; such a life would not be a human life. The basic trust at the bottom of human life is a mark of mind itself.

It is very easy to misunderstand what Wittgenstein is doing in *On Certainty,* because it is so tempting to see him there putting forward certain philosophical theses in order to combat those proffered by Moore. Under the spell of this temptation, one might believe that in *On Certainty* he is asserting that we live within world-pictures, that these pictures are neither true nor false, and so forth. Such "conceptual relativist" claims look very philosophical; so it might seem that Wittgenstein is responding to the Cartesian challenge with a "nonfoundational" theory of knowledge, a theory presupposing a metaphysics all its own. He himself worried about this way of appropriating his remarks, as we see in these sections from *On Certainty:*

421. I am in England. —Everything around me tells me so; wherever and however I let my thoughts turn, they confirm this for me at once. —But might not I be shaken if things such as I don't dream of at present were to happen?

422. So I am trying to say something that sounds like pragmatism.

Here I am being thwarted by a kind of *Weltanschauung.*

In these remarks one sees Wittgenstein attempting to put distance between himself and all the standard philosophical responses to Cartesian skepticism. He recognizes that the images he deploys (*Weltbild,* for example) can be literalized into philosophical constructions; the remarks he has made can be heard as intimating a kind of latter-day pragmatism, for example: the truth is what is good for us to believe. But he insists that to do so is to thwart his real intention; it is to be seduced by a particular *Weltanschauung,* one which assumes that the response to a philosophical puzzlement must be the promulgation and defense of a philosophical thesis. And, of course, it is just that assumption that Wittgenstein so vehemently rejects, for that assumption is but a corollary of the literalization of mind and speech that lies at the root of the Cartesian conception itself. If, as the Cartesian philosopher insists, all thought is representation, if all image is literal picture, then the remarks in *On Certainty* and in all the other books by Wittgenstein must be at least *pieces* of a metaphysical view of the world.[7] What else could they be?

The hermeneutic for the later work developed above in chapter four gives us an answer. The image of knowledge deployed against the Cartesian in *On Certainty* is just that: an *image*. It is not to be taken as Wittgenstein's own epistemological or metaphysical postition. Its sole function is to be an illuminating object of comparison to the familiar representational and foundational image of knowledge assumed both by the Cartesian skeptic and by his opponents like G. E. Moore. Because Wittgenstein's nonfoundational, nonrepresentational image is, as he thinks, every bit as charming and as plausible as the Cartesian— perhaps even more plausible—its acknowledgment by us gives us freedom from our habitual ways of thinking and from the philosophical rat runs that those habits entail. The object of comparison developed in *On Certainty* can change the epistemologist's way of looking at what is there:

> I wanted to put this picture before your eyes, and your *acceptance* of this picture consists in your being inclined to regard a given case differently; that is, to compare it with *this* series of pictures. I have changed your *way of seeing*. (z, sec. 461)

The acceptance of the image of knowledge found in *On Certainty* is not the commitment to "conceptual relativism" or some other such philosophical thesis; acceptance of it just means that one's mind is released from the powerful cramp of the Cartesian picture. One now does not have to think that knowledge *must be* that way.

On Certainty must be set within the context of the whole of Wittgenstein's later work, the point of which is to free us from *all* captivity to pictures (cf. PI, sec. 115). Against the traditional philosophical pictures of knowledge as accurate representation and the medium of knowledge as the re-presenting proposition Wittgenstein deploys the image of the *Äußerung,* the immediate expression of trusting action; and against the foundations picture he deploys the image of the *Weltbild,* resting on a mythology not itself open to test and verification. Both these alternative Wittgensteinian images are in the final instance intended to loosen the grip of the conception that our relationship to what is there around us is fundamentally one of representation. Both are attempts to intimate the possibility that we do not stand over against the world, setting it up in view before us in the abstract representation of thought. To the extent that these new images take hold, we are free of the Cartesian alienation from the world and restored to the possibility of harmony with it.

The methodology of Wittgenstein's later work rests upon his vision of soundness in understanding and in life. His remarks in *On Certainty* have as their intention to break the grip of the Cartesian *Weltanschauung*. But they are not philosophical *theses*; they are not attempts to represent—not even attempts to represent the place of soundness from which they themselves come. (Certainly *not!*) They are gestures. Or, to change the image to one of Wittgenstein's own, they are a kind of utterance (*Äußerung*). They take hold of (OC, sec. 510) that other place; they are its natural instinctive expressions. Their intention is to show what cannot be said.

III

SO MUCH for Wittgenstein's response to the Cartesian demand for an unshakable foundation for knowledge and life. It is now time to examine his response to Descartes' second major bequest to the philosophical tradition: the identification of the self with a mental substance only contingently embodied in a physical organism. The *locus classicus* of Wittgenstein's discussion is the middle sections of the *Philosophical Investigations,* especially those dealing with the possibility of a "private language." Here he tacks back and forth before the wind, approaching and reapproaching the Cartesian conception from several directions. We must limit our attention to a few of his remarks; as in the previous section, our only intention is to trace some of the contours of Wittgenstein's thinking by seeing him in concrete encounter with his *bête noire*. In this struggle, as in *On Certainty,* he depends finally upon radically nontraditional modes of reasoning and response; his fundamental aim is to alter the sensibility of the Cartesian philosopher trapped in the bonds of rationality-as-representation.

Why should the possibility of a "private language" be the focus of Wittgenstein's remarks? Because, first of all, such a possibility is required by Descartes' philosophical account of the person as noncorporeal mental substance; and also because in the notion of "private language" one can see most clearly the influence of the conception that in one way or another underlies the whole Cartesian program: rationality-as-representation. It is not necessary here to trace in detail the progress of Descartes' thought that leads him to affirm the "real distinction" of body and mind; a quick sketch will suffice. Once he had committed himself to the notion that all thought is representation, and hence to the philosophical primacy of epistemology, it was inevitable that "body" and "mind" should come to seem metaphysically distinct since the epistemological status of reports about my body is quite different from that of "reports" about my mental states. Since, given rationality-as-representation, both "I am more than six feet tall" and "I am in pain" are *reports*—literal representations of some reality—and since the relationship of the first report to such epistemological notions as certainty, empirical verification, and the like is so radically different from the second, Descartes drew the conclusion that they must be reports about metaphysically quite distinct realms. The first is a representation of "the world," the realm of physical objects, whose essence is extension; the second is a representation of "the mind," whose essence is thought. And I, of course, am *thought,* for I can doubt (conceive the falsehood of) all representations of my physical characteristics; but my inner representations are indubitable.

Given this metaphysical dualism of body and mind, a "private language" becomes inevitable. It is indubitable that I frequently express in language what I am feeling; pain, for example. I thus apparently "report" on what sensation I am having. If I am, as Descartes imagined, essentially "mind"—mental substance only contingently (if at all) connected to a physical organism—then what does the semantics of my familiar sensation language look like? What is the analysis of a "report" like "I am in pain"? Descartes would never doubt, of course, that one is saying (representing) *something* when one says that one is in pain; so what does the word 'pain' mean in such a report, and how does it get its meaning?

The notion of a "private language" provides an answer to both questions. First, in such a "language" the meaning of a word like 'pain' is given by its being the name of a *private object,* an immediate and distinct modification of consciousness; a distinct occurrence, so to speak, in the inner theater of my mind. Second, the word gets its meaning because *I name* that private object 'pain'; I associate that word with that object. Because a private object is so private—because only I can see the stage on which the objects appear—the meaning of a private object term like 'pain' is also private. Since only I can see the object I have decided to call 'pain' (and so on for all the sensations), my sensation language is wholly a private one: "The individual words of this language are to refer to what can only be known to the person speaking; to his immediate private sensations. So another person cannot understand the language" (PI, sec. 243).

We have already seen how the notion of a grammatical picture plays a crucial role in Wittgenstein's understanding of traditional philosophy, and here such a picture is very evident. The conception of a "private language" rests upon "a particular picture of the essence of human language" (PI, sec. 1). According to this picture, the individual words of a language are names of objects. Every word in a language has a meaning, and that meaning is the object that the word names. Sentences are articulated combinations of such names. When a child learns a language, a great part of his learning is the proper correlation of words (sounds, marks on paper) with the objects these words name.

This picture of the essence of language is the same as that found in the *Tractatus,* and it is also found in the *Confessions* of St. Augustine; Wittgenstein begins the *Investigations* with an attack upon its Augustinian expression. Thus the response to the idea of a Cartesian "private language" can be seen as a part of Wittgenstein's general response to the object/name grammatical picture of the essence of language. But the presence of that picture in the psychological context of expressing what one is feeling is especially important, for there one can see what gives the picture its powerful hold on our attention. What is it that forces this grammar upon us here? Why should we believe that 'pain' is the name of an object, much less the name of a private object? By now, the answer is not far to seek. We cannot doubt or deny that we do sometimes express in language what we are feeling; I do sometimes complain to my friends that I have an awful headache, for example. It is rationality-as-representation that forces us to construe all such complaints as *reports, descriptions, representations;* thus it is that conception which fertilizes the ground for the seed of the object/name picture. Once we are sure that "I am in pain" is a report—and, given rationality-as-representation, what else could it be?—it seems inevitable that 'pain' is the name of some sensation. And because, through another and more subtle working of rationality-as-representation (one which, by forcing us to see all our thoughts as representations and thus in need of justification, led to the whole Cartesian program), we have already surrendered to a metaphysical dualism of body and mind, how can we not believe that the sensation named by 'pain' is a private "mental" object? Thus we see that rationality-as-representation is the true root of "private language"; so Wittgenstein's response to the idea of such a language is ultimately a response to the deep conception of rationality (and hence human being) that nourishes it. As in all his later work, Wittgenstein is trying to break the grip of a vision of thought and life that determines the very character of Western philosophy—indeed, Western culture—itself.

How does he struggle against the hold of that vision? It is useful to consider here, as an "object of comparison," Norman Malcolm's classic account of Wittgenstein's remarks on "private language" appearing in his 1954 essay "Wittgenstein's *Philosophical Investigations*."[8] Since Malcolm was a student and close friend of Wittgenstein's and since his clear and interesting argument seems to reveal what Wittgenstein was after, his account has assumed a particular historical importance. It has set the tone for later reconstructions, however they have diverged from it in detail. Malcolm understands a "private language" to be "one that not merely is not but *cannot* be understood by anyone other than the speaker. The reason for this is that the words of the language are supposed to 'refer to what can only be known to the person speaking; to his immediate private sensations'."[9] Wittgenstein also speaks of "the language which describes my inner experiences and which only I myself can understand" (PI, sec. 256). In his characterization of private language Malcolm intends his phrase "*cannot* be understood" to be read "*necessarily* cannot be understood." Later in his paper he claims that if a language is private (in his sense) then "it is a logical impossibility that anyone else should understand it or should have any basis for knowing whether I am using a particular name (in that language) consistently." [10]

Malcolm believes that in the *Investigations* Wittgenstein develops and deploys two attacks on the idea of a private language, the "internal attack" and the "external attack." His statement of the "internal attack" has generated the most attention. In the "internal attack" one postulates a "private language" and then deduces that it is not a language. [11]

Let us consider, says Malcolm, the situation envisioned by those who defend the possibility of a private language, in particular the pos-siblity of a private sensation language. In a natural language like English undoubtedly there is a "connection" between the word 'ball' and those round things, often red in color and made of rubber, that are played with by children and cats. This "connection" enables a speaker of English to refer to a ball with the word 'ball'. It is what helps to make a certain phonetic sequence a word rather than a noise. Now balls are public objects, of course, but there must be analogous "connections" between certain words and "private" objects like sensations. That is, there must be some sort of "connection" established between 'pain' and pains in order that a speaker of English be able to refer to the latter by means of the former.

Malcolm construes the "connections" between words and the world to be *rules*. It is a linguistic rule that connects balls to 'ball' and elephants to 'elephant'. But how, he asks, can one give oneself a rule connecting a sensation to a name? Malcolm wants to show that the rules of a "private language" could not be rules at all (and, therefore, that a "private language" could not be a real language). What are the essential features of linguistic rules that the "rules" of a "private language" lack? First of all, if something is to be a linguistic rule of a language L, then it must be the sort of thing that can be either followed or ignored by a speaker of L. [12] It would be a queer sort of linguistic rule that ruled out *nothing* and so could not be heeded or violated. But Malcolm goes further than this. Not only does he claim that the rules of L must be the sort of thing that can either be followed or ignored by a speaker of L; they must be the sort of thing that can be ignored (violated) *unbeknownst to the speaker.* It must be possible for a speaker to think that he is following a particular rule of L when in fact he is not. Malcolm believes this characterization of linguistic rules to be a gloss on Wittgenstein's remarks in section 202 of the *Investigations*.[13]

> 202.   And hence also "obeying a rule" is a practice. And to *think* one is obeying a rule is not to obey a rule. Hence it is not possible to obey a rule "privately": otherwise thinking one was obeying a rule would be the same thing as obeying it.

It is this second feature of linguistic rules that, according to Malcolm, shows that the "rules" of a "private language" cannot be genuine linguistic rules at all. For consider the typical account of language genesis envisioned by the Cartesian believer in "private language": a man, perhaps cut off from his fellows, notices a certain sensation, is intrigued or horrified by it, and decides to give it a name. He wants to be able to refer to the sensation in the future and to be able to note to himself or to his friends its recurrence. So the man names the sensation by focusing his attention on the phenomenological character of the sensation and by giving himself the following linguistic rule (call it 'R'): "I will call *this* sort of sensation 'pain' and will hereafter call the same sort of thing 'pain' whenever I want to refer to it."[14] To follow this linguistic rule correctly is, it seems, to give a meaning to the word 'pain'. That is, R established the necessary "connection" between the word 'pain' and the sensation. And in this case, to follow R *correctly* means to apply the word 'pain' *only* to sensations of a particular character, not to colors or tastes or to sensations like tickles. Now it is just here that Malcolm's Wittgenstein attacks. According to him, R does not allow for the second necessary feature of linguistic rules, i.e., it is not possible to make a distinction between a speaker's having followed R correctly and his only having *seemed to himself* to follow R correctly.[15] Thus, linguistic "rules" like R are only *impressions* of rules, and the possibility of a speaker's having violated R unwittingly (the second necessary feature of linguistic rules) is an empty hypothesis. Hence R is not a linguistic rule; and, since being rule-governed is a necessary condition of a language, no "language" that depends upon the formation and use of "rules" like R is a genuine language. But, according to Malcolm, all "private languages" do depend upon "rules" like R; hence no "private language" is a genuine language.

Malcolm believes that his argument is merely a tidy restatement of the one at work in section 258 of the *Philosophical Investigations:*

258.   Let us imagine the following case. I want to keep a diary about the recurrence of a certain sensation. To this end I associate it with the sign "E" and write this sign on a calendar for every day on which I have the sensation. —I will remark first of all that a definition of the sign cannot be formulated. —But still I can give myself a kind of ostensive definition. —How? Can I point to the sensation? Not in the ordinary sense. But I speak, or write the sign down, and at the same time I concentrate my attention on the sensation—and so, as it were, point to it inwardly. —But what is this ceremony for? for that is all it seems to be! A definition surely serves to establish the meaning of a sign. —Well, that is done precisely by the concentrating of my attention; for in this way I impress on myself the connection between the sign and the sensation. —But "I impress it on myself" can only mean: this process brings it about that I remember the connection *right* in the future. But in the present case I have no criterion of correctness. One would like to say: Whatever is going to seem right to me is right. And that only means that here we can't talk about "right."

Throughout his essay Malcolm assumes that he is presenting Wittgenstein's response to the idea of a "private language." His is an essay in exegesis, he believes, not an exercise of invention.

But is it? From the outset Malcolm's argument is predicated upon a traditional conception of philosophy. His response is to try to show that the Cartesian proponent of "private language" is in error, that the Cartesian claim about the privacy of our sensation language is false. Malcolm constructs an argument to this effect, an argument which turns upon a certain necessary condition for meaningfulness in a language. Thus he is, consciously or unconsciously, enunciating a philosophical truth about language, thereby committing himself (and, on his account, Wittgenstein) to the defense of a philosophical thesis.

That Wittgenstein rejected this conception of his work has already been argued. In responding to the constructions of philosophers Wittgenstein looked for nonsense, not error; and his intention was to show this nonsense by altering sensibilities in the direction of the sound human understanding. The incompatibility between a sound understanding and rationality-as-representation means that a "scientific" philosophy, itself predicated on the Cartesian literalization of mind into representational intellect, is not a proper vehicle for such an alteration. A philosophy of argument—thesis and counterthesis—is itself a specimen of the nonsense he condemns. So Malcolm's account, however interesting or comforting, must be a misconception of Wittgenstein.

What, then, is the nonsense of "private language," and how does it show itself? A complex process of persuasion is underway in the remarks on "private language," the object of which is breaking the hold of certain grammatical pictures. Consider the heart of Malcolm's account of the "internal attack," the famous "diary passage" in section 258 of the *Investigations*. Here we see not argument, but reminder; not thesis, but suggestion; showing, not saying.

For Wittgenstein the notion of a "private language," since it is a direct result of accepting the object/name picture of language, is defined by reference to what might be called a "private object." In section 243 he characterizes a "private language" as one "the individual words of which are to refer to what can only be known to the person speaking; to his immediate private sensations." The "private object" is something that can be known to exist or to be of a certain character by only one person, its possessor. If sensations are private objects, then the phenomenological character of a certain sensation is something that can only be known by the person who has the sensation. Thus, under this assumption, if a man names a sensation of character *K* 'pain', only he can know the character of the sensation he undertakes to call 'pain'. It might or might not be the same as the character of the sensation his friend undertook to call 'pain'. Thus the man might rightfully doubt that he and his friend call the same sort of sensation 'pain'. He might even doubt that his friend names anything at all by his use of the word 'pain'. The Cartesian, of course, claims that sensations like pain are private objects.

Wittgenstein's response to the Cartesian is to make a grammatical remark, to remind us of an undeniable fact about the everyday language-game we play with 'pain'. He uses our standard, everyday language-game as an "object of comparison." First of all, he focuses the Cartesian's attention on the consequences of the assumption that sensation words of natural language name private objects. The consequence he is most anxious to stress is that if sensation words named private objects, then one would need a criterion of identity in order to reidentify one's own sensation. If sensation words named private objects, there would arise a problem of the correct recognition of a sensation previously noted and named. It would always be possible to doubt that the sensation one now feels an inclination (perhaps even an *overwhelming* inclination) to call 'pain' is of the same phenomenological character as the sensation one earlier used as a paradigm of pain. This philosophical doubt is always possible because there is, *ex hypothesi,* no way to check the correctness of one's recognition—except through memory, which may at any time deceive one (this latter fact is the point of Wittgenstein's remarks in section 265, culminating in his famous remark about buying several copies of the same newspaper in order to check the correctness of a news story).

To get his "private language" going, the diary-keeper of section 258 must effect a "connection" between a sensation (assumed here to be a private object) and a name, such that the name becomes the name of that sort of sensation. And this "connection" must be such that it can consistently be made in the future. (Wittgenstein, section 258: "— But 'I impress it on myself' can only mean: this process brings it about that I remember the connection *right* in the future.") But there would be no certain way of telling (section 258: "no criterion of correctness") whether the future uses of the name are consistent with the paradigm "association" of name and sensation (object) that supposedly effected the "connection" between the name and the sensation (object). Therefore, philosophical doubt is always possible. One might at any time in the future legitimately begin to doubt whether one was in "pain" or was having some other sort of sensation.

Wittgenstein wants to remind (cf. PI, sec. 127) the Cartesian that in the ordinary language-game we play with 'pain' (and other sensation words), it is *not* possible to say that one is not sure, has doubts about, whether one is in pain. That is simply *not* how the language-game is played. He makes this clear at section 288:

If he [the believer that sensations are "private objects"] now said, for example: "Oh, I know what 'pain' means, *viz.,* it means the sort of sensation I focused my attention on when I gave a definition of the word 'pain'; what I don't know is whether this, that I have now, is pain"—we should merely shake our heads and be forced to regard his words as a queer reaction which we have no idea what to do with. (It would be rather as if we heard someone say seriously: "I distinctly remember that some time before I was born I believed. . . .")

That expression of doubt has no place in the language-game; but if we cut out human behaviour, which is the expression (*Ausdruck*) of sensation, it looks as if I might *legitimately* begin to doubt afresh. My temptation to say that one might take a sensation for something other than what it is arises from this: if I assume the abrogation of the normal language-game with the expression of a sensation, I need a criterion of identity for the sensation; and then the possibility of error also exists.

Notice what Wittgenstein does and does not do here. He does point out the difference between our ordinary language-game and the language-game that must be played by one who believes that sensations are private objects. He does not argue that one or the other language-game must be wrong. He is content to point out their difference. He does not try to answer the kind of Cartesian skeptic who might say, "Well, yes, you are right. Things are much worse than I thought. Not only can I never know what sort of sensation (if any at all) you call 'pain'; I cannot even be sure that my own use of this name is consistent."

Wittgenstein is making essentially the same response in this remark:

Always get rid of the private object in this way: assume that it constantly changes, but that you do not notice the change because your memory constantly deceives you. (PI, p. 207)

As in sections 258 and 288, Wittgenstein is reminding the one who believes that sensations are private objects that he can always doubt that he is consistently following the "rule" that, on the "private language" account, gives meaning to the name of a sensation. And he also wants to make the Cartesian recall that no doubt is possible in our everyday language-game for sensation talk. He wants to make him see that on his account of sensations one *can* "assume that [the private object] constantly changes" without one's notice, while with the standard language-game of sensation this is a senseless assumption. In the standard language-game one does not have, nor does one need, a criterion of identity for a sensation.

There is no philosophical *argument* here; there is merely a reminder of certain undeniable facts.

> We want to replace wild conjectures and explanations by quiet weighing of linguistic facts. (z, sec. 447)

When Wittgenstein makes a point, assembles a reminder, or quietly weighs a linguistic fact, the purpose is always to draw attention to a certain feature of a grammatical picture or a "way of seeing," never to argue that the way of seeing is right or wrong. Here he draws attention to a consequence of "private language" that puts it at odds with our everyday language-game of sensation talk. His intention is to get us to notice the difference, to reflect upon it. Is he using our ordinary language-game as a standard of sense? Not in any philosophical way. Our ordinary language-game is an object of comparison (pi, sec. 130), employed so as to call our attention to a difference we might be tempted to overlook. The guiding assumption operating here is that, confronted with the difference, we will somehow be changed; we will be less charmed by the alien language-game, more likely to ignore it and go on. This object of comparison, this reminder, when combined with all the other reminders and alternative images Wittgenstein assembles in the *Investigations,* makes possible our freedom from the seductive charm of the Cartesian picture. Like his other remarks, the remarks about memory, rules, correctness, and the like deployed against the notion of a "private language" cannot be understood as philosophical *theses.* They are not arguments, nor are they pieces of some metaphysical view. They are for the most part *truisms,* but truisms arranged in such a way that we are brought to our senses and returned to our normal lives and world.

As we have noticed before, the true ground of Wittgenstein's response to the philosopher never itself appears on the stage. That ground I have been calling his vision of the sound human understanding, and it is that vision which ultimately functions as the standard of sense and nonsense. That vision underlies his employment of certain language-games as objects of comparison; that vision guides his arrangement of certain linguistic reminders into a perspicuous presentation. It is the balance within which linguistic facts are weighed. That vision grounds his therapeutic philosophical practice and is the object toward which he seeks, always indirectly, to direct our attention. It is the indescribable, unrepresentable place from which he sees and speaks.

Again we are brought to see his fundamental antipathy toward rationality-as-representation. The nonsense in the idea of a private language is just a special case of the conception that leads to the nonsense of metaphysical philosophy itself. Unbewitched by rationality-as-representation we would not be led to the Cartesian search for unshakable foundations for our representations and thence to the dualism of body and mind. Without the blinkers of that conception of thought's essence we would not construe every intelligent utterance as a report about some reality, internal or external: thus we could avoid the grip of the object/name picture of the grammar of our sensation language.

In examining the *On Certainty* material we saw how Wittgenstein refused to follow the Cartesian tradition in believing that the basis for our knowledge of reality must itself be an instance of knowledge. He characterized the linguistic expressions of our most fundamental ways of seeing as *Äußerungen,* which he compared to expressions of trust (not trustworthiness). They are, he said, like reaching out and taking hold of something directly (oc, sec. 510); they are not mediate representations of a distant yet ungrasped reality. At the bottom of the impersonal language-games of evidence, reason, and argument that constitute our world-picture is something like a trusting grasp, and *Äußerungen* are the natural expressions of that closing of the hand. When we are not hoodwinked by rationality-as-representation, such images—for they are nothing more, and nothing less—can also have their play in our language-game of sensation.

Expressions of pain, desire, fear, hope, and the like, are often best seen as *Äußerungen,* not as descriptive reports on some inner reality.

> 585. When someone says "I hope he'll come"—is this a *report* about his state of mind, or a *manifestation* (*Äußerung*) of his hope? —I can, for example, say it to myself. And surely I am not giving myself a report. It may be a sigh, but it need not. If I tell someone "I can't keep my mind on my work today; I keep on thinking of

his coming"—*this* will be called a description of my
state of mind. (PI, sec. 585)

Here he compares the verbal expression of the hope to a *sigh,* the
instinctive expression of his state of mind, not a report on it. The
Äußerung literally *presents* the state of mind; it doesn't *represent* it. In
such a case there is no gap between the hope and its natural expression
in language.

The same trenchant observation is made near the beginning of his
remarks on "private language."

> 245.   For how can I go so far as to try to use language to get
> between pain and its expression (*Schmerzäußerung*)?
> (PI, sec. 245).

In the preceding section Wittgenstein has been puzzling over the private language questions of how words "refer to" sensations. To a believer in private language there is a mystery in how the connection of
word to sensation, private object to name, is actually forged. But this
"mystery," says Wittgenstein, is actually just a question about how human beings are taught to use our sensation language.

> Here is one possibility: words are connected with the primitive,
> the natural, expressions of the sensation and are used in their
> place. A child has hurt himself and he cries; and then adults
> talk to him and teach him exclamations and, later, sentences.
> They teach the child new pain-behavior.
> "So you are saying that the word 'pain' really means cry-
> ing?" On the contrary: the verbal expression of pain replaces
> crying and does not describe it. (PI, sec. 244)

In this passage we can again see the deep roots of private language
in the picture of rationality-as-representation. Confronted with Wittgenstein's "possibility," the interlocutor's question—"So 'pain' means
crying?"—elegantly reveals his controlling assumption that language
always "means" something, i.e., that it is always a re-presentation of
something else: a fact, a state of mind. Since language-thought is always re-presentation, sensation language must be talk *about* sensations, reports on the inner landscape. But in Wittgenstein's image lan-

guage can present as well as re-present, and sensation language can be seen as a way to present to others the reality of one's pain. The verbal expression is learned as a substitute for instinctive ones like groans; it is not, in the first instance, a report on a ghostly something—it is the thing itself, embodied. Thus, as section 245 realizes, there is in this primary case no way to come between the pain and its *Äußerung,* for the two are essentially connected; rather, to put it cryptically but accurately, the two are one. The *Äußerung* of pain is the pain presented.

This image of sensation talk gives no purchase to the idea of a private language. That idea depends upon there being in every context a gap between word and thing, name and object; and *that* idea flows naturally from rationality-as-representation. But the image of the *Äußerung* closes the necessary gap. 'Pain' no longer seems a Tractarian name contingently and privately welded to a mental object. By breaking the paralyzing hold of rationality-as-representation, thus allowing the image of the *Äußerung* free play, Wittgenstein has undercut the charm of the philosophical idea of a private language.

Furnished with the image of the *Äußerung* we can now see some of the true weight carried by the reminders assembled in the "diary" passages of the *Investigations.* We have already seen that their intention is to demonstrate the difference between our ordinary language-game of sensation and the one imagined by the believer in private language. It is now clear that this difference grows from a fundamentally different imaging of the relationship of language-thought to reality. The image of the *Äußerung* gives one a way of seeing some fundamental forms of language as the natural outgrowth of certain primitive gestures and expressions; it allows one to see this language as a mode of presentation, a mode of embodiment. On the other hand, the idea of a "private language" depends upon a conception of language as essentially representation mediating the contact of a spectral consciousness with the inner or outer world. Thus the idea of a private language ultimately rests upon the conception of thought, language, person, and reality we have called rationality-as-representation.

And just here one can see how the image of the *Äußerung* also gives one a powerful weapon against what Donald Davidson has aptly called "the third, and perhaps the last" dogma of empiricism: the distinction between scheme and content.[16] Once one reflects upon the fact that there are some uses of language that are not necessarily best thought of as the re-presentations of some worldly content in the medium of some conceptual-linguistic scheme, then the grip of the powerful distinction is loosened. The *Äußerung*, since it is presentation, not re-presentation, shows language that is not separated from the world. In, for example, the linguistic presentation of pain in the *Schmerzäußerung*, language and world are one, so to speak; and while this instance alone does not demonstrate that the entire distinction between scheme and content is just a dogma to be discarded, it does destroy the distinction's claim (fed, of course, by rationality-as-representation) to be *the* model in terms of which language is to be understood. And once the image of the distinction between scheme and content has been shown to be that, an image, then one is free to begin to reflect upon other images in its place, some of which may be as philosophically untraditional as those of Davidson and Derrida. And moreover, as those names intimate, once the distinction between scheme and content has become questionable, so can the even more fundamental and traditional distinction between language and world begin to seem a put-up job.[17] The point is that the attack on private language, which is an attack on the hegemony of the image of language as inherently representational, carries one into the heart of our philosophical tradition since Descartes; if the attack is successful, then that whole tradition becomes questionable. Rationality-as-representation itself totters.

To bring to attention, as Wittgenstein so forcefully does, the difference between a private language and our ordinary language-game of sensation talk is thus to attend to the possibility that rationality-as-representation may not lie at the bottom of our lives. It forces us to consider the possibility that the reality of our practice may not square with our most powerful philosophical preconceptions; in particular, it makes one consider that some very fundamental forms of language may not be representational at all. Thus it may loosen the hold of the Cartesian picture, so that other images may be given play as well. This is not to use our ordinary language-game as a philosophical standard of sense; neither is it to construct an argument that things must be this way or that. Wittgenstein is content to focus attention upon the difference, for his aim is not a change of one's philosophical views. The ultimate goal is a loss of "views" altogether, a way of thinking that gives a variety of images free play, literalizing none of them into metaphysical pictures. Like all of Wittgenstein's work, the remarks on private language are an attempt to free us from the toils of a single image, a single sensibility.

This section's discussion of Wittgenstein and "private language" has been extremely brief, to say the least, but my intention has not been to expound the whole of his response to the Cartesian legacy of mind-body dualism. Rather, I have tried to illustrate something of the nature of that response, showing how philosophers like Malcolm misread Wittgenstein's favorite techniques of philosophical criticism. First, the passage about the diary finds him deploying a language-game as an object of comparison; in this case our ordinary language-game of sensation talk is set up against that of the Cartesian, in which self-doubt about whether one is in pain is possible. And second, we see Wittgenstein using an illuminating image at odds with a philosophically traditional one. The image of the *Äußerung,* the utterance which is the very presentation of sensation, its embodiment, is used as an alternative to the image of language as representation.

Neither of these techniques is putting forth a philosophical thesis in opposition to those of the Cartesian; that would be to play his game, and lose. The division between Wittgenstein and Descartes goes much deeper than a difference in philosophical views. It is a difference in sensibility itself, a fundamental difference of vision. The standard reading, exemplified in our discussion by Malcolm, fails to take account of Wittgenstein's radically nonphilosophical sensibility; thus it fails to point to the vision of mind and life that is the true ground of his remarks against the Cartesian. Private language is *nonsense* for Wittgenstein, and the ground for such judgment is his vision of the sound human understanding—a vision shown to him and one that, in his remarks, he is trying to show to others.

IV

CARTESIAN philosophy has determined not only philosophers' ruminations but the shape of a culture. Willy-nilly we are ruled, individually and collectively, by the Cartesian ideals of truth-as-representation, abstraction, self-forgetfulness, and narcissism. We are ruled by them even as we seek to throw off their dominion by force of will. We find it impossible to understand how there could be an alternative mode of thinking and living, unless it would be to stop thinking altogether. Having lost that direct encounter with the numinous and the mundane that was a characteristic of the "religious" sensibility that preceded our "scientific" one, we are now the captives of our own powers of abstraction and representation.

That is why the spirit of Wittgenstein's later work is so foreign to us. His remarks proceed from a sensibility thoroughly at odds with rationality-as-representation and its progeny. His remarks are like remarks coming from a different culture: we understand the words, but not the sense; we cannot find our feet with them. Shaped as we are by our Cartesian expectations, we strain to hear them as metaphysical bits and pieces; we expect him to enter the philosophical wars to fight under a flag we can recognize. But he will not. That's why his remarks remain fascinating even as they evaporate from our hands. It is a sort of "conversion" (OC, sec. 612) that Wittgenstein is after: a conversion to a new way of seeing everything (oneself, one's world, philosophy); a way of seeing that is not itself philosophical, that is not itself just a "way of seeing." It is now time to say something directly about that sound human understanding which is the object of his endeavors.

CHAPTER 6

Ethics without philosophy

T HE FUNDAMENTAL intention of Wittgenstein's thinking, in both its
periods, is its attempt to incarnate a vision of the healthy human
life; the transmission of a moral vision—the attempt to reveal its character and make it potent—is the true burden of all his philosophical
work." Thus the bold claim of our first chapter; it is now time to draw
together the strands of our discussion and to show the contours of that
sound human understanding and life Wittgenstein sought to exemplify.
Because no thinker, not even the very greatest, can call forth the un-
thought ground of his own work, Wittgenstein's later vision remains
hidden in the work itself; and only time can show, or fail to show, a
thinker's grasp of just those elements (unseen, perhaps, but ready to
hand) which can make a turn in thought and culture possible. With

only a few decades' distance, a complete account of Wittgenstein's extraordinary sensibility, doing full justice to the subtleties that can make
all the difference in such matters, is out of the question. In this final
chapter we can hope only to illuminate themes already hinted at, pointing out important continuities and shifts, and connecting the vicissitudes of his vision to changes in his relation to the philosophical tradition itself. The pictures we now draw in Wittgenstein's margins will
certainly get some things wrong: a faulty line here, too garish a color
there. Nevertheless, they must be drawn, in spite of their inadequacies, for we need images of that world beyond the page toward which
his remarks point and in which the real discovery in philosophy has
been made (PI, sec. 133).

I

THE ETHICAL intention of the *Tractatus* is readily apparent. We have,
indeed, the author's own word that the point of that early book is ethical: it aims to show where the sense of life is to be found. That sense is
not to be found in the world, nor is it to be found in thought. The world
is nothing but a collection of contingent states of affairs, altering concatenations of eternally existent simple objects; these contingent configurations are utterly independent of one another; belief in the causal
nexus is superstition. In this atomistic world there is no sense of life to
be found; there is only what happens. Neither is the sense of life to be
found in thought, for thought is always thought about the world. The
essence of thought is representation; so any thought is just the attempt,
successful or unsuccessful, to re-present some state of affairs, with
language as the medium within which this re-presentation takes place.
Where then *is* the sense of life to be found? In the metaphysical self,
which, as the limit of the world, lies outside it, just as the eye lies outside the visual field it defines. The world-limiting self defines its field
too: the world is always *my* world. It is my world because it is penetrated by my *will;* it is my world, that is, because it is problematic—
happy or unhappy—for me. The sense of life is given form by good
willing, that willing which makes the world a happy one. But this ethical willing is not the ordinary sort: it has nothing to do with agency; I
am, in fact, completely powerless to alter the flow of what happens in
the world. Will, the bearer of good and evil, is an *attitude* toward the
world, a particular way of seeing it; and good willing is a way of seeing

the world so that it has a life-sustaining sense. Then despair is over-come, suicide (the elementary sin) is avoided, and the world is a happy one. To be happy, then, is to see the world aright; it is a movement within the willing self which is the limit of the world.

The nature of this all-important movement was a great mystery for the author of the *Tractatus*. It was a transformation of a "way of seeing" the world, but it was not a movement of thought per se, for thought can do no more than re-present a contingent state of affairs. Even to think all true thoughts (the apotheosis of science) would give one nothing more than a re-presentation of the world, not its sense. So it seems that thought and will, representation and good willing, have absolutely nothing to do with one another. But that cannot be. There *must* be some philosophical way to connect thought and will, since they are undoubtedly connected in our ethical experience.

That way is the doctrine of showing, of course. The world-altering insights that cannot be thought or said can be shown. The sense of life is found outside the realm of thought, in the world-limiting willing self, and the self is *shown* that sense. The good will that gives life its sense is made possible by the showing of *das Mystische,* a showing which occurs only when the metaphysical self is fully self-conscious and so surveys the world *sub specie aeternitatis*. What is shown to the self then is a kind of practical knowledge: knowledge of how to see the world aright, of how to assume the correct attitude to it. There is a sense to life, all right; there is a way to will the good (happy) world. But the nature of this sense, the content of the practical knowledge that makes the good will possible, cannot be represented; it can only be shown, whether in poem, parable, or philosophical treatise. And what is always shown to the metaphysical self is the necessity and possiblity of its own heroism, its own power. The world is *my* world: I *can and must* make it happily mine by my own choice of attitude toward it. *Wovon man nicht sprechen kann, ...*

No claim is made here that this Tractarian vision is ultimately co-herent; I am convinced that it is not. It does, however, paint a very powerful ethical picture. One could say, perhaps more precisely, that in the text and subtext of the *Tractatus* a very deep and appealing *im-age* of the ethical life shows itself, an image found in many mytholo-gies. It is, as was pointed out in chapter two, the image of heroic as-cent to a godlike status. Salvation is achieved by an intellectual ascent to the self-consciousness of the metaphysical self vouchsafed by the

Tractatus; this self-consciousness—knowing oneself to be the godhead of the independent I—shows the self that it is the first and final maker of meaning. The world is *my* world: not only do I think out the senses of the propositions in which the world shows itself; I also in my attitude make that world either happy or unhappy. Value is somehow *given* the world by the heroically free metaphysical self which is its limit, so for the self-conscious self the happy world is as close as its own willing.

Once the world is seen for what it is *sub specie aeternitatis*—a limited, contingent whole bounded by the willing self—then the self can assume the right attitude toward it; the world can be seen aright. And to see it aright is to see its inevitable limitation, in two senses. It is first of all to see that the sense of life lies, not in the world itself, but in the willing self that limits it; and that is to see that one's happiness is within—indeed, *is*—one's own power. ("I am safe, whatever happens.") And that means a limitation of the world in a second sense, for it reveals the futile "worldliness" of most human effort. Most people try to secure their lives *within* the world; they adopt the common standards of the world—security, power, ease, wealth, and the like—and use them as arbiters of the sense of their lives, of their happiness or unhappiness. The good life is the life of ease, power, and affectation; unless I have those things, my life is a shambles. But to look for the sense of life in the world is to put oneself on the royal road to despair, since all worldly distinctions are gifts ("graces of fate") and cannot be reliably secured. Only when one can renounce the world of abstract intellection and material comfort, as did Kierkegaard and Tolstoy, can it become the happy world—and that because it is now the world of the happy self.

This image of the ethical life, its form and content, was not a passing fancy for Wittgenstein. As we have seen, his life shows its profound and enduring influence: giving away his large patrimony; teaching for six years in the peasant schools of Lower Austria; working as a gardener's assistant at a monastery near Vienna. Even the "Lecture on Ethics," composed soon after his return to Cambridge in 1929, is still essentially Tractarian in its themes and substructure. The philosophical-ethical vision adumbrated in the *Notebooks* and the *Tractatus* determined the character of Wittgenstein's life for a decade; it took a revolution in his thinking to dislodge it. That revolution, which led to the later work, marked a change in his relationship to philosophical thinking itself and brought in its train substantial alterations to his vision of soundness in thought and life.

II

THE MOST striking difference between the earlier work and the later is the absence of an explicit ethical intention after 1930. Gone are remarks about "what is higher"; no longer do his works climax, as did the *Tractatus,* in a flurry of dark sayings about the good or evil will. Their absence does not mean, however, that no ethical point is being pressed there. In the later work there is still a vision of human soundness at the center of things, and because it is a vision that makes possible the discernment of fundamental good and evil in thought and life, one can legitimately deem it ethical. This vision is the ultimate ground of all his philosophical criticism; it is the perspective from which nonsense is judged and it is the sensibility toward which all his work urges us. Without our recognition of this vision's hidden yet fundamental role, Wittgenstein's later work loses its integrity, becoming the disjointed pieces of a philosophical system, the rough ore from which we must smelt the gold of philosophical thesis and argument.

Why, if this is so, do we find no overtly ethical considerations after 1930? Because there has been a profound change in Wittgenstein's relationship to philosophical thinking itself. The ethical vision of the *Tractatus* is a philosophical one: it is not rational—thought and ethics have only a boundary in common—but it is still philosophical. It is, so to speak, still philosophical in *form;* it depends for its expression upon such concepts as the metaphysical self, will-as-attitude, the separation of fact and value, and the like. For all its criticism of earlier philosophy, the *Tractatus* still wants to be metaphysical; it still wants to be able to see things *sub specie aeternitatis,* even if the view from this perspective pushes ethics into mystery and turns one into a silent sage. The metaphysical impulse still has status, even if Wittgenstein is wary of its excesses within the tradition: the ladder, he says, must be climbed before it is kicked away.

The later work, however, rejects the metaphysical impulse itself. To attempt to see things *sub specie aeternitatis* is symptomatic of a diseased understanding; the impetus to metaphysical philosophy needs to be cured, not given its head. His later work wants to dispense with a philosophical form for his determining vision, not just (as in the *Trac-*

tatus) with its rational content. Wittgenstein wants to prevent his constituting ethical sensibility from seeming a philosophical thesis, to prevent it from becoming just another "way of seeing." That vision must, therefore, be hidden: shown, not said at all. The moment it appears on the page it assumes a philosophical form in our apprehension; it becomes a product of the philosophical mind, to be dissected, evaluated, and appropriated in a particular way.

Since it is that philosophical mind which is the later Wittgenstein's true antagonist, he (like Kierkegaard) must present his vision "indirectly." He must find a way of thinking and writing that exemplifies his sensibility without representing it. The vision must never become literalized; it must never lend itself and its power to the sensibility it seeks to overthrow. As we have already discovered, that familiar and tyrannical sensibility which pushes us toward a metaphysical life is rationality-as-representation, the conception of thought's essence that identifies it with representation: the literalization of mind into intellect. When this ideal of thought, which is also an implicit ideal of the person, holds sway, every image becomes a picture, every utterance becomes a description, every gesture becomes a statement; in short, metaphysics is king and I become the spectral knower derided by Kierkegaard (and exalted in the *Tractatus*).

Under the spell of rationality-as-representation we sublime (PI, sec. 38) thought and language. We mythologize them into mysteries of representation. When language and thought become mystical in this way—when they become mythological powers of literal representation—then so does the ethical become a mystery too. Since it belongs to the realm of practice, and since will seems to have little or nothing to do with the passive representation of reality, the connection between thought and action, between the seeing eye and the bearer of good and evil, becomes problematic. This is precisely what has happened in the *Tractatus,* and we have examined the ways Wittgenstein tried to resolve this puzzle. He makes there a virtue of necessity, separating ethics from thought and bringing in the mysterious notion of showing to explain the sparks that sometimes get struck between them.

When language and thought are demythologized, as happens in the later work, then so does ethics lose its air of mystery. No longer does the philosophical form of the ethical vision impose restraints on what can be said about its content; but the restraints are still in place, now the result of our disposition to construe the vision as a philosophical view. The necessity for showing remains, therefore, although its significance is very different. In both the earlier work and the later, rationality-as-representation is the precipitating factor. In the *Tractatus* that conception was an important feature of the book's subtext, and the author's (partial) captivity to it led to the bind that made the doctrine of showing a necessity. In the later work rationality-as-representation has become the ultimate target of philosophical therapy, the virus that produces the diseased, metaphysical understanding; and showing is necessary in order to prevent its infection of the therapeutic vision itself. Here showing is not, as in the *Tractatus,* a philosophical doctrine; it is a defense against doctrine, a way of undercutting the impulse to make philosophical doctrines out of everything. In the *Tractatus,* the doctrine of showing is necessary because rationality-as-representation has the upper (but not quite the only) hand; in the later work, showing (no longer a doctrine) is necessary so that rationality-as-representation cannot regain its former advantage.

The radical transformation of Wittgenstein's relationship to rationality-as-representation may make it seem that there is no continuity at all between the ethical visions of the earlier and the later work, but that is a mistake. In both there is a defining emphasis on the limits of "thought"; the sound human understanding recognizes the limitations on its own powers of representation. In the *Tractatus,* where thought is identified with representation, this limitation is understood as a boundary inherent in the nature of thought itself. Before the sense of life can come clear, one must see the world as a limited whole, i.e., recognize the intrinsic limit on one's powers of representation. Because that discovered limit is the metaphysical willing self, the limitation of thought thus makes room for that movement of the will which can make the world a happy one. In Wittgenstein's variant of the Kantian position, recognition of the limitation of the intellect's power is a necessary condition of the willing self's mystical freedom to give the world (his life) the sense he wishes it to have: Kant's limitation of knowledge in order to make room for faith. The ladder of the *Tractatus* is climbed to a place where the will is at last unshackled; the moral life is wholly cut free from anything discovered by the *Naturwissenschaften.*

In the later work no longer is the limitation on representation seen as intrinsic in the nature of thought itself; rather, it is seen as the limitation of a certain image of thinking. The later Wittgenstein has deliteralized the notion of representation itself, and that makes it possible for him to see through the kind of thinking which constitutes metaphysical philosophy. By the time he began the *Philosophical Investigations* Wittgenstein had lost confidence in the Tractarian representational account of language and thought. Not, as sometimes is maintained, that he balked at the unwarranted generality of the early theory, having come to see that only *some* sentences are literal representations of facts; rather, he had lost confidence in the philosophical notion of literal representation itself.

Here we approach the center of the later vision, especially as it functions in his criticism of philosophy. Metaphysical philosophy is the attempt to represent how things are *sub specie aeternitatis*. Even philosophy that is not explicitly metaphysical, that does not systematically deploy a set of fundamental explanatory categories, is very likely to be metaphysical at bottom: it still assumes that it makes sense to talk philosophically about "the way things are." The notion of representation—the literal re-presentation of reality in the medium of thought or language—is basic to all traditional philosophy, whether "metaphysical" or "analytic." It may even seem to be basic to thinking itself. The sensibility of the later Wittgenstein is defined, from a philosophical point of view, by its break with this notion of literal representation; his abhorrence of metaphysics, of traditional philosophy itself, rests upon his having seen through the notion of representation upon which it rests. The fundamental nonsense of traditional philosophy is the nonsense of representation and the sensibility it defines.

This is likely to seem absurd for a number of reasons. What could it mean to speak so blithely of Wittgenstein's having seen through the notion of representation? One plausible way of trying to explicate Wittgenstein's skepticism is clearly inadequate. He certainly is not a skeptic about representation in the sense that he believes that no representation is ever adequate (or, known to be adequate) to its object. That sort of epistemological skepticism, with which we are very familiar from the Cartesian tradition, may be serious or trivial depending upon whether the gap between representation and reality is claimed to be large or small, unbridgeable or temporary. Notice, however, that the notion of representation itself is not challenged here; only our powers of representation. Epistemological skepticism assumes that literal representation of reality makes sense; Wittgenstein's skepticism concerns the notion of representation itself.

What, then, is the nature of his skepticism? For an answer, let us return to the notion of a grammatical picture. In chapter four we saw that the captivity to such pictures, interpreted as literal representations of the superfacts on which our grammar rests and to which it conforms, is a primary mark of the metaphysical philosopher. We stressed in our discussion there the crucial role of rationality-as-representation as the literalizing agent, turning the inevitable images of our grammar into pictures, thus binding the philosopher to a particular way of looking at his world. One of Wittgenstein's favorite techniques for liberation is to deliteralize a particular picture by putting it into contact with other, and incompatible, images also found in the grammar (one sort of "perspicuous presentation"). We stressed in our discussion that this process of deliteralizing must be complete, i.e., the point of the exercise is not to trade one literal picture for another, but to break the hold of picturing itself. This gives us a key for thinking about what it is to break with the philosophical notion of literal representation: it is to give all images their due as images; it is to allow mind to play freely among a multitude of images, using those that are appropriate at a given time, literalizing none of them into pictures.

Philosophers have had a hard time with images. Two courses of action are typical: first, to (try to) eradicate images from thinking altogether, insisting that they are at best negligible and at worst an impediment to understanding; and second, to literalize images into metaphysical pictures. The two are often parts of the same process: having tried, unsuccessfully, to dispense with a particular image, the philosopher at last comes to accept it as an insight into the nature of things. Neither of these approaches accepts the integrity of the image as image. The first sees it as the accidental product of a faculty of fantasy, a prettification of something that could be better presented without the embroidery furnished by the image. The second accepts the necessity of the image but makes the image into a picture, a literal representation. Both are, in their different ways, attempts at literalization. The first, impatient with "mere images," explicitly wants a way of speaking that is literal. The second seems more tolerant, but it accepts images in philosophy only if they can be read as pictures, not "mere images."

Wittgenstein is the enemy of such literalization. His enmity to the literalizing intellect is a defining mark of the sensibility that expresses itself in the later work. It is the heart of his antipathy toward rationality-as-representation since that conception of thought literalizes all thinking into re-presentation. The sound human understanding, the end of all Wittgenstein's philosophical efforts, is one in which the image has its own integrity; where mind has not been literalized into intellect.

What does it mean to respect the integrity of the image? First of all it is, as we have already implied, to have recognized the necessity of images. They are not just embroidery; neither are they just heuristic aids to literal thinking. The play of images is natural to the mind. Our language—the most natural manifestation of mind—is full of them. (How many images does just that sentence contain? Does anyone believe that all its constituent images could be removed, leaving its sense intact?) In addition to recognizing the necessity of the image, respect for it means a refusal to take it literally. We can easily understand what it is to take an image literally. If I mention the pain of my breaking heart and a listener suggests I consult a cardiologist, he has taken literally what was only an image. It is not so easy to characterize what it is *not* to literalize. When Hopkins speaks of the falcon as "kingdom of daylight's dauphin," no one is such a dolt that he would look to the sky for a prince's crown; but what exactly is the image supposed to do for us? Is it literal in some shorthand way, to be cashed out as making a series of claims about the bird's regal silence, its apparent indifference always ready to erupt into plunging rapacity, and the like? Is an image just condensed representation? I think not.

To give an image its own integrity is to *use* it in a particular fashion. It is to use it as a way of seeing; the image becomes a way to *see through* the object to which it is applied. Ordinarily, of course, we do not see through what we see. That is, we take it for what it prima facie claims to be, and that means we take it for what a certain conception of it presents. When we look at a bird in flight, that is what we see: a bird in flight. Although we are using certain concepts (even certain images) to make sense of—to constitute—what we are seeing, we are not aware of them and their influence. Because they are powerful, familiar, and useful, we use them utterly unconsciously. To take an image or a concept literally is just this sort of failure to see it at work; literalness identifies an object with a certain conception of it, an identification so strong and so unconscious that the conception becomes invisible as such.

To give an image its own integrity is to keep it constantly in mind as an image. It is not to lose sight of the lenses, so to speak, through which we are always looking. When the image is seen for what it is, mind is made aware of its own role in the process of thinking; the seeing eye, to use the *Tractatus* image, becomes directly aware of its own existence through the recognition of its own necessary participation in the process of visualization. It sees its own lenses.

To keep the image in mind is necessarily to *see through* what we see. When we see something literally, failing to see the lens through which it is seen, we see it in some determinate way: as a bird, for example. The reality before us is identified with the dominant conception: that *really is* a bird. When, however, mind is aware of itself in the process of seeing, the object that is seen is also seen through. We see through the thing as initially given (bird) to another (thing-viewed-as-bird); the thing itself floats free from identification with the way it is seen.

Let us return to Hopkins's image of the falcon as the crown prince of the kingdom of daylight. The use of that image by the poet is a way of helping us to see through what we ordinarily see. It is a way of deliteralizing and thus expanding our perceptions. If it is well chosen and perspicuously presented, the poetic image can help us to see the image that we usually fail to perceive in our ordinary way of seeing only the thing. If we suddenly see the dauphin of the kingdom of daylight sailing there in the heavens, if that image takes hold of us and for a moment disappears as a "mere" image, then upon our return to our everyday conceptions we become newly aware of *their* status. By means of the extraordinary image, we are forcefully reminded of the role of those everyday conceptions in determining what we see; thus we can see through the ordinary objects of our sight. The temporary appropriation of the poetic image deliteralizes all our seeing, at least for a time.

And in that deliteralization is a corresponding expansion. Once it is brought home to us that the world is much richer than our everyday conceptions of it, we can never be quite so complacent in our ordinary ways of seeing, feeling, and acting. There are worlds yet unconceived in our familiar forms of life.

It is in this connection that Heidegger speaks of the poet's images as *spectacles*, as exhibitions or performances that let something show itself in order to be seen.[1] For him the image is not a copy; it is an unconcealing event. As the god is present in his festival—present but not re-presented—so is the world present to us in the images of the poet. The god is more than the spectacle that shows his presence, of course, and the world is more than the images with which it is constituted; but without their festivals the gods could not appear at all. So it is with images: with every image something shows itself; and without that image it would not be seen. Every new image reveals a new world, but every revealing is at the same time a concealing.[2] Since no image can manage to show all there is to be seen, the pursuit of new and illuminating images cannot end. Poetry is never over with.

Thus it would be a gross error to characterize a poetic image as an indirect or shorthand representation. It is no kind of representation at all. The philosophical notion of representation is itself an image of literalness: the re-presentation of the thing itself in thought or language; the magical encapsulation of the world in mind's amber. The poet wants to free us from literalness, and that means freeing us from taking the image of representation itself literally. The poet's sensibility has lost the temptation to identify the world with any image of it: his images always, and even intentionally, fail to close their hands around the realities themselves. The world—manifold, indefinitely various, self-concealing, and self-revealing—is there in the poems themselves, but not literally in the images that constitute them. The poet wants to *present* the world, not re-present it. He wants to get us to see ourselves in all our seeing, to break the grip of the self-forgetfulness of representation. The poet's images are not statements; they are reminders, reminding us, putting us in touch with all the images through which we see, deliteralizing our perceptions.

Philosophical therapy is not exactly poetry, of course, but both flow from the same deliteralizing sensibility. The metaphysical philosopher is susceptible to being captured by grammatical pictures interpreted as literal representations of the superfacts underlying language. To be freed from such captivity it is necessary to be freed from the literalizing sensibility that promotes it. In Wittgenstein's later philosophy, as with poetry, the intention is to give the image its due, and thus to shake us out of the confidence we lend to our philosophical notion of literal representation. Once we have come to see the image in everything, once we have recognized ourselves in every process of seeing, we begin to see through what we see. To speak of seeing through is to use a psychological idiom; appropriately, I think, for the change that takes place is like the change that occurs when one's psychological sensibilities are deepened. To the person who has achieved a certain depth of psychological insight, having come to understand that "everything is what it is *and* another thing," the whole world is changed. No longer is there an easy confidence in one's perceptions or self-perceptions; one is always looking for hidden, manifold significances: the skull beneath the skin. Seeing is accomplished only by seeing through; literalness is replaced with depth, with oblique reflection.

So it is with the sensibility of the enlightened philosopher: to see is to see through. Metaphysical philosophy itself is seen through because we can see through the image upon which it ultimately rests: rationality-as-representation. No longer is the attempt to speak *sub specie aeternitatis* taken for granted; in fact, it is seen as nonsense, laughable because in it one forgets oneself in one's thinking. Kierkegaard's remark about the comic presuppositions of metaphysical thinking is apposite; the humor of which he speaks is rooted in our self-forgetfulness as metaphysicians. We don't laugh at ourselves because we don't see through our own self-forgetful self-deceptions; when we do, our philosophical theses and arguments become literally nonsensical, food for laughter, not thought. The fly is finally out of the fly bottle.

This emphasis on the self-forgetfulness of metaphysical objectivity, and on the intrinsic self-awareness of the deliteralizing sensibility, reminds us of the threat of narcissism. Has Wittgenstein, trying to free us from metaphysical self-forgetfulness, plunged us instead into self-enchantment? Can mind, which is constantly aware of itself, escape the fate of Narcissus lost in his own perfect reflection? Are self-forgetfulness and self-enchantment an inescapable dialectic, or is there some form of life and thought that avoids both?

It is certainly true that narcissism is as real a danger to the sound human understanding as is self-forgetfulness, and its peril can be overcome only if self-consciousness has its proper status as a *moment* of mind, not its final end. The roots of narcissicism, like those of absent-minded objectivity, lie in the *metaphysical gaze*. To have seen one's own reflection and to have been enchanted by it, it is first of all necessary that one has been *looking*. In philosophy, and in the forms of life constituted by it, the paradigmatic mode of relationship to reality is vision: it lies out there to be viewed, understood, *known*. Is it any wonder that, having been first transformed into the metaphysical seeing eye, the human being should fall so readily into the mythical fate of Narcissus?

But this insight into the roots of narcissism enables us to see how the sound human understanding can escape its toils, because that understanding no longer appropriates reality solely in the mode of vision. The recognition of image—mind itself—in every act of seeing is, far from being the beginning of a narcissistic quasi-Kantianism, instead the beginning of the end of the metaphysical gaze itself. Once the inescapable image has been recognized *even in the idea of representation itself,* then the hold of that image is broken and mind (now human being, not just the ghostly representing consciousness) is free to move among the realities that nourish it, entering the world as the unhooked trout reënters the stream, effortlessly moving from depth to depth, from sunlight to shadow and back again, at home in its all-encompassing element.

So the sound human understanding is characterized by a sort of action, action which is not self-forgetful, nor is it self-enchanted. No longer is the human being separate from his world, blithely living in his representations of it or narcissistically scrutinizing them; he is present *in* it, not *to* it, nor it to him. But these dark sayings need illumination.

III

WE HAVE spoken again and again of Wittgenstein's vision of the sound human understanding and life, the true center of his philosophical work, early and late. We have named the defining characteristic of that sound understanding: a sensibility which, deliteralized and deliteralizing, makes possible for human beings a certain kind of presence *within* their world. The sound understanding is, without narcissism, self-conscious of its own determining presence in all its activities; thus it always sees through what it sees. This sensibility is comfortably at home among the manifold images that constitute mind and its grasp. None of those images is literalized into picture; none becomes the understanding's captor. Rather, mind plays freely among a variety of images, moving from one to the other, gathering illumination with a variety of lenses. The more we see, the more we see through; the more we see through, the more we see. And the more we see, in this sense, the more we can move and be moved within what is seen; the more we are restored to our world, and it to us.

The sound human understanding is, obviously, not philosophical. It has seen through metaphysics to the magical image of re-presentation beneath it, and it has placed other images alongside it: language as tool, as game, as music. None of these images is a metaphysical picture; yet all these lenses gather light. No wonder Wittgenstein's writing is so full of metaphors and similes; his is an attempt to return mind to its natural element, the wash and swirl of images. The range of images his later work presents—all of which have their places; *different* places—helps to deliteralize the idea of representation itself. Like the alchemist's, his work is an *opus contra naturam:* speaking as a philosopher to philosophers, he must deliteralize the literalizing sensibility which makes philosophy possible. Thus his later work is ultimately exhibition, not representation. In the mind his writing reveals—vivid, image-laden, constantly unsatisfied, unphilosophical—we see the sensibility he envisions: the sound human understanding.

But what of the healthy human life? Why should we call this benchmark conception of the sound human understanding also a vision of the sound life? In the later work there is *thinking* without philosophy, certainly; but ethics? Nowhere does one find discussions of the moral principles which underlie and justify modes of conduct; there are no arguments to specific ethical conclusions, nor are there meta-ethical investigations of the truth conditions for such judgments. Neither popular nor philosophical ethics is explicitly present in the later work; yet we have insisted upon the ethical content of his vision. Why?

Our use of 'ethical' here harks back to the *Notebooks* and the *Tractatus*. There ethics has to do with the discovery of the sense of life, not with immediate problems of conduct.

> Ethics does not treat of the world. Ethics must be a condition
> of the world, like logic. (NB, p. 77*e*)

An ethical vision is one that shows where the sense of life is to be found, revealing that condition of the world which can make it a happy one. In the later work there is clearly an ethical vision in this sense, for that work gestures decisively toward a certain way of determining life's sense and nonsense. Sense and nonsense are, of course, Wittgenstein's fundamental terms of philosophical criticism; and the sense and nonsense of thinking and of life have something of the same grammar. Nonsense in thinking is produced when mind is literalized into intellect and metaphysics becomes king; nonsense in living is the product of those same literal modes of thought. Certain forms of life rest upon metaphysical foundations, i.e., foundations which explicitly or implicitly incorporate the legitimacy of metaphysical thinking. For Wittgenstein those forms of life are nonsense. They obscure where the sense of life is really to be found, diverting one's energies into paper chases.

To take only the most obvious example, consider academic philosophy itself. Wittgenstein frequently expressed abhorrence at his own role as a professor: "He believed that a normal human being could not be a university teacher and also an honest person." [3] He also commonly encouraged his favorite students to give up their professional aspirations in philosophy in favor of working on a ranch or farm, or managing a mine; indeed, several of his students followed his advice. As a professional philosopher, expected in one's courses to wrestle with the issues and exemplars of the tradition, one is in constant danger of a professional deformation, an infection by that disease of the understanding which produces the nonsense of literalization. Moreover, the academic environment itself, a place of ease and affectation, where the self-enclosure of abstract thinking is encouraged, breeds the *hubris* that despises or patronizes the common lot of most men and women. Thought, because it is literalized into a way of seeing *sub specie aeternitatis,* is cut off from action; it is gone on holiday.

Wittgenstein's own tenure in academic life, interrupted by frequent excursions to Vienna, by periods of solitude in Norway and Ireland, and by war work in an infirmary and a laboratory, was predicated upon the hope that his own thinking, in spite of the incomprehension with which it was greeted, could do some good. He had, as he believed, a certain talent for thinking in a way which showed the nonsense and emptiness of much of what passes for thought of the highest order; and he was compelled to use that talent while it lasted, refusing to bury it in the ground.[4] That the immediate result of his teaching was the growth of a certain jargon and a cult of personality was a source of great distress to him.

The repugnant characteristics of professional academic philosophy are not, of course, uniquely confined to such a form of life. In *any* life one is threatened by the diseases of the understanding—"If in the midst of life we are in death, so in sanity we are surrounded by madness" (RFM, p. 157)—and in any ordinary life one's victories against them are tenuously held. The literalization of mind's constituent images, the self-enclosed self-forgetfulness of metaphysical intellection, the loss of immediate connection between thought and action—all these can overtake anyone at any time. The struggle against philosophical bewitchment is, for most of us, unending; and in it we need the help of our friends. Thus Wittgenstein's later work, like the earlier, is itself intended as an *ethical deed*. It is an aid to thinking (PI, p. x); but, more precisely, it is also an aid to living. That later work exemplifies a way of thinking, a sensibility that is also a way of life; its deepest intention is that that sensibility and that form of life prevail. In November of 1944 he wrote in a letter to his friend Norman Malcolm:

> What is the use of studying philosophy if all that does for you is to enable you to talk with some plausibility about some abstruse questions of logic, etc., if it does not improve your thinking about the important questions of everyday life, if it does not make you more conscientious than any . . . journalist in the use of the *dangerous* phrases such people use for their own ends. You see, I know that it's difficult to think *well* about 'certainty', 'probability', 'perception', etc. But it is, if possible, still more difficult to think, or *try* to think, really honestly about your life & other people's lives. And the trouble is that thinking about these things is *not thrilling,* but often downright nasty. And when it's nasty then it's *most* important.[5]

Because the form of life urged upon his friends by the later Wittgenstein flows naturally from his vision of the sound human understanding, we are justified in calling that vision an ethical one. Our consideration of the *Tractatus* revealed a connection between the philosophical form of his ethical vision there and its content, and a similar connection is present in the later work. In the *Tractatus* the sense of life can come clear only when the limits of thought are recognized and felt, only when the world is abandoned as the source of happiness and unhappiness. In the later work the sense of life is possible to see only when it is not sought, for "*the* sense of life" is a metaphysical fantasy, a specimen of self-forgetful (or narcissistic) thinking. There is no "*the* sense"; there are just those forms of life that are nonsensical, and those that are not. The later writings exhibit the sensibility constituting any sound form of life, not least in their silence about their true object.

IV

BUT IS such heroically strict silence really necessary? Is there no way other than example to present the form of life characteristic of the sound human understanding? In spite of Wittgenstein's own legitimate worries about saying what must be shown, in this case the risk of direct speech is worthwhile, since otherwise too much of the vision, the center of gravity of all the later work, remains private and idiosyncratic, liable both to indifference and to the wildest misinterpretation. Also, there is at hand a tradition already familiar to philosophers in terms of which an approach to the sound human understanding is possible, at least in an initial way. We will begin by reflecting upon a few truisms about the evaluation of actions.

Human beings undertake to do both particular discrete actions (like eating a cookie) and whole courses of action (like studying for the priesthood). In their own terms actions can be done well or ill: I can choke on my cookie; and my study can be botched and lackadaisical. More important, actions can be judged morally in terms of their sources in the vices and virtues of human character: the cookie may be eaten out of gluttony; the priesthood sought for status and power. If there is such a thing as the sound human understanding, one would expect it to be a source of reflection and action analogous to human character; and that is just what I have been arguing: the sound human life flows from the sound human understanding as virtuous action flows from a virtuous character. But is there a way of acting specifically characteristic of such soundness? One which would allow us to distinguish Wittgenstein's "sound human understanding" from other, and competing, ideals of character? The answer must be *no,* since that way of putting it makes the sound human understanding seem just another philosophical construction: a comprehensive set of terms and principles within which ethical thinking and living must be done, comparable to Aristotle's account of the life of virtue. But the sound human understanding gives one neither a final and unambiguous moral vocabulary nor an algorithm for choice under ethical uncertainty. In the sound human life there is still an abundance of fundamental moral struggle, and no promise that easy answers, or any at all, will be forthcoming. As Wittgenstein emphasized in his conversations with Rush Rhees, wherever powerful moral consideration pulls against powerful moral consideration, bitter and irremediable tragedy can be one's lot; and there is no hint in his remarks that the sound human understanding could furnish one with a mode of reflection and action that could avoid anguish and loss.[6] The sound human understanding is not a moral panacea.

But in another sense the answer to our question is *yes:* there is a form of life characteristic of the sound human understanding. In order to understand it, however, we must first reflect in some detail upon the form of life inherent in its opposite. As we have seen, the diseased human understanding is dominated by rationality-as-representation; the metaphysical gaze, the seeing eye of the *Tractatus,* is its paradigmatic expression. Vision becomes the fundamental metaphor for one's relation to reality, with the view *sub specie aeternitatis* the apotheosis of such seeing; and because the sense modality of vision always incorporates distance between seer and what is seen, reality always lies apart from the thinker. Thus, on this picture, thought is conceived as a kind of seeing, the thinker's re-presentation of the distant world in some medium. Given such a picture of subject, world, and thinking, there is, as we have noted above, a constant dialectic between self-forgetfulness and self-enchantment, between objectivity and narcissism. We are at any time liable to have forgotten ourselves in a headlong attempt to secure the view *sub specie aeternitatis* or to have become so aware of ourselves in our seeing that we are damaged by self-fascination and the temptations to heroic self-assertion.

What is the connection of such a picture to action, to a distinctive form of life? The key lies in the natural assumption that intelligent action in the world must rest upon a prior theoretical understanding of it, i.e., upon *representations* of that world in thought. However the mysterious link between thought and action is forged, it is assumed that *we act out of our representations;* my action is guided by those pictures of reality I have constructed. For example, when I face an ethically significant choice, such as whether to leave my wife to pursue medical research or to stick by her and abandon my scientific ambitions (Wittgenstein's own example; cf. Lydgate in George Eliot's *Middlemarch*), the key to my decision will (it is alleged) lie in my representations of the relevant reality: right action depends upon rightness of representation; inaccurate representation will, ceteris paribus, result in the wrong choice. Two sorts of representations are involved. In the first place we seek representations of fundamental moral truths; we try to map those principles of practical reason which are the ultimate constraints on the will. (Is it wrong to lie? Do I owe justice even to the barbarians?) Second, we seek accurate representations of the settings for moral action, including relevant descriptions of the persons concerned. (Is that really a lie? Is he really a barbarian?) In the form of life dictated by rationality-as-representation, ethical life is the search for action predicated on right representations; it is a change rung upon the Socratic claim that virtue is knowledge.

Growing out of such a form of life are two distinct responses, each of which is characteristic of an important segment of contemporary culture; we may call them, using the terms unambitiously, *realism* and *relativism*. Both, it is important to stress, depend upon the assumption that thinking consists in the re-presentation of reality; both, that is, take the image of thought-as-representation *literally,* as a true picture of metaphysical reality.

Realism has both a sophisticated and a naïve form. Naïve realism takes the familiar representations of its culture, time, ethnic group, or whatever, for granted; it does not question the moral vocabulary, the principles of ethical choice, the distinctions between "us" and "them," which it inherited from the elders. Such a realism is, at least in our world, inherently unstable; it is always liable to get pushed into a more sophisticated realism (or, indeed, into relativism) by exposure to the fact of radically different vocabularies, principles, and tribal distinctions. Once Paree has been surveyed, things down on the farm can never look quite the same. Reflection upon the fact of such diversity in theory and practice forces one to consider one's own representations of reality as just that: re-presentations, not the things themselves.[7] A sophisticated realism first accepts this construal and then argues that its representations are true, or at least *approximately true,* or, at the very least, show a *convergence toward truth.*[8]

But a sophisticated realism is not the only possible response to the difficulties of the naïve true believer; we are painfully familiar with the movement to relativism as a result of the same forces. The relativist, feeling the pinch of the visual metaphor, has taken seriously the necessary distance between the various realities and our representations of them; and, reflecting further upon the various epistemological difficulties inherent in verifying the match between scheme and content, reality and representation, he has decided that no set of representations can claim a privileged status of accuracy. There are, of course, degrees of relativism, ranging from the most radical (anything goes) to the more modest claim that, while some views can be ruled out of court, nevertheless among certain sets of mutually incommensurable representations no rational choice is possible. Unlike the sophisticated realist, the relativist is moved to deny that one is ever justified in asserting that one's most fundamental representations of moral reality converge upon an accurate rendering.

Applied to ethical matters, realism and relativism pull, naturally enough, in different directions. The danger of realism is the danger of taking one's representations for the realities themselves; bluntly put, realism runs the risk of *idolatry,* the worship of an image. Because the diseased human understanding has literalized the image of thought-as-representation, and thus has opened itself in consequence to the literalization of mind's other images, it is emboldened to act on the basis of those images, secure in their truth as renderings of reality. The realist, naïve or sophisticated, has adopted some set of moral principles, some moral vocabulary, as the truth. The naïve realist doesn't admit the possibility of change, of course, while his sophisticated colleagues do; but both, as realists, agree that some moral representations have a grasp (complete or partial) on the moral realities themselves. In this conviction certain images (of human excellence, human degradation) are hypostatized; those images are thus made into metaphysical representations, into pictures of the truth. The blindness, resting on pride, that identifies some images with reality itself is a kind of idolatry.[9] It is worship of an image; worship in the fullest sense, because one's life and practice are governed by the images one has made metaphysical. One serves an image, a conception of reality, just as one might serve a god. One entrusts one's relations to oneself and one's fellows to the care of these metaphysical images: one sees what they direct one to see; one acts as they command. The very clarity of vision they produce, however, is purchased at the cost of their single-minded ignorance of ambiguity and doubleness. They see with one eye, sharpening definition by flattening out depth. They empower decisive action, but they court sincere and intelligent moral tyranny.

If an idolatrous dogmatism is the risk of realism, the dangers of relativism are either a debilitating loss of moral energy or the collapse of ethical sensibility into an arbitrary willing. In the first case, the recognition that one's most fundamental representations, those conceptions out of which one's actions and attitudes naturally flow, lack rational justification against other incommensurable representations, can sap one's commitment to one's moral ideals. After all, if my belief that human beings have rights against being treated in certain ways cannot be rationally upheld against the incommensurable view that subordinates the individual to the good of some larger whole, why then should I put myself at risk for the sake of that belief? Lacking a firm ground for my representations, self-conscious action on the basis of them can seem silly or boorish; and thus it becomes easy to slip into a kind of moral impotence, ceasing to care very much about moral matters and probably content to slide along with the moral complacency of my time and place.

In the other case, relativism can lead, not to enervation, but to an energetic self-assertion. Here the realization that fundamental truth is not to be had encourages one to *make* that truth by force of will. Fundamental representations, whether epistemological or ethical, cannot be grounded in rational inquiry; so they must be grounded in human choice, either individual or communal. It does not take a great deal of imagination to recognize the possibility of the will to power thus masquerading as moral conviction; indeed, it may as well come out of the closet, since no one can claim a better-grounded principle anyway.

It is worth noticing, by the way, how both these reactions to relativism are varieties of narcissism, forms of self-enchantment. The first accords to some extent with the classic image of dreaming Narcissus, bewitched into paralysis by the vision of his own reflection. Once one has noticed that one's representations are indeed one's *own* representations in some unalterable way (i.e., one cannot attribute them just to the world itself), one can easily be lulled into apathy or incapacitating self-doubt by reflection upon one's presence in those representations. On the other hand, a relativistic self-assertion is another sort of self-enchantment in which the necessity of one's own presence in all one's representations becomes an occasion for bumptious self-expression rather than mute self-absorption.

So the diseased human understanding produces a strong impetus toward either idolatry or narcissism. Both these pathologies of thought and action are, it will be noticed, direct results of rationality-as-representation, for it is that literalizing sensibility that underwrites the metaphysical gaze and turns the world of my moral action into an object, present *to* me, to be appropriated through my re-presentation of it. Now, we may readily agree that both realism and relativism are dangerous; neither a dogmatism that trades ambiguity for decisiveness nor a relativism that courts self-paralysis or self-aggrandizement is an appealing prospect. But if these pathologies are the legacy of the person subject to rationality-as-representation, what is supposed to be the alternative? It is all very well to speak darkly of the sound human understanding, which has seen through the image of representation itself, but what would such a form of thinking and living be like? What would it be to have broken with literal representation and thus to appropriate one's experience—to *live*—in a radically different way?

There seem to me to be two ways in which the form of life characteristic of the sound human understanding can be approached. One is
deflationary, and much easier to understand because it employs notions
already familiar to philosophers; the other is more radical, and much
more obscure. I shall present both, and then try to adduce some considerations for thinking that the second, for all its obscurity, is closer to
Wittgenstein's own heart.

The less radical way of characterizing the sound human understanding identifies it with a variant of the pragmatism of William
James and John Dewey.[10] The pragmatist's advice to the philosophical
tradition is to forget about the Cartesian-Kantian dream of trying to
map the conditions under which representations of the world are possible, most accurate, and the like; indeed, the pragmatist encourages the
philosopher to drop the image of *representation* altogether. Think of
knowledge as effective practice in service of one's ends, not as accurate
representation; think of ideas and concepts as tools, not as pictures.
The pragmatist gives a sense to our notion of "seeing through" the image of representation by his suggestion that the static spectatorial conception of knowledge be replaced by one which stresses the centrality
of *action*, not vision; thus the pragmatist's vocabulary emphasizes
"dealing with" the world, or "coming to terms" with it. The philosopher's obsession with the human being conceived as *knower* of the
world is eliminated within the pragmatist's sound human understanding; instead, attention is drawn to human beings *acting* within their
world to meet needs and desires. By means of this shift, many (if not
all) of the traditional distinctions and arguments of philosophy (ana-
lytic/synthetic; realism/relativism; *Naturwissenschaften/Geisteswis-
senschaften*) are mooted; the "real discovery in philosophy" has been
made, the one that brings transcendental philosophy itself to a peaceful
end (PI, sec. 133).

This pragmatist construal of the sound human understanding has
every right to be considered a form of life as well as a form of thought.
(Indeed, one of the manifest intentions of pragmatism it to destroy the
appeal of that very distinction.) The sound human life, construed prag-
matically, would be tolerant, experimental, optimistic, forward-look-
ing, unconstrained by outmoded intellectual or practical patterns, and
so forth. It would, according to men like James and Dewey, free us to
preserve the good of the past while remaining outside the clutches of
its various rigidities; and the sound human life would give us confidence in a better future, a confidence unshadowed by fears of

skepticism (and its political correlate, anarchy) or dogmatism (with its offspring, tyranny). The sound human life points toward an ever-increasing liberalism, the wider and wider extension of that conversation among equals which J. S. Mill thought essential to civilization itself. The collapse of the distinction between the natural and the moral sciences, for instance, would free us to pursue moral and political life experimentally; it would, by forcing us to abandon our dogmatism and to recognize the symmetry of moral and scientific learning, prepare in us that tolerance for the new and strange which is the precondition of progress in any area. While pragmatism certainly does not provide us with substantial moral principles suitable for the resolution of concrete dilemmas (in fact, it calls into question the place of such principles in ethical thinking), in every important respect it deserves to be called a way of life. Since a distinctive form of life—open, tolerant, democratic—flows naturally from the sound human understanding, the central vision of Wittgenstein's later work is, on this interpretation, indeed an ethical vision, a vision of the healthy human life.

This description of pragmatism, brief and sketchy as it is, does provide an interpretation of the central features of the notion of the sound human understanding we have gleaned from Wittgenstein's work. Let us consider three by way of illustration. First, we have seen the fundamental importance to that understanding of what I have heretofore called, somewhat darkly, a "nonliteralizing sensibility." In chapter four we examined in some detail the role of grammatical pictures in Wittgenstein's account of philosophical perplexity, seeing there how their construal as literal representations of the superfacts upon which our grammar rests inevitably lures the philosopher into endless and fruitless metaphysics; and we also saw how Wittgenstein's own literary and rhetorical techniques (language-games, perspicuous presentations) are designed to break the hold of these literalized images, thus freeing the mind to play among a variety of images and literalizing none of them. Earlier in this chapter I have argued that such a capacity to give all images their due, using them as lenses to gather and focus light in mind's constant search for illumination, is the mark of a distinctive sensibility, one that sees through whatever it sees; and I have further claimed that it is the gift of such a sensibility to have seen through the very image of representation itself, thus freeing one from the coercion of that conception of human thought (and human excellence) I have called *rationality-as-representation*.

Pragmatism seems to give some concrete sense to these claims. By focusing our attention on action (effective practice in service of needs and desires) rather than on contemplative theorizing, the pragmatists were trying to undercut the notion of knowledge as an accurate picture of the facts, replacing it with the image of knowledge as a useful tool for a certain job. Crudely, knowledge is habitual behavior that gets us what we want. Since a screwdriver need in no way be a representation of anything in order to drive screws, the notion of representation begins to look fishy when knowledge is seen in terms of an aid to effective practice. Thus the notion of representation comes to be seen as *one* way of thinking about knowledge, not *the* way; the image of knowledge-as-representation is *seen through,* so to speak. No longer is one constrained by the single image of re-presentation, literalized into the essential nature of what it is to know; and once, given another turn of the screw, representation itself (the re-presentation of a thing in a ghostly medium of consciousness) is seen as *an* image rather than *the* picture of thought, one's whole attitude toward images is changed. None will ever be able to assume a final dominance, because, by seeing through the image of representation *tout court,* one has lost one's naïve trust that any image can literally represent. The pragmatist thus tries to stop thinking in terms of representation; he will try his best not to have any *pictures* of the world, though at any point he will of course be using various images as aids for his effective practice, as lenses for gathering and focusing light. The sensibility of the pragmatist therefore can lay some claim to being the instantiation of the nonliteralizing sensibility characteristic of the sound human understanding.

A second feature of the Wittgensteinian vision that is given concrete expression in pragmatism is the end of philosophy. We have seen again and again in this book that the sound human understanding is incompatible with metaphysical philosophy; in the healthy human life one will have given up the temptation to try to view the world *sub specie aeternitatis*. Pragmatism also seeks the end of traditional (i.e., transcendental) philosophy, because it sees both the aim of such thinking and the distinctions that keep it going to be products of the representational account of knowledge. Once that account is seen through, there will be no foundations for science, for ethics, for politics to establish; no distinctions to guard or to destroy; no boundaries to draw— in short, nothing distinctive for the philosopher to do. The view of things *sub specie aeternitatis* becomes merely that form of life possible for us at the ideal limit of inquiry, and it is worse than silly for a philosopher in his armchair to believe that he could here and now even *aim* at such, much less produce it. So the "real discovery" that ends philosophy and that is so much a part of Wittgenstein's vision of soundness seems also to be a feature of pragmatism.

Finally, there is a third feature of pragmatism that seems to provide an interpretation of an aspect of the sound human understanding. That is its tendency toward direct and unimpeded action. We have seen that Wittgenstein believed that philosophy somehow stood between a person and the world that really matters; he counselled his best students to give up their ambitions for careers as philosophers, and his own professional life seems to have been a burden to his conscience.[11] His ideal seemed to be, later as well as earlier, a life devoted to direct action in service to others: the life of a mine manager, a farmer, a laboratory assistant, a hospital orderly. But for the philosopher, convinced that any course of virtuous action must be based upon rational representations of the way things are, such a life is doubly difficult. In the first place, the search for those rational representations is endless; one will never get around to doing all that one could because the obsessive concern that such doing be grounded in the right representation will require the bulk of one's time and energy. The philosopher is a professional thinker; he is laying up treasures of theory, and there is where his heart will be as well. Like the Pharisaical lawyer, he will be interested in the theoretical question "But who *is* my neighbor?"; and no simple story is likely to satisfy. Second, those representations for which the philosopher searches will not only deflect his endeavors and sap his energies, they will actually screen him from the world he is seeking to know. His representations will, because they are limited and partial, blind him to the limitless variety of things and therefore impede his ability to shape his actions to the unique individual needs that confront him. His very search for the ethical view *sub specie aeternitatis* blinkers him in regard to the specific neighborliness required of us all, neighborliness which strips through all representations (Samaritan, Jew) to bind up wounds with oil and wine.

With its openness and its experimental attitude, pragmatism seems to be an antidote to such pathology. Because it has put aside the delusion of representing the world, it will not encourage fruitless transcendental speculation; it will, rather, encourage thinking directly related to action. And because it will not accept any image as a metaphysical picture, pragmatism is less vunerable to overlooking the unexpected and specific occasions for virtue.

So, pragmatism seems to offer the best way of making sense of Wittgenstein's notion of the sound human understanding. It exemplifies the three central features we have discussed—the nonliteralizing sensibility, the end of philosophy, the empowering of direct action—and, what is more, it avoids the two defining pathologies of the diseased sensibility. For the pragmatist, neither realism nor relativism is an option, since both rest upon the literal representationalism he rejects. Furthermore, pragmatism is a way of life as well as a way of thinking, so it gives, as we have said, substance to my claim that the vision of the sound human understanding for Wittgenstein is an ethical notion.

Should we, therefore, consider Wittgenstein to be a latter-day pragmatist, a colleague to James and Dewey whose difference from them is mostly a matter of idiom, itself explainable in terms of the cultural and temperamental differences between the robust Americans and the hypersensitive Viennese? Given the largely underutilized resources of the pragmatist tradition, such an interpretation of Wittgenstein would not damn him with faint praise, to be sure; but I am inclined to think it would be seriously in error. His vision of the sound human understanding goes, I believe, much deeper than pragmatism both in its originating impulse and in its critique of philosophical culture.

One may begin to see this by questioning the basis of the pragmatist's assaults on the commonplaces of philosophy. On what grounds does the pragmatist reject the scheme/content distinction, Cartesian doubt, the Kantian search for transcendental justifications, and the like? What, according to the pragmatist, is wrong with these pillars of our intellectual tradition? Two quite different sorts of answers have been offered. First, some pragmatists, notably Peirce, have attacked philosophy from the vantage of *better* philosophy. Peirce's critique tried to show internal problems with the metaphysics of the past, but he himself had certainly not lost the metaphysical impulse, as his later work shows. Pragmatism in this incarnation becomes a kind of antimetaphysical metaphysics, a better mousetrap; we may call such a critique of the tradition a *philosophical* pragmatism. A second response to our questions is much more brusque: "What's wrong with (e.g.) the scheme/content distinction is the last three hundred years of philosophy!"[12] This response is less interested in demonstrating internal incoherences than in pointing out atrocious consequences. What better argument against the Kantian program could there be than to point out the confusion, folly, and intellectual overkill it has occasioned? This short way with the tradition is more characteristic of James and Dewey, at least in some of their moods, and it takes more seriously than philosophical pragmatism does the end of philosophy as a distinct mode of thought.[13] It shows a healthy-minded *impatience* with philosophy: push it aside as the mistake it was, and get on with the important work before us.

It is clear that Wittgenstein is not a philosophical pragmatist. His critique of the tradition is, as I have argued several times, made from a position totally outside it; he has completely surrendered the metaphysical impulse, not traded it in for a newer model. But his critique is not a pragmatism of the second sort, either. That is, while it is quite true that the pragmatist themes we have canvassed are characteristic of the sound human understanding, I believe that in Wittgenstein's case they originate in a dissatisfaction with the tradition deeper than that which motivates the pragmatist. To put it bluntly, the sound human understanding is for Wittgenstein something of a *religious* notion; it is, unlike pragmatism, a sensibility in which mystery—*das Mystische*—is an essential component.

I will begin my necessarily indirect and circumstantial argument for this more radical reading of Wittgenstein by recalling some of his own remarks. In the early 100s of the *Philosophical Investigations* Wittgenstein offers a famous series of remarks about philosophy; these remarks, which are explicitly deflationary in intention, reach their climax in such jabs as:

> Philosophy is a battle against the bewitchment of our intelligence by means of language. (PI, sec. 109)

> What we [Wittgensteinian antiphilosophers] are destroying is nothing but houses of cards (*Luftgebäude*) and we are clearing up the ground of language on which they stand. (PI, sec. 118)

Such remarks seem to show that impatience with the tradition characteristic of the pragmatist: the problems of philosophy are a series of air castles raised upon foundations of linguistic misconstrual; once the errors are rectified, the problems will blow away. Once, for example, we recognize the arbitrariness and the dire consequences of taking knowledge to be literal representation, the Cartesian-Kantian program can be cheerfully abandoned to the historians of ideas. That program was not, and is not, our *fate* as Western thinkers; it was just a mistake, one which we no longer need to make.

But then, as if intentionally to forestall such optimism, Wittgenstein inserts these remarks into his deflationary critique:

110.   "Language (or thought) is something unique"—this proves to be a superstition (*not* a mistake!), itself produced by grammatical illusions.

And now the impressiveness (*Pathos*) retreats to these illusions, to the problems.

111.   The problems arising through a misinterpretation of our forms of language have the character of *depth*. They are deep disquietudes; their roots are as deep in us as the forms of our language and their importance is as great as the importance of our language. —Let us ask ourselves: why do we feel a grammatical joke to be *deep?* (And that is what the depth of philosophy is.)

Section 110 is especially interesting. It begins with a quotation that wonderfully exemplifies the philosopher's commitment to rationality-as-representation: language-thought is of a piece; it is one thing, unique, i.e., the medium for the representation of reality. But even after we have been able to see through such a claim, seeing it as founded upon certain grammatical illusions, we cannot just dismiss it. It is, says Wittgenstein, a superstition, not a mistake. That is, its hold on us is a deep one; our bewitchment by language here is not merely fortuitous, as if in choosing between two unmarked doors we had chosen the tiger rather than the lady.

What is the difference between a superstition and a mistake? Consider a familiar example of a superstition: it is bad luck to spill salt; but if one does, one can avert or mitigate the misfortune by throwing a pinch of the spilled salt over one's left shoulder. Such a ritual would seem a silly, not to say incredible, mistake if interpreted causally: science shows us absolutely no nomological connections between spilling salt and suffering misfortune, nor does it show any connections between the throwing ritual and the avoidance of ill luck. But, of course, the ritual is not such a mistake, and we can see this by reflecting upon the fact that highly intelligent people who are perfectly aware of the lack of demonstrable causal connections between spilled salt and bad luck nevertheless still find themselves uncomfortable when they don't perform the throwing ritual. We mark this by calling it a *superstition;* and that means that something in the occasion of spilling salt has a *Pathos* (impressiveness) that grips us, and the ritual is a response to that *Pathos.* (I retain Wittgenstein's own word, *Pathos,* since the best English equivalent, "impressiveness," does not hold the same resonance as the German.) Perhaps in this case the *Pathos* is connected to our awareness of salt as savor and as preserver: as easily as we carelessly let spill these valuable crystals, so easily can we let spill the things that give our lives savor and that preserve us from spoilage; and the throwing ritual is a way of acknowledging our carelessness and our determination to do better. But whatever the source of the *Pathos,* the important consideration is that in the ritual is a response to some deep feeling.

To call something a superstition, however, is not just to remark its connection to some deep feeling; a superstition is a particular sort of response to such *Pathos.* We can see this by recalling a case discussed in Wittgenstein's remarks on Sir James Frazer's *The Golden Bough.*[14] The anthropologist Frazer considers an instance in which a person ritually stabs the portrait of his enemy; he assumes that some causal efficacy is being supposed by the one who stabs. Frazer sees the ritual as one of *magic* inasmuch as it is an attempt to coerce nature toward specified ends (in this case, the death of the enemy). Thus he can dismiss the ritual as "primitive" because as coercion it is unscientific; we can discover no nomological connections between the picture-stabbing and the enemy's death. But Wittgenstein suggests that there is another way of seeing the ritual. It could be, rather than magic, a *religious* ritual. That is, it may be an attempt to acknowledge, rather than coerce. The stabbing ritual itself may be the point, not what that performance is supposed to produce. "It aims at some satisfaction and it achieves it. Or rather, it does not *aim* at anything; we act in this way and then feel satisfied" (f, p. 31). Frazer, we may say, treats the stabbing ritual as a superstition, whereas Wittgenstein does not.

We can now specify somewhat more clearly what distinguishes a superstitious response to *Pathos:* it is the connection of superstition to magic. A superstition remarks not only a deep impressiveness in some things; *it also responds to that impressiveness with a magical attempt at control.* We call something a superstition when the means of control it invokes are magical ones, i.e., the means are attempts at coercion and control of nature that are in some way profoundly inappropriate, perhaps because they are causally inefficacious, perhaps for some other reason. The salt-throwing ritual is a superstition to the extent that some magical connections are being appealed to in order to forestall the anticipated misfortune.

Wittgenstein says in section 110 that the metaphysical philosopher's claim is a superstitious response. It is, that is to say, a magical response to *Pathos,* to a deep impressiveness in things. And even when the metaphysical claim is demythologized—when it is seen to depend upon certain grammatical illusions—the *Pathos* does not disappear; it merely retreats to those illusions and to the philosophical problems they create for us. These are deep disquietudes, as he acknowledges in section 111; so it would be a terrible error to treat them, as the pragmatist suggests, as mistakes, as remediable errors in judgment. No, if the metaphysical superstition is merely repressed, it will (like a neurosis) be sure to return to haunt us in some other form. Wittgenstein is not a pragmatist of any variety, because he refers the philosophical impulse to a depth, to a *Pathos,* that is missing in the narrative the pragmatist tells about the genesis of the tradition. For Wittgenstein, the diseased sensibility of rationality-as-representation is not an accident, nor is it a mistake; its hold on us goes much deeper than that. It is, to return to an earlier theme, *nonsense,* not error. And that means that the process of its eradication must cut very deep indeed.

But what is the hold of rationality-as-representation? What gives this nonsense its bewitching power? Here is a suggestion. Rationality-as-representation, and therefore metaphysical philosophy, is a superstitious response to the *Pathos* of the existence of the very world itself. We know that both in the *Tractatus* and at the time of the return to Cambridge astonishment at the existence of the world was very close to the center of Wittgenstein's ethical reflections:

6.44   It is not *how* things are in the world that is mystical (*das Mystische*), but *that* it exists.

6.45   To view the world *sub specie aeterni* is to view it as a whole—a limited whole.

Feeling the world as a limited whole—it is this that is mystical. (TLP)

For me the facts are unimportant. But what men
mean when they say *"The world is there"* lies close to
my heart. (WWK, p. 118)

And there, in my case, [whenever I want to fix my
mind on what I mean by absolute or ethical value] it always happens that the idea of one particular experience
presents itself to me which therefore is, in a sense, my
experience *par excellence.* . . . I believe that the best
way of describing it is to say that when I have it *I wonder at the existence of the world.* (LE, p. 9)

These passages, especially those from the late twenties, illustrate
not only a characteristic recognition of a *Pathos* inherent in the existence of something rather than nothing but also a particular response to
that *Pathos*. In the "Lecture on Ethics" he calls it *seeing the world as a
miracle,* an acknowledgment of its mystery as such; and he contrasts it
with a very different response, which he there calls "scientific." The
scientific response does not admit to mystery as such; anything can be
comprehended, given world enough and time.

The truth is that the scientific way of looking at a fact is not the
way to look at it as a miracle. (LE, p. 12)

It is clear in the Lecture that Wittgenstein believes that ethics has
nothing to do with the scientific approach. An ethical sensibility—one
which is capable of making and understanding "absolute" judgments
of value—will be a sensiblity open to miracle; the recognition that
"the world is there" will produce wonder and humility, properly ethical sentiments, not scientific curiosity.

In respect of the connection between the ethical and the mysterious, I believe that Wittgenstein's mind changed little between the
early thirties and his death. If anything, his perception of the connection deepened, making him more and more reluctant to speak of it in a
philosophical context where it was so likely to be misunderstood, for it
is obvious that the tradition of metaphysical philosophy in the West is
antithetical to seeing the world as a miracle. That tradition, in fact, is
best understood as a Faustian attempt to *deny* any essential mystery in
things, to turn all mystery into riddle, into a problem soluble with
enough effort and insight.[15]

Consider these extraordinary remarks about Isaac Newton, made in 1942 by John Maynard Keynes and recorded by the mathematical physicist Freeman Dyson:

> Why do I call Newton a magician? Because he looked on the whole universe and all that is in it *as a riddle,* as a secret which could be read by applying pure thought to certain evidence, certain mystic clues which God had laid about the world to allow a sort of philosopher's treasure hunt to the esoteric brotherhood. . . .[16]

If Keynes is correct about Newton, and I think that he is, he is even more right about the metaphysical tradition in which Newton appropriately is placed. That tradition defines itself as the attempt to comprehend everything, to stand back from anything and to represent it in its relationships to everything else. It is the tradition of the metaphysical gaze, the view *sub specie aeternitatis,* where that means the absence of mystery, the light of full understanding.

> The aim of philosophy, abstractly formulated, is to understand how things in the broadest possible sense of the term hang together in the broadest possible sense of the term.[17]

The world is a riddle, and it is our responsibility to solve it.

These reflections at last give us, I believe, a way of locating for Wittgenstein the true status of rationality-as-representation and its alternative, the sound human understanding. Rationality-as-representation, and therefore the metaphysical culture it constitutes, is a *magician's* response to the *Pathos* of the world's existence; it is, to return to the theme of section 110 of the *Investigations,* a *superstitious* response to that *Pathos* because it aims at control rather than sheer acknowledgment. Confronted by the stark there-ness of all there is, we in the West have most often reacted with curiosity, not astonishment. We have thought we could understand what is there, and thereby control it. The *Pathos* of the world has been an occasion for will, *our* will, to make the world stand still and submit to our understanding and to our aims. If only, so the story goes, I can know the world, know it as it is *sub specie aeternitatis,* then I have made it as available to my aims as possible. I have heroically overcome it, and can make it mine. Rationality-as-representation—the notion that thinking just *is* a way of fastening upon the things as they are—thus properly appears as an expression of this Faustian response; it goes hand in glove with will, the will to power, and with a form of life (scientific, technocratic) shaped by that will. And Wittgenstein's abhorrence of rationality-as-representation is his abhorrence of this whole magical, superstitious, irreligious form of life. It goes much deeper than the pragmatist's rejection of a mistaken and counterproductive conception of knowledge. Wittgenstein's abhorrence is the expression of a religious commitment; it is the expression, that is, of a fundamental and pervasive stance to all that is, a stance which treats the world as a *miracle,* as an object of love, not of will. The sound human understanding is the mark of such love, for it is a feature of love that it never literalizes any perception; love is always ready to go deeper, to see through whatever has already been seen. From the perspective of loving attention, no story is ever over; no depths are ever fully plumbed. The world and its beings are a miracle, never to be comprehended, with depths never to be exhausted. Thus the sound human understanding is essentially a religious response to the *Pathos* of existence, not a magical or superstitious one. It is a response that makes sheer acknowledgment, not control, central. The world is a mystery, a miracle; such an attitude, incommensurable with the impetus to metaphysics in a culture constituted by rationality-as-representation and the will to power, approaches all things as holy, as inexhaustibly deep, unencompassable, manifold, and, strange as it seems, lovely. It is an attitude that could accurately be called a form of *worship,* if that designation were not so likely to mislead.[18] But is is not an *idolatrous* worship, for no image is ever confused with a god. Past all necessary but partial images, the world—not the riddle-world of science but the world whose very existence is a miracle—is the holy other. The unknowable *Ding-an-sich,* no longer a philosophical idea as in Kant, has become a religious conception.

Considering an example or two may perhaps remove some of the darkness from my description of such a religious sensibility. Who responds to the world in the way I have just described? The great poet or, more generally, the great artist comes first to mind. For the poet the world is certainly a miracle, an occasion for wonder, not curiosity. The poet's aim is not to understand the world but to acknowledge, to hallow, and to celebrate it. In the attempt to do so, he is constantly raising up and sloughing off a welter of images, for no way of letting something be seen will ever be adequate to his intention. No way of seeing can be literalized into the final representation of the reality there before me; rather, every image, especially the image of re-presentation itself, must be seen through and replaced with another.

Moreover, the poet's aim is not a manifestation of the will to power. His intention is not to subdue the earth; on the contrary, he wants to be the place where the earth has its own way. As Rilke puts it, the poet is not the one who wills, but who is willing: willing to let the earth rise up in him invisible.[19] And such willingness is not at all narcissistic. The poet is not the maker of meaning; he is not imposing value or significance, nor is he fascinated with his own images, in which what is valuable or significant shows itself. Rather, he wants to be the place where the poem happens. He wants to hollow himself out, to create a space within so as to give the earth the resonance that lets us hear, partially and temporarily, the earth's own song.

Two examples of such artistry come to mind. The first is Keats's ode "To Autumn," extraordinary for the kind of selfless attention to the finite (the gathered crops, the gnats that rise at evening from the river shallows), which lets us see, not *beyond* the familiar and mundane but endlessly *into* it. A second is Rembrandt's series of self-portraits. What is most remarkable about this series of almost sixty paintings is its lack of narcissism. These self-portraits are neither self-glorifying nor sadomasochistically self-hating. They simply present, justly and truly, the record of a man's circumstances and fantasies over a lifetime; and the subject happens to be the painter himself. To the great artist it is a matter of indifference what individual is given attention in his images: self, other, the gnats by the river are for him all the same. It is the *quality* of the attention that matters in poetry. To love oneself—to give to oneself a truly profound and just attention—is no easier than to love any other part of the world.

With the reappearance of love in the argument, we come to a second example of the sensibility I have described and to the point where we can at last see the full justice of calling Wittgenstein's notion of the sound human understanding an *ethical* vision. Indeed, we can now even trace some connections between that vision and one of the streams of ethical reflection in the West, an ethical tradition that has fallen on hard times in the last century or so. We may call it, somewhat limply, an ethic of love; it contrasts with the ethic of principle that has dominated moral philosophy since Kant.[20]

The best recent example of such an ethic known to me is found in

Iris Murdoch's remarkable essays collected in *The Sovereignty of Good*.[21] In these essays, attention—"a just and loving gaze directed upon an individual reality"—supplants will as the focus of ethical life.[22] From the eighteenth century on, ethics has been obsessed by problems of will. "How shall I act?" seems to most of us the paradigmatic ethical question, and it seems only to admit answers formulated in terms of general and substantial first principles; "Act only on that maxim which you can at the same time will to become universal law" or "Act always so as to produce the greatest good for the greatest number." On this conception, moral life requires moral knowledge, and moral knowledge means the knowledge of the true moral principles. It is not difficult to see the connections of this conception of ethics to rationality-as-representation, since these wonted ethical principles must be true, i.e., must represent the Form of the Good, or the a priori structure of practical reason, or the like. The moral life presents itself as a riddle to be solved, and the key to the solution lies in our discovery of the right principles of action. Notice the obvious centrality of the will in this account: we face the moral realities before us as a set of obstacles to be surmounted, or as a maze to be run, or as a set of tasks to be fulfilled, or as a set of decisions to be computed and taken. Moral life becomes a sort of technical, even technological, problem. The other person becomes a setting for moral action, an object which, in the pursuit of my own purposes, I must treat in ways specified by the principles which constitute "the moral point of view."

In contrast to this, Murdoch's attempt is for a moral sensibility that is not technological. Moral life is a matter of deeper and deeper penetration into the vicissitudes of one's life and the lives of one's fellows; love is the central concept in morals because it names that capacity to go ever deeper in attention, to find more and more reality to wonder at in whatever individual one confronts. Love is constantly seeing through, not just seeing; it is constantly developing new images for appraisal and understanding, enlarging mind's stock of lenses for gathering and focusing light. Such a sensibility violently distrusts any ethical principle designed to guide the will, for two reasons. First, any principle can become an idol; it can through its generality blur the very individual realities that give moral reflection its characteristic importance and difficulty. And second, a focus on action-guiding principles makes will the center of the moral life, thereby introducing the "behaviourist, existentialist, and utilitarian" picture of the moral agent:

It is behaviourist in its connection of the meaning and being of action with the publicly observable, it is existentialist in its elimination of the substantial self and its emphasis on the solitary omnipotent will, and it is utilitarian in its assumption that morality is and can only be concerned with public acts.[23]

In the moral consciousness of such an agent there is no place for affirming the fundamental ethical significance of seeing the world as a miracle, of seeing it as a series of occasions for love—inexhaustibly rich and various attentions to the realities—rather than as a setting for the exercise of one's will.

In our ordinary thinking, the moral life is essentially public, in two senses. It is, first, concerned with what publicly happens, with actions and reactions; and, second, it has essentially to do with large-scale social structures and relationships. For us, that is, ethics is inseparable from what we call *politics*. The locus of moral reflection in our day is the public man, moving among strangers, as it were, searching for principles applicable universally, independent of those particularities of need and desert that loving attention may reveal. For us, *moral* has come to mean *impersonal,* for in our day the public has become the impersonal.[24] The *polis* is gone, and politics means something quite different from what it did to Aristotle.

For an ethic of love, however, the locus of the moral life is in the individual perspective, not the public. First, moral progress may on occasion be measured in the quality of a person's reflection, not in overt action.[25] And more importantly, according to such an ethic the height of virtue is not the following of universal (hence impersonal) principles. Consistency in action is not the supreme moral excellence, as any lover knows. Loving perceptions of an individual do not give rise to universalizable first principles of action; in that sense they do not provide something immediately recognizable as an *ethic*. Those perceptions are occasions, not for personal deliberations about duty or happiness, but for direct and unmediated response, whether to meet a need or provide a benefit. And these are responses born of wonder, not calculation; they treat the other as a mystery worthy of love: worthy, that is, of the most constant, patient, undemanding, and exacting individual attention, which will nonetheless never exhaust the reality that is there.

In her essays Murdoch is recalling the efforts of various Jewish and

Christian thinkers to locate the moral life within a fundamentally religious sensibility: a sensibility that is constituted by the acknowledgment of the essential mystery of things and by a response to that mystery that is self-effacing and loving, not willfully Faustian. She is also sounding a theme common to Aristotle and some other of the Greek moralists in their emphasis on the ethic of character. For Aristotle, living well is a matter of practical reason; it is knowing how, not knowing that. Substantial moral first principles are otiose for the man of virtue; his judgment—his perspicacious attention to the individual realities confronting him—is the source and standard of the moral life.

So the sort of Greek-Judaeo-Christian ethic of love and character expounded by Murdoch (an ethic of which, of course, only the barest bones have been exhibited here) gives us an interpretation of the sound human understanding that cuts deeper than the pragmatist interpretation while still keeping its best features. Very significantly, this deeper account allows us to place Wittgenstein's work within a long tradition. For all its originality in conception and execution, and for all its plain and secular idiom, Wittgenstein's later philosophy is at its core a return to an important moment of the Western religious vision, namely, that moment which exalts the essential sacredness and mystery of all things, which demands an astonished worship as the proper response to that mystery, and which identifies worship of God with an infinitely patient, detailed, and self-surpassing attention to the individual realities facing one, which is love.

V

SO MUCH for an attempt to describe a form of thought and life that can give substance to the notion of the sound human understanding. What reasons, if any, do we have for thinking it ought to be attributed to Wittgenstein? Certainly there is no direct evidence available that would support my claims. Wittgenstein's published work contains nothing like the account I have given; in fact, I am sure that for a variety of reasons—some of which have to do with the danger of saying what should only be shown—he would have rejected outright the idiom in which my claims are made.[26] Nevertheless, I do believe some substantial considerations can be advanced in support of my account. I will briefly canvass four.

In the first place, my interpretation can provide an intelligible account of those features already independently identified as constitutive of the sound human understanding. Three of the most important are, as we have seen, the nonliteralizing sensibility, the end of philosophy, and the restoration of direct, unimpeded action. Why, one may ask, should the ideal of human soundness have been delineated in these terms? If I am right, these features are central to Wittgenstein's work because of their essential connection to that ethical sensibility which sees the world as a miracle rather than as a place for Faustian self-assertion of intellect and will. The nonliteralizing sensibility I have described as giving each image its due as an image yet petrifying none into pictures. While neither tentative nor ironic in the instant of assertion, such a sensibility yet maintains a certain essential distance from whatever is asserted. There is constantly the freedom to move away from what is first perceived—there is always the opportunity to see through whatever is seen—and this freedom lends a particular tone of voice to whatever is said, a tone of voice which reveals a mind self-conscious of its own constituting and limiting activity in every disclosure of reality. Yet this self-consciousness is, remarkably, neither heroic nor narcissistic. If metaphysical philosophy speaks with a certainty that indicates pride or with an irony that reflects self-enchantment, the voice of the sound human understanding has the timbre of humility.

That humility marks Wittgenstein's ideal response to things, a response that, recognizing the essential mystery of the world, *acknowledges* that mystery; it does not seek to deny or to control it. This sensibility is constantly aware of the insufficiency of any particular conception; it feels the inexhaustible depth of every reality, and gives itself over to that work of patient attention which begins to reveal those depths. And this form of life is more than just the fallibilism of the pragmatist, however difficult the two may be to distinguish in practice. For the sound human understanding, the acknowledgment of the world's mystery is not just to say, "Of course, my best judgment in the matter may turn out to be mistaken." Rather, it is the consciousness that one's—anyone's—best judgment actually *is* insufficient to the realities at hand. It's not just to be aware that one's most scrupulous judgments may still need revision; it is to be conscious of the inherent hatefulness of judgment itself, to be aware of how shot through with Faustian *will* any judgment is. The distance of the sound human understanding from its assertions is moral, not epistemological. Because it has recognized itself in every judgment, seeing there a presence that inevitably constrains and distorts the reality that is judged, such an understanding is more than fallibilist. It is founded upon a deep (I have called it religious) sense of the self-concealing mystery of all things. Because of that mystery, every image commands respect, since any image may disclose some truth; any lens, however cloudy or distorted, may gather and focus some of the radiance that streams around it. But respect means respect *as an image;* none is literalized.

How can that be? Must not some conceptions be literal if the notion of the nonliteral is to have any bite? But, rightly understood, literalness is a moment, not a metaphysical state. We may recall here Wittgenstein's own image of the shifting riverbed in *On Certainty* (sec. 96–99): although the course of a river may always be slowly changing, at any given moment the bed in which the water flows is fixed. So it is with the images through which we appropriate the world. At any given time some set of these images is actually in operation; we are using them to gather light and to illuminate what we see. We are, that is, using them "literally." But something happens to us when we come to see the image in whatever we see. Once we have been awakened to the ubiquitous presence of mind, no literal perception will remain literal forever. Once mind has become aware of itself in its constituent images, no one of those images will capture its full and permanent attention; rather, mind's attention to the realities that surround it will constantly shift, centering now in this image, now in that one. As it is centered in one, the world will be seen, literally, in that particular way; but the riverbed is always shifting: soon the stream of consciousness will flow through another image; another lens will gather and focus the light. Mind is, after all, a capacity for illumination; and all images have their places as images. All gather some light; none gathers all.

To the sound human understanding, therefore, "literal" perception is always the first moment in seeing. Anything is first of all seen *as* something; some image, conception, idea gives form to what is seen, disclosing it to our vision. But to the sound human understanding that disclosure, literal in its appearance, is always just about to be supplanted by another. We are always about to see through what is seen. Only the image of thought as re-presentation, unrecognized as an image and fed by the Faustian will to fix and control the realities, could make the "literalness" momentarily characteristic of mind's activity into a metaphysical ideal. Once the world's unencompassable mystery is acknowledged, no way of seeing will be hypostatized. All will be recognized as moments of mind, puny disclosures of a reality so rich and manifold as to make our judgments an impudence, if not a sacrilege.

Thus the account I have given seems to provide a ground for that nonliteralizing sensibility which is so central a feature of the sound human understanding. From here it is no trouble to see that it also provides a ground for Wittgenstein's fervent desire that philosophy come to an end. Metaphysical philosophy—the attempt at the clear gaze *sub specie aeternitatis*—is inherently incapable of acknowledging the world as a miracle. The philosopher par excellence is one who sees the world as a riddle, not a mystery. Thus, the end of metaphysical philosophy is not for Wittgenstein, as it might be for a pragmatist, just the passing of a particular and ill-conceived cultural phenomenon; rather, it is the end of a fundamentally irreligious response to the *Pathos* of reality. It is a disease, a superstition, a bewitchment, a death trap.[27] Its end is a deliverance from evil. Such passionate characterizations as these can only be accommodated within a conception that connects the sound human understanding to deep ethical and religious sentiments.

Finally, the congruence of my interpretation of Wittgenstein's vision with what I have called an ethic of love allows us to understand why he believed the sound human understanding would make possible a certain sort of action. Once one has seen through the illusions of rationality-as-representation and has realized that moral reflection consists in infinitely patient attention to the individual realities, not the discovery and application of first principles of action, then one is freed to that task. Direct and unimpeded action for the concrete good of one's neighbor becomes possible, after all, only when that neighbor has been *noticed*. Such notice will be impossible when one's attention is consumed by the search for general ethical principles or for the more-and-more-adequate abstract representations of that neighbor whom—I assure you!—I want to serve. No, love of neighbor requires that we abandon the global for the local, the abstract for the concrete, the willful for the self-effacing. That kind of action has as its provenance the sound human understanding as I have described it.

In addition to accommodating these three central features of the sound human understanding, my interpretation has some textual support. I have already discussed in some detail sections 110–11 of the *Philosophical Investigations,* showing how Wittgenstein's use there of such notions as superstition and *Pathos* indicates his conviction that the roots of the diseased human understanding go very deep indeed: "There are deep disquietudes; their roots are as deep in us as the forms of our language and their significance is as great as the importance of our language." Moreover, his characteristic use of such epithets as 'disease', 'superstition', and 'bewitchment' to describe metaphysical philosophy indicates in another way the intensity that attaches to the vision of the sound human understanding; my interpretation of the nature of that vision makes such intensity plausible.

It is also important to recall that my interpretation connects up with some of the fundamental ethical themes of the early work. In developing the interpretation in section four of this chapter I have already had occasion to set out most of the crucial passages from the *Tractatus*, the "Lecture on Ethics," and the conversations with the Vienna Circle.[28] I will not repeat them here. Suffice it to say that the interpretation of the sound human understanding as a form of life which is, in my terms, essentially religious rather than magical allows us to see another very deep connection between the early Wittgenstein and the later; without, of course, denying the very real changes that had taken place as well. In the early work there is, without doubt, a deep sense of the world as a miracle—to feel it as a limited whole is the touch of *das Mystische* (TLP 6.45)—but there this religious sensibility is overlaid with the metaphysical perspective that marks the direct influence of Russell, Frege, and, through Schopenhauer, Kant. In the *Tractatus* rationality-as-representation is still alive; so the metaphysical gaze is still the author's official point of view, producing in this case a brilliant but unstable system that must at the end denigrate the rigorously representational rationality which gave it birth. Moreover, in the *Tractatus* the sense of *das Mystische* is connected to the heroic self-consciousness of the willing self, the godhead of the independent I; and this gives that early sensibility a narcissistic cast. In the later work Wittgenstein had come to see rationality-as-representation as a powerful superstition, so there is no attempt at a metaphysical construal of his vision. It remains entirely off the page, safe from the literalizing philosophical intellect, but making itself felt nevertheless. To summarize, in both the early and the later works there are passages that support my interpretation, and the continuity itself is further support.

This brings me to a third consideration in favor of my interpretation of the sound human understanding: it provides a way of seeing the continuance of those idiosyncratic "Christian" themes so obvious in Wittgenstein's life in the twenties. In our discussion of the *Tractatus* in chapter two we remarked the very great influences of Tolstoy and Kierkegaard on the young Wittgenstein. Reading Tolstoy's redaction of the

Gospels was a decisive event of those wrenching years; its influence, in conjunction with others, led to Wittgenstein's surrender of his patrimony and to years of teaching in the peasant schools of Lower Austria. Without trying to attribute to Wittgenstein any standard form of religious belief, it does seem clear that his extraordinary actions reflect his commitment to the "Christian" values Tolstoy found in the Gospels: love of neighbor, especially the poor and untutored; rejection of personal wealth and affectation; pursuit of simplicity. And these ideals charted the course of Wittgenstein's life for a decade.

Where did they go after 1929? Did the religious sensibility we have seen in his work and even more clearly apparent in his life, disappear or significantly diminish? I believe not. I believe that his later vision of the sound human understanding and life is the transmutation of that early sensibility. In its adamant refusal to countenance the metaphysical gaze there are present both the Tractarian acknowledgment of the world's miraculous existence and an ethic of love which continues the Tolstoyan service to the poor. By interpreting the sound human understanding as a religious vision we preserve a place for these important features of his thought and character; otherwise their ostensible disappearance is an anomaly.

Finally, I will mention a fourth consideration, more problematic than the first three, to support my interpretation, namely that it is consistent with what we know of Wittgenstein's life after 1930. While there are no events comparable in drama to the rejection of his inheritance or to the decision to abandon philosophy for primary-school teaching, his life after the return to Cambridge was certainly not that of a typical professor of philosophy. Consider these indications. From Malcolm's *Memoir* we know of Wittgenstein's hatred for academic life itself; we also know of his strenuous attempts to dissuade his favorite students from becoming professional philosophers. He took no part in the professional associations of philosophers. He sought no wide recognition inside or outside his university. He refused to eat at High Table. He dressed simply and lived frugally. During the 1939–45 war he worked as a hospital orderly and as a laboratory assistant. He resigned his chair at an early opportunity. He was merciless to himself and his friends in an attempt to put by cant. He *lived* ideas; his struggles with his thoughts were moral agonies. These facts, and others equally striking to be found in the several memoirs of his Cambridge life, indicate not only a man very far from the conventional; they show, I believe, the continued presence of a powerful religious sensibility.

Because he always felt the pressure of the vision of the sound human understanding, and because that vision had for him a religious intensity and meaning, his life shows some of the characteristic contours of the prophet and the evangelist. Convinced of the corruption of the present, he gestures toward a deliverance, a form of life that has done with the nonsense of philosophy.

Wittgenstein was an outsider, in self-image and in reality. (He once, in pain and anger, spoke of himself as a *Vogelfrei,* a bird legal to be shot by anyone.)[29] He fully expected to be misunderstood: "The only seed I am likely to sow is a certain jargon."[30] He was, as he said, thinking and writing for men and women of a culture radically different from his own. What pushed Wittgenstein outside the pale? What was the source of his prickly and defensive intensity, the ground of his heroic efforts in thinking? I believe part of the answer is the religious vision of the sound human understanding, which I have tried to describe. As with Kierkegaard, the impact of that vision moved Wittgenstein outside the normal patterns of his culture. Like Kierkegaard, he was a prophet celebrated as an eccentric, an evangelist touted as a great intellect. Small wonder that neither lived a happy life.

Even taken together, none of the four sorts of considerations I have presented conclusively demonstrates the correctness of my interpretation of the sound human understanding. It remains an interpretation, and a speculative one at that. Nevertheless, Wittgenstein's work and his life encourage such speculation. His intensity, his sense of mission, his bitter frustration (early and late) with the misapprehension of his work's true intention, the peculiar form and authority of the work itself, all these and more manifest a thinker outside the normal categories of the Western philosophical sensibility. To enter his sensibility, to become privy to the sound human understanding, requires from us an extraordinary act of imagination. Most of our efforts will misfire, of course; perhaps this book is a paradigm case. Such leaps must be made, however, if his work is to have the chance to effect the liberation he intended.

VI

BEFORE BRINGING this chapter to a close, a few loose ends remain to be tied up. The first, because it is so dangerous, is especially important to make right. It is an utter misconception to identify my account of the sound human understanding with a denigration of thinking. One might be tempted to believe that a sensibility that sees the world's existence as a miracle, and that acknowledges the presence of mystery as such, would despise thinking altogether. On a quick reading such a form of life as I have described might sound like anti-intellectual religious enthusiasm, or a strange variant of Zen. But this is a total misconception. Wittgenstein does not despise thinking; he despises attempts at magic that pass themselves off as thinking.

Thinking is as necessary to human beings as breathing or eating. The danger in thinking is the danger of prideful will: rationality-as-representation. When thinking becomes an attempt to fix reality in an attempt to control it, i.e., when it becomes an expression of the will to power, then it has become a form of magic, properly to be despised. And there is no doubt that sometimes thinking has a magical character: then the world is conceived as a cow to be milked, and by concentrating my intellectual energies I can get her to hold still and deliver.

But that is not the only form thinking assumes. There can be a thinking that is a mode of love, not will. Thinking then becomes a self-surpassing attention to what is there, attention which with its patience and industry acknowledges the endlessness of its tasks of discovery and response. The origin of such thinking is not curiosity or desire, but wonder; its aim is not science or technology, but disclosure and just reply. Such thinking acknowledges mystery by recognizing the continual need to see through whatever thinking has shown. The tasks of love spiral endlessly onward, and there is always more in any individual to be understood and answered to.

If the model of the first sort of thinking is the philosopher or the technocrat, the model of the second is the lover's active care for his beloved. And that model shows us how very far away from mindless enthusiasm or the void of Zen Wittgenstein's ideal lies. To give the active care worthy of a lover, to continue to focus one's attention so as to bring depth from depth, and to respond to those disclosures with justice and affection, these goals demand from us the very richest resources of mind. Good will is not enough; a scrupulous, flexible, strenuous application of all our powers of thought is required. It is *hard* to tell what is there in the other. We must *work* to notice whatever is before our eyes.

Although in my description here I have been using an idiom ('care', 'attention', 'response') most at home in characterizing our relations with our fellows, there is equally a thinking about the natural world that is a form of love. The artist again provides the clearest case. A painter like Cezanne, for example, shows in his work a patient attention to mountains and apples that is much the same as the attention of the lover to his beloved. In his paintings the phenomena of the natural world are revealed as things that repay wonder and contemplation in a measure which astounds the careless. They become, in their beauty, occasions for that joy which can take us outside ourselves and our willful pursuits. From the case of the artist it is not too long a step to a scientist whose thoughtful probing of nature is in service of wonder rather than will. Science too can become an occasion for joy rather than exalted self-feeling. Not every scientist must be, as Keynes calls Newton, a magician (perhaps Einstein was not). The sound human understanding may take any of the world as its proper object.

So it is a grave error to believe that my account of the sound human understanding underrates in any way the value of hard thinking. Indeed, there is room within that account for the most rigorous practice of natural science. Any thinking—art, science, moral reflection—can have a proper quality of attention. One is reminded in this connection of some sentences in the preface of the *Philosophical Remarks:*

> I would like to say 'This book is written to the glory of God', but nowadays that would be chicanery, that is, it would not be understood. It means that the book is written in good will, and in so far as it is not so written, but out of vanity, etc., the author would wish to see it condemned. He cannot free it of these impurities further than he himself is free of them.

Those remarks reflect thinking that knows its true nature. Whatever the matter of such thinking, its spirit shows its source in the sound human understanding.

The discussion so far should have made clear that the ethical vision of the sound human understanding offers no scope for the familiar and dreary debates about ethical realism and relativism, since both positions in these debates depend upon rationality-as-representation. Relativism makes sense only when set over against a realist position, and realism clearly involves taking literally the image of thought as representation. Once the sound human understanding has made it possible for one to see through every image, including that fundamental one, neither realism not its ostensible opposite will make much sense.

But that way of mooting the issue may seem a bit of a cheat, for there *is* something like ethical relativism in the neighborhood. Against the realist the ethical relativist has wanted to insist that no set of ethical terms and principles is or could be final; in this sense, says the relativist, none is or could be *the truth*. (And this is more than the weaker fallibilist claim that none could ever be *known* to be true.) In this rejection of finality the sound human understanding is one with relativism, for to such an understanding there is always more to be seen in any reality than that which has already shown itself. Given the patient attention of love, any image through which something is seen may be replaced with another, perhaps incommensurable, one. The truth, understood as the view *sub specie aeternitatis,* is an idol of the will to power; and as such it has no place in Wittgenstein's later sensibility.

This loss of truth (in the sense of finality) does not mean, however, that any sort of ethical reflection is just as good as another. From "Nothing is true" it does not follow that "Everything is permitted." We can see this by reminding ourselves that what is crucial in ethical reflection is the quality of attention that comprises it. In reflecting upon the formulation and application of the ethical terms, principles, and judgments of a person or a culture we can discriminate care from carelessness, patience from haste, scruple from self-interest, courage from fear, and the like; and these qualities of attention are just what is at issue. Not, of course, that there won't be ground for dispute here—after all, ethics is not mathematics, and in particular cases it may be difficult to tell, say, patience from cowardice or carelessness from a healthy intolerance for dead tradition—but at least we know what the dispute is about. We are given an ideal in the sound human understanding, albeit an ideal of *process* rather than *result;* and in terms of that ideal we can comfortably make some of the discriminations that the realist fears so to lose. Not everything will be permitted.

Like any ideal, this one offers no guarantee of protection against the barbarian or the sociopath, but to realize this is itself probably a good thing since we seem to need reminders of how fragile the web of civility is. And, of course, the ideal just sketched does not rule out "irremediable" ethical dissonances, as when one is confronted with incommensurable sets of ethical terms and principles arrived at by means of reflection, which are, so far as one can tell, equally scrupulous and fair. Insofar as it is sensible to say anything about such a hypothetical case, it seems at most an argument for an initial tolerance toward new ways of seeing familiar and cherished phenomena, not an excuse for throwing up one's hands. Perhaps, so the argument goes, there is another, equally scrupulous, way of reflecting upon the every-day elements of my life, and perhaps I would be better for consulting both.

But what if these different but equally attentive ways of seeing are deeply, fundamentally at war? Here again one is hesitant about saying anything in the absence of a concrete example, but certainly nothing rules out a priori such conflict. If it happened we would, I suppose, be utterly baffled, and not a little afraid. That such does *not* happen, or not happen very often, may just be a condition of human society. Just as we need air in order to live, but could lose it, so perhaps we need enough "agreement in form of life" (PI, sec. 241) to rule out such fun-damental and paradoxical conflict, or at least to keep it within man-ageable limits.[31] It is worth noting here that such "agreement" seems very much the rule rather than the exception. While we are occasion-ally puzzled about what to do, especially when trying to fit convictions to complex and tricky cases, surely we do not ever seriously consider that our most fundamental moral opposites—the racist, the anti-Sem-ite, the child pornographer—have arrived at their forms of life through a process of reflection and deliberation just as patient, scrupulous, and disinterested as our own. Certainly not! And, just as surely, we do not take seriously the protest that perhaps in these cases it is only our own ethnocentric moral prejudices that blind us to the courage of the anti-Semite or the scrupulosity of the pornographer. "'But, if you are cer-tain isn't it that you are shutting your eyes in face of doubt?'—They are shut" (PI, p. 224).

However that may be, the possibility of doubt and conflict at the periphery shows us in another way that the sound human understand-ing is not a moral panacea. The sound life will still contain uncertainty, danger, and pain; and the brief remarks offered in mitigation above are only the simplest of reminders. Enough has been said, however, to show that the conviction that any set of ethical reflections can and should be seen through does not leave one with a vicious ethical rela-tivism; instead one is left with ethics without philosophy: a new sen-sibility, not just a new position on the same old landscape.

Another loose end deserves a final comment. It has been a constant theme of this book that there are significant, largely overlooked continuities between the "early" Wittgenstein and the "later." The foremost continuity I have urged is, of course, the presence of an ethical vision at the center of his work in both periods. Now that the later vision has been more fully described, perhaps it would be useful to note again, and in another way, some of its relationships to the earlier. In some ways the visions are very similar; in others they are very different. Continuity is not, of course, identity.

In both periods the fundamental ethical affection is constituted by the way the self views the world that lies before it; the key to ethics is in a particular *way of seeing things*. In the *Tractatus* the sense of the problematic world is resolved by the good willing of the metaphysical self which is the world's limit; and that willing, as we saw in chapter two, is an *attitude* of the self to its world. The world becomes happy when the self which limits it becomes happy, and the self's alteration from unhappiness to happiness is a movement *within the self*. The aim of ethical reflection is to make possible such a movement of the attitudinal will, thereby giving the world a sense.

In the later ethical vision there is also a *way of seeing* that is crucial: the sound human understanding sees the world as a miracle, not a riddle. The key to ethics still lies in an *attitude* toward the world which one confronts. One can appropriate that world through a mode of will, or one can see it as an occasion for loving attention and response. As in the Tractarian account, *das Mystische* plays an important role here. In the earlier vision, it is the recognition of the metaphysical self as the world's necessary limit which makes possible the showing of the mystical and thereby empowers the self's good willing. *Das Mystische* is essentially connected to the self's seeing the world as miraculously *there,* "as a limited whole" (6.45).

6.44   It is not *how* things are in the world that is mystical,
         but *that* it exists.

For the sound human understanding there is, as we have seen, an apparently similar linkage of the ethical to the mystical there-ness of the world. Only the person who sees the world as a miracle can respond to it with love rather than with the will to power. Early and late, then, there is in Wittgenstein's thinking a crucial connection between the ethical life and a way of seeing and acknowledging the miraculous existence of the world.

But these similarities should not blind one to some very important differences. The ethical vision of the *Tractatus* is still narcissistic and willful. Consciousness of the world is essentially connected to a simultaneous consciousness of the metaphysical self which is the world's boundary, *and it is the self which is the source of the world's meaning*. Discovery of the sense of life is a function of the *willing* self; the world becomes happy as a result of a mysterious movement *within the self*. The world is *given* a sense as a result of the self's will (attitude); the metaphysical self is the final maker of meaning.

This narcissistic grounding of the sense of life in the willing self stands in real tension with those elements in Wittgenstein's early thinking which are due to the Christian influences of Tolstoy and (in some of his writings) Kierkegaard. Those elements stress God, not the self, as the source of the sense of life. According to this Christian conception, to go and serve the poor in Lower Austria is not the result of an act of will; in fact, it is precisely the *surrender* of one's will to God's. But to be consistent with the vision of the *Tractatus* Wittgenstein must have interpreted that surrender of will as itself heroically willful. In this he more resembles Kierkegaard that Tolstoy, for Kierkegaard more blatantly stresses the grounding of the life of faith in the individual's choice. The account in *Fear and Trembling* of Abraham as the knight of faith, for instance, specifically characterizes faith as a *movement* beyond the movement of infinite resignation, thus emphasizing its connection to the will. Indeed, the image of Abraham which emerges from the book is the image of the hero beyond the heroism of Greek tragedy. He is the man willing to assert himself not just against his own inclinations, in service of a higher moral law; he is willing to assert himself *as an individual* (note the heightened self-consciousness) against the moral law itself, in virtue of the absurd. To compare this absurdly heroic knight of faith to the mystically willing self-conscious happy self of the *Tractatus* is not at all farfetched, but both egregiously lack the humble selflessness so much a part of the Gospels. (I suspect, by the way, that some of the unhappiness and guilt Wittgenstein continued to feel as a schoolteacher was due to his recognition of the inherent willfulness of his ostensibly "Christian" decisions.)

In the later vision this tension is resolved. To see the existence of the world as a miracle, is to see *that mystery* as its meaning. There is no call for the will to power to *give* a meaning to it; indeed, to see the world as a miracle, as an occasion for love, prevents the will to power from exercising itself. There is here no narcissistic self-consciousness; nor is there self-forgetfulness. The self is naturally aware of itself, but there is no puffed up sense of omnipotence. Here one can clearly see the loss of Heroic Ascent as the Wittgensteinian image of salvation and its replacement with another. The metaphysical self brought to consciousness in the *Tractatus* is thoroughly heroic. In its quest for the sense of life, that self has had to overcome the world; by intellectual effort it has ascended from its ordinary self-conception (finite, vulnerable, a part of world) to put on the power and freedom of a god: the godhead of the independent I. The merely finite, whether in thought, desire, or style of life, has been put by. In the *Tractatus,* therefore, the godlike is the transcendent; it is that perspective which stands above the finite and surveys it *sub specie aeternitatis.*

But the later work shuns such transcendence. The world is not heroically to be overcome; rather, it is to be acknowledged and disclosed. The finite (the "merely" finite) is to be given a quality of attention capable of continually seeing through whatever is seen, thus acknowledging the world's essential mystery and refusing the prideful attempt to view it *sub specie aeternitatis.* The image of the godlike in the later work is Love, not Will; Depth, not Height. The godlike vision goes deeper down into things; it does not rise above them. Attention is directed outward to the individuals there before one. The sense of life is not found because it is heroically sought; certainly it is not created by the willing self. Indeed, the issue of discovering the sense of life doesn't even get formulated in the later work, since to do so would make its discovery one more task to be accomplished by the philosophical intellect–heroic will, comparable in *Tractatus* terms to making the world a happy one. Rather, it comes to one in the midst of those actions which are responses to the infinitely patient attention of love.

There are, therefore, two deep tensions in the *Tractatus.* There is the tension between the intensity of Wittgenstein's ethical feelings and his theoretical commitment to rationality-as-representation; there is also the tension *within* his early ethical vision between narcissism and Christian self-surrender, between will and love. We can now see, I hope, how these two tensions are fundamentally one. Rationality-as-representation, which leads through the picture theory to the doctrine of showing, is itself an aspect of the will to power; it is a form of self-aggrandizement. This lets us see the deepest basis of Wittgenstein's conviction of both the importance and the perversity of the *Tractatus.*

The problem in that book is not just the picture theory as an oversimple account of language; on the contrary, that theory is wonderful precisely because in its lucidity it crystallizes the impetus to literal representation and thus precipitates the will to power—the metaphysical self, the transcendental ego—which is behind it. The book is the apotheosis of metaphysical philosophy; and Wittgenstein's eventual repulsion from it is moral, not theoretical.

Both tensions in the *Tractatus* are resolved in the later vision of the sound human understanding, for in that vision of the world as miracle, love has overcome will. The abandonment of rationality-as-representation which marks the advent of the later work is not, therefore, just the loss of a philosophical doctrine; it indicates, rather, the resolution of a tension at the very heart of Wittgenstein's life. That resolution finally made possible ethics without philosophy.

We may conclude with a final rejoinder to a final objection. Surely, the objection runs, the sound human understanding here attributed to Wittgenstein remains philosophical, even metaphysical, in spite of frequent assurances to the contrary. After all, what could be more philosophical than a vision which stresses the insufficiency of an appearance to capture reality; what could be more metaphysical than the miraculous world, this new sort of *Ding-an-sich,* which cannot be exhausted in any image? Moreover, the sound human understanding is equally philosophical when it disavows the will to power. What is that but a moral judgment which, like any such, demands a philosophical justification?

There is something to this objection, but words and distinctions and judgments are not in themselves either philosophical or not. Everything depends upon the tone of voice with which they are uttered, and upon the form of life in which they are set. Here it may not be possible to describe the difference that is crucial. One wants to account for the fact that in Wittgenstein's sensibility none of the standard philosophical distinctions (some of which I have certainly traded upon in this chapter) have their ordinary force. It is as if the distinction between, say, appearance and reality is stripped of its philosophical import only to be revealed as a moral injunction or a religious insight. To reflect upon the necessity for seeing through whatever is seen is not, as with ordinary philosophy, to be struck with a conundrum or a curiosity; rather, it is to take up a certain attitude toward things, to enter a particular form of life. And that form of life is not philosophical.

And if one were now to insist that it *is,* whether Wittgenstein admits it or not, then one will have missed just the point the later work insists upon, for that work is an attempt to show that philosophy is determined by a particular sensibility, one which is not inevitable. That one cannot describe it without using some of the terms central to its antithesis is a problem only if one lacks any acquaintance with practices and attitudes that will let these terms have resonances other than the usual.

No thinker or critic can guarantee such resonances, of course. Incomprehension is quite real; the pupil's capacity to learn may come to an end before the point of the exercise has been grasped. Ethics without philosophy is an unfamiliar form of life, a specimen of social practice at odds with the deepest impulse of our technological culture. To the extent that such a form of life is lost to us, Wittgenstein must remain an enigma.

Thus we are brought to reflect in another way upon his insight that at the bottom of our lives is doing, not seeing (oc, sec. 204). A sensibility is inseparable from a form of life; consciousness is not a king, to have its will done whatever the circumstances. The sound human understanding is not our achievement. It is possible for us only because a form of life is, and that possibility is not the result of our will. We do not *decide* to stop doing philosophy; it just happens that we can. The sound human understanding is an occasion of grace, not heroic triumph.

NOTES

CHAPTER 1: The recovery of Wittgenstein's thinking (text pages 1–9)

1. PR, p. 7. Abbreviations used in citing Wittgenstein's works and selected other references are listed on pages ix–x.
2. PI, p. x.
3. J. Bennett, "Purposeful Reminders," *Times Literary Supplement,* June 20, 1975 (no. 3,824), p. 693.
4. R. Rhees, *Without Answers* (London: Routledge and Kegan Paul, 1969), p. 169.
5. PI, p. x. One is reminded of the first paragraph of the preface to the *Tractatus:* "Perhaps this book will be understood only by someone who has himself already had the thoughts that are expressed in it—or at least similar thoughts."
6. It was the work of Stanley Cavell that first made me aware of the importance of "terms of criticism" in understanding the spirit of a philosopher's work. See "Austin at Criticism," *Philosophical Review* 74 (April 1965): 204–19.
7. Martin Heidegger, *Kant and the Problem of Metaphysics,* trans. James S. Churchill (Bloomington: Indiana University Press, 1962), pp. 206–7. I have altered the translation slightly.

Chapter 2: Ethics in the *Tractatus:* showing and saying (text pages 11–73).

1. See TLP, 4.022, 4.12, 4.121, 4.1212, 4.122, 4.124, 4.125.
2. See TLP, 6.12, 6.124, 6.13, 6.1201, 6.122, 6.2, 6.21, 6.22.
3. See TLP, 5.62, 6.421, 6.44, 6.45, 6.521, 6.522, 7.
4. For references and further details, consult W. and M. Kneale, *The Development of Logic* (Oxford: Clarendon Press, 1962), chs. 7–11.
5. Anthony Kenny, *Wittgenstein* (London: Allen Lane/Penguin, 1973) contains a good discussion of these matters. See pp. 43ff.
6. NB, p. 2.
7. The "Notes on Logic" is printed as Appendix 1 of NB; the notes dictated to Moore are printed as Appendix 2.
8. Most philosophers *have,* of course. For a typical example, see James Griffin, *Wittgenstein's Logical Atomism* (London: Oxford University Press, 1964).
9. Laszlo Versenyi, *Socratic Humanism* (New Haven: Yale University Press, 1963).
10. Richard Rorty, *Philosophy and the Mirror of Nature* (Princeton: Princeton University Press, 1979).
11. Jay F. Rosenberg, *Linguistic Representation* (Dordrecht: D. Reidel, 1974), p. 1.
12. I am indebted to Richard Rorty for this way of putting the matter.
13. Thomas Nagel, *Mortal Questions* (Cambridge: Cambridge University Press, 1979), p. 209.
14. Letter to Russell (#35) in RKM.
15. RKM, p. 82.
16. Letter to Russell (#26) in RKM.
17. This letter, translated by B. F. McGuinness, appears on p. 16 of G. H. von Wright's historical introduction to Wittgenstein's *Prototractatus* (Ithaca: Cornell University Press, 1971).
18. Allan Janik and Stephen Toulmin, *Wittgenstein's Vienna* (New York: Simon and Schuster, 1973).
19. See Janik and Toulmin.
20. G. H. von Wright, "Biographical Sketch," in Norman Malcolm, *Ludwig Wittgenstein: A Memoir* (London: Oxford University Press, 1958), p. 5.
21. Janik and Toulmin, p. 201.
22. Leo Tolstoy, *A Confession, The Gospel in Brief, and What I Believe,* trans. A. Maude (London: Oxford University Press, 1940), p. 124.
23. Tolstoy, *A Confession,* p. 18.
24. Preface to *The Gospel in Brief,* p. 118.
25. Malcolm, *Memoir,* p. 71.
26. Søren Kierkegaard, *Concluding Unscientific Postscript,* trans. D. F. Swenson and W. Lowrie (Princeton: Princeton University Press, 1941), p. 223.
27. Søren Kierkegaard, *The Point of View for My Work as an Author,* trans. W. Lowrie (New York: Harper and Row, 1962), p. 24.
28. NB, p. 73.
29. NB, p. 77.
30. Here I have deviated from the Pears/McGuinness translation. For an explanation,

see G. E. M. Anscombe, *An Introduction to Wittgenstein's Tractatus,* 2d ed. (New York: Harper and Row, 1965), p. 167n.

31. In the *Tractatus* and *Notebooks* accounts of the metaphysical subject there is everywhere the influence of Schopenhauer. Like Wittgenstein, he wrestled with the post-Kantian difficulties of making sense of the self, and in response he developed a form of transcendental idealism that in many ways is the ancestor of Wittgenstein's untraditional solipsism. Others have done a fine job of showing the details of Schopenhauer's influence on the early Wittgenstein. See, for example, Janik and Toulmin, *Wittgenstein's Vienna,* and P. M. S. Hacker, *Insight and Illusion* (Oxford: Clarendon Press, 1972). It is not necessary to deflect the argument of this chapter to recapitulate their results; it is, however, important for us to keep the Schopenhauer influence in mind, since it indicates an originating tradition for the *Tractatus* wider than merely the influences of Frege and Russell.

32. Cf. TLP, 5.133, 5.134, 5.135, 5.136, 6.1361.

33. I am pleased to note the congruence of some of my conclusions with those of Peter Winch in "Wittgenstein's Treatment of the Will," in his *Ethics and Action* (London: Routledge and Kegan Paul, 1972). We arrived at these conclusions independently.

34. See above, p. 29.

35. Tolstoy, *The Gospel in Brief,* p. 118.

36. Ibid.

37. See above, sections two, three, and four, of chapter two.

38. LLW, p. 7.

39. That is the subject of Uhland's poem.

40. See p. 15 above for a summary of the things that are shown.

41. Von Wright, "Biographical Sketch," p. 10.

42. Ibid.

43. For details see W. W. Bartley, III, *Wittgenstein* (Philadelphia and New York: J. B. Lippincott, 1973).

44. Tolstoy, *A Confession,* p. 67.

45. Tolstoy, *The Gospel in Brief,* p. 193.

46. See Bartley, *Wittgenstein,* for details.

47. Kierkegaard, *Postscript,* p. 118.

48. Tolstoy, *A Confession,* p. 30.

49. This remark is attributed to Wittgenstein's friend, the Cambridge mathematician and philosopher F. P. Ramsey.

50. Leo Tolstoy, *Twenty-three Tales,* trans. L. and A. Maude (London: Oxford University Press, 1906).

51. Ibid., pp. 200–201.

52. My friend Tom Turner first called my attention to the image of ascent in the *Tractatus,* thus provoking my attempt to tie together ethical form and substance. The translation of the Heraclitus fragment is from James Hillman, *The Dream and the Underworld* (New York: Harper and Row, 1979), p. 25. Hillman's work on images has been very useful to me throughout this book. I am particularly indebted to *Revisioning Psychology* (New York: Harper and Row, 1975).

Chapter 3: The "Lecture on Ethics" (text pages 75–102)

1. For details, see W. W. Bartley, III, *Wittgenstein* (Philadelphia and New York: J. B. Lippincott, 1973), p. 104.
2. G. H. von Wright, "Biographical Sketch," in Norman Malcolm, *Ludwig Wittgenstein: A Memoir* (London: Oxford University Press, 1958), p. 11.
3. Ibid., p. 13.
4. Of course, as was pointed out in chapter two, Wittgenstein's sensibility was a divided one. Rationality-as-representation never had his complete allegiance, even in the *Tractatus*.
5. This information is due to the introductory note to the Lecture which appeared in the *Philosophical Review* 74 (January 1965).
6. G. E. Moore, *Principia Ethica* (Cambridge: Cambridge University Press, 1903), p. 3.
7. A third experience—guilt—is mentioned later in the Lecture.
8. The translation is by Max Black and is printed with the Lecture in the *Philosophical Review*.
9. Wittgenstein himself connected this experience to a play he saw in Vienna in 1910. See Malcolm, *Memoir*, p. 70.
10. An English translation was published: *Problems of Ethics* (New York, 1939).

Chapter 4: Showing and saying in the later work (text pages 103–160)

1. George Pitcher has an essay comparing Wittgenstein and Carroll, "Wittgenstein, Nonsense, and Lewis Carroll," *The Massachusetts Review* 6(1965).
2. Lewis Carroll, *Through the Looking-Glass*, in *The Annotated Alice*, ed. Martin Gardner (New York: Clarkson N. Potter, 1960), pp. 279, 281–2.
3. Søren Kierkegaard, *Concluding Unscientific Postscript*, trans. D. F. Swenson and W. Lowrie (Princeton: Princeton University Press, 1941), p. 109.
4. Cited in the preface of BB, p. viii. The translation is by Rush Rhees.
5. Stanley Cavell, "Aesthetic Problems of Modern Philosophy," in Max Black, ed., *Philosophy in America* (Ithaca: Cornell University Press, 1964), reprinted in Stanley Cavell, *Must We Mean What We Say?* (New York: Charles Scribner's Sons, 1969), pp. 85–86.
6. Other sorts of judgments of sensibilities themselves are possible, of course. See below for examples.
7. This is pointed out by Stanley Cavell in "The Availability of Wittgenstein's Later Philosophy," *Philosophical Review* 71(1962), reprinted in Cavell, *Must We Mean What We Say?*, pp. 44–72.
8. This remark occurs in a notebook written in 1934 or 1935. It is found in vol. 50 of the Cornell edition of the *Nachlass*.
9. D. Pears, "Wittgenstein and Austin," in *British Analytical Philosophy*, ed. B. Williams and A. Montefiore (London: Routledge and Kegan Paul, 1966), p. 39.
10. Wilfrid Sellars, *Science, Perception and Reality* (London: Routledge and Kegan Paul, 1963), p. 1.
11. These remarks about the nature of practical reasoning in connection with incom-

mensurable forms of life are indebted to Professor Alasdair MacIntyre's presentation to Richard Rorty's NEH Summer Seminar at Princeton in July 1979. I am
grateful to Professor MacIntyre, but I am sure he would endorse neither my
sketchy account nor the use to which I put it.

CHAPTER 5: Wittgenstein and Descartes (text pages 161–201)

1. Wilfrid Sellars, *Science, Perception and Reality* (London: Routledge and Kegan
   Paul, 1963), p. 1.
2. Søren Kierkegaard, *Concluding Unscientific Postscript,* trans. D. F. Swenson and
   W. Lowrie (Princeton: Princeton University Press, 1941), p. 118.
3. *Descartes' Philosophical Writings,* trans. Norman Kemp Smith (London: Mac-
   millan and Co., Ltd., n.d.).
4. Immanuel Kant, *Critique of Pure Reason,* trans. Norman Kemp Smith (New
   York: St. Martin's Press, 1965), B 39, note.
5. G. E. Moore, "A Defence of Common Sense," in Moore, *Philosophical Papers*
   (London: George Allen and Unwin, 1959).
6. See, for example, OC, sec. 11 ff. and 21 ff.
7. The importance of *images* in Wittgenstein's thinking will become clearer in the
   next chapter.
8. Norman Malcolm, "Wittgenstein's *Philosophical Investigations,*" *Philosophical
   Review* 63(1954):530–59. The essay is reprinted in G. Pitcher, ed., *Wittgenstein:
   The "Philosophical Investigations"* (Garden City, N.Y.: Anchor Books/Double-
   day and Co., 1966), pp. 65–103; my references will be to the pages of the Pitcher
   volume.
9. Malcolm (Pitcher, ed.), p. 66.
10. Ibid., p. 70.
11. Ibid., p. 75.
12. Ibid., p. 74.
13. Ibid.
14. Ibid., pp. 74–75.
15. Ibid., p. 74.
16. Donald Davidson, "On the Very Idea of a Conceptual Scheme," *Proceedings of
    the American Philosophical Association* 47(1973–74):5–20.
17. Richard Rorty, "The World Well Lost," *Journal of Philosophy* 69(Oct. 26,
    1972):649–65.

CHAPTER 6: Ethics without philosophy (text pages 203–256)

1. Martin Heidegger, "'. . . Poetically Man Dwells . . .'," in Martin Heidegger, *Poetry, Language, Thought,* trans. Albert Hofstadter (New York: Harper and Row,
   1971), p. 226.
2. Martin Heidegger, "On the Essence of Truth," in *Martin Heidegger: Basic Writings,* ed. David F. Krell (New York: Harper and Row, 1977), p. 132.
3. Norman Malcolm, *Ludwig Wittgenstein: A Memoir* (London: Oxford University
   Press, 1958), p. 30.

4. Ibid., p. 94.
5. Ibid., p. 39.
6. See "Some Developments in Wittgenstein's View of Ethics," which follows the printing of LE in the *Philosophical Review* (1965).
7. Certainly this conclusion does not follow from the fact of moral diversity. It is a nice question why it is the conclusion drawn by most philosophers.
8. For a discussion of convergence, see Hilary Putnam, *Meaning and the Moral Sciences* (London: Routledge and Kegan Paul, 1979), p. 20.
9. I am indebted to my friend Gerald Casenave for a conversation that provoked this way of putting the matter.
10. I am indebted to Richard Rorty's work for making me see the importance of the pragmatist tradition. His book *Philosophy and the Mirror of Nature* (Princeton: Princeton University Press, 1979) is especially valuable.
11. See Malcolm's *Memoir,* passim, for examples.
12. I have heard Richard Rorty make this sort of pragmatist rejoinder to the tradition.
13. Such antiphilosophy is not invariably present in James and Dewey, to be sure. Both occasionally succumbed to the temptation to try to give the philosopher something special to do.
14. See F, p. 31. In my discussion I go beyond what Wittgenstein explicitly says in his remarks. He draws no explicit distinction between religion and magic, for example.
15. The following very brief description of the Western philosophical tradition as an exemplification of the will to power has obvious affinities to Heidegger after the *Kehre,* so I am hesitant to assert my belief that I arrived at these ideas independently. The same is true for my notion of the nonliteralizing sensibility, which apparently has some connection to late Heidegger's call never to take any account of beings to be an account of Being. Certainly I can make absolutely no claim to Heidegger's erudition or to his original genius, so if we do agree, it just goes to show that a *potzer* can luck out every once in a while. At any rate, having recently discovered late Heidegger I have helped myself to some of what I could use. There is, I believe, much more to be done in making the comparison between Heidegger and Wittgenstein, work which I omit here because it would distract from my argument.
16. Freeman Dyson, *Disturbing the Universe* (New York: Harper and Row, 1979), p. 8. The text of Keynes's lecture was published as John Maynard Keynes, *Newton, the Man,* Royal Society of London "Newton Tercentenary Celebrations, 15 July 1946" (Cambridge: Cambridge University Press, 1947).
17. Wilfrid Sellars, *Science, Perception and Reality* (London: Routledge and Kegan Paul, 1963), p. 1.
18. It is liable to mislead because it encourages us, in what Heidegger calls our "onto-theological" tradition, to see the world as a superobject present to hand. It is also liable to mislead us into looking beyond the finite by encouraging us to think of worship as defined in terms of the supernatural kind of object worshipped rather than in terms of the quality of attention brought to the finite and ordinary. Some-

times, I believe, the later Heidegger, with his talk of "only a god can save us," falls into the latter misunderstanding.

19. Heidegger, "What Are Poets For," in *Poetry, Language, Thought,* p. 141.
20. Here again I am in the debt of Richard Rorty and the members of the NEH Summer Seminar of 1979.
21. Iris Murdoch, *The Sovereignty of Good* (London: Routledge and Kegan Paul, 1970). She acknowledges the great influence of Simone Weil.
22. Murdoch, p. 34.
23. Murdoch, p. 9.
24. John Rawls's magisterial *A Theory of Justice* (Cambridge, Massachusetts: Harvard University Press, 1971) is an example.
25. This is a point stressed by Murdoch in her example of the mother-in-law.
26. That in itself does not bother me overmuch. I suppose I agree with Heidegger that some violence toward a classic text is necessary in order that its message be partway freed from the inevitable encrustations of incomplete understandings (including, perhaps, the author's). But that is the wrong way to put it, since what seems like violence—it does, after all, cause pain and distress—can actually be a form of patient attention which refuses to take anything for granted. Not every act of homage has to take the object of admiration on its own terms. All of us know, in fact, that it is one of the chief graces of love that it often refuses to assent to the favorite self-image of the beloved.
27. PI, sec. 110, 309; RFM, p. 57, 157.
28. See above, pp. 233–34.
29. Malcolm, *Memoir,* p. 57.
30. See Cora Diamond, ed., *Wittgenstein's Lectures on the Foundations of Mathematics* (Ithaca: Cornell University Press, 1976), p. 293.
31. See Clifford Geertz, "Religion as a Cultural System," in Michael Banton, ed., *Anthropological Approaches to the Study of Religion* (London: Tavistock Publications, 1965).

INDEX

University Presses of Florida is the central agency for scholarly publishing of the State of Florida's university system. Its offices are located at 15 NW 15th Street, Gainesville FL 32603. Works published by University Presses of Florida are evaluated and selected for publication by the faculty editorial committees of Florida's nine public universities: Florida A&M University (Tallahassee), Florida Atlantic University (Boca Raton), Florida International University (Miami), Florida State University (Tallahassee), University of Central Florida (Orlando), University of Florida (Gainesville), University of North Florida (Jacksonville), University of South Florida (Tampa), University of West Florida (Pensacola).

This book was composed in Times Roman by the publisher on a CCI-400™ front-end phototypesetter. It was photoset on a Mergenthaler Linotron-202™ by G&S Typesetters, Austin, Texas.

Library of Congress Cataloging in Publication Data

Edwards, James C., 1943–

   Ethics without philosophy.

   "A University of South Florida book."
   Includes bibliographical references and index.
   1. Wittgenstein, Ludwig, 1889–1951—Ethics. 2. Ethics—History—20th century. I. Title.
B3376.W564E38   170'.92'4   82-2830
ISBN 0-8130-0706-2   AACR2